Women and Judaism

JEWISH STUDIES IN THE 21ST CENTURY

The Hebrew Bible: New Insights and Scholarship
Edited by Frederick E. Greenspahn

Women and Judaism: New Insights and Scholarship
Edited by Frederick E. Greenspahn

Women and Judaism

New Insights and Scholarship

EDITED BY

Frederick E. Greenspahn

NEW YORK UNIVERSITY PRESS

NEW YORK AND LONDON

NEW YORK UNIVERSITY PRESS
New York and London
www.nyupress.org

© 2009 by New York University
All rights reserved

Library of Congress Cataloging-in-Publication Data

Women and Judaism : new insights and scholarship /
Edited by Frederick E. Greenspahn.
p. cm. — (Jewish studies in the 21st century)
Includes bibliographical references and index.
ISBN-13: 978-0-8147-3218-2 (cl : alk. paper)
ISBN-10: 0-8147-3218-6 (cl : alk. paper)
ISBN-13: 978-0-8147-3219-9 (pb : alk. paper)
ISBN-10: 0-8147-3219-4 (pb : alk. paper)
1. Women in Judaism. 2. Jewish women—Religious life.
3. Feminism—Religious aspects—Judaism. 4. Jewish women—History.
5. Jewish women in literature. 6. Jewish literature—Women authors.
I. Greenspahn, Frederick E., 1946–
BM729.W6W658   2009
296.082—dc22   2009017393

Manufactured in the United States of America
c   10 9 8 7 6 5 4 3 2 1
p   10 9 8 7 6 5 4 3 2 1

Contents

PART III. CONTEMPORARY LIFE

PART IV. LITERATURE

II

Acknowledgments

The explosion of Jewish Studies scholarship has been one of the most dramatic developments in American Jewish life during the past half-century. There are programs of one sort or another at hundreds of universities. The Association of Jewish Studies, which is the professional organization of professors in the field, has a membership that is approximately equal to that of the organizations for Reform or Conservative rabbis, with annual meetings that routinely attract close to a thousand participants. Yet, as Ellen Frankel, editor-in-chief of the Jewish Publication Society, has observed, "Jewish laypeople and rabbis remain uninterested in what Jewish scholars study and publish"; instead, rabbis "continue to teach what they themselves learned in seminary or even earlier . . . even though many of the ideas . . . have been discredited by contemporary scholarship" (*Sh'ma*, March 2004).

If Frankel is right that "Scholars have yet to demonstrate that what they're up to is good for the Jews," then surely the dramatic insights pertaining to women is one area where their work has much to offer. It would be hard to find any other field within the constellation of Jewish Studies that is as relevant to contemporary Jewish life. Because women obviously constitute half of the Jewish people, their experience represents half of Jewish culture, even if that half has typically been overlooked. Recovering their experience, therefore, amounts to recovering half of Jewish civilization. But its value goes much further, because it can also provide information and insights that pertain to a host of issues that afflict contemporary Jewish life. Studying Jewish women can help to separate myth from reality, clarify the distinction between custom and law, and explore possible alternatives to the present way.

It would obviously have been impossible to include every relevant topic within a single volume and still keep it to a reasonable length. However, these chapters, written by some of the leading scholars in their respective fields, address many of the most prominent topics in such areas as Jewish history and law, literature and theology. They are offered here in the conviction that Jewish scholarship has much to contribute to enriching Jewish life and addressing current concerns. Moreover, ignoring scholarly insights and information can actually impede progress by making it more difficult to resolve pressing problems and thereby creating anxiety where there need be none so that potential solutions are overlooked.

This series, *Jewish Studies in the 21st Century*, is the product of many people's effort and support. It began with the vision of Herbert and Elaine Gimelstob, who provided the resources that have made it possible. From the beginning, Jennifer Hammer has been generous with her time and expertise, helping to turn a vision into reality; along the way, the staff at New York University Press has ensured that the results take the highest possible shape. Ellen Frankel gave the project clarity by sharing her knowledge and experience, along with her deep commitment to our goals, and Teresa Maybee invested yeoman service toward making the nuts and bolts of this effort work. Others who participated in the realization of this volume included Jessica Spitalnic Brockman, Avigail Rock, and Marianne Sanua. And, *aharona aharona haviva*, Barbara Pearl made my goals her own, providing support, insight, and assistance every step of the way while creating the supportive environment that has made this endeavor enjoyable as well as constructive.

Introduction

IIIIIIIIIIIIIIIIIIIIIIIIIIIIIIIIIIIIIIIIIIIIIIIIIIIIIIII

Four Approaches to Women and the Jewish Experience

Judith R. Baskin

Although women have always constituted half of the Jewish population and have played essential roles in ensuring Jewish continuity and the preservation of Jewish beliefs and values, it is only since the 1970s that their contributions and achievements have received sustained scholarly attention. This burgeoning research into women and women's experiences is a result, in great part, of the development of women's studies as a theoretical discipline and of the significant increase, beginning in the 1970s, in the number of women who earned doctoral degrees in various fields of Jewish Studies. Using gender as a category of analysis, these scholars and increasing numbers of their colleagues have begun to investigate Jewish women's domestic, economic, intellectual, spiritual, and creative roles in Jewish life from biblical times to the present. Studies of the conceptions and portrayals of women in every genre of Jewish literature, including the legal documents that have determined patterns of Jewish life for centuries, are also ongoing. Similarly, female writers and poets, as well as female readers, from various Jewish milieus have attracted unprecedented scholarly attention.

This volume details these new developments in academic research about Jewish women and suggests future directions in a range of fields, including biblical studies, rabbinics, literature, history, and sociology. In her chapter, for example, Esther Fuchs delineates the varied ways in which Jewish feminist scholars of the Hebrew Bible have approached and analyzed biblical images of women, while Dvora Weisberg and Judith Hauptman consider innovative feminist analyses of the representations of women in rabbinic texts. Sara Horowitz and Nehama Aschkenasy, in their chapters, discuss the literatures that contemporary Jewish women have created in North America and in Israel. Historians, too, have returned to a range of primary documents to reveal women's central social and economic contributions to sustaining the Jewish family in many different times and places, as well as evidence of their intellectual and spiritual lives. Renée Levine Melammed, Chava Weissler, and Harriet Pass Freidenreich address the situations of Jewish women in the medieval Muslim world, in early modern Europe, and during the first decades of the 20th century in Central Europe.

Since the 1970s, many Jewish women, of all ages and backgrounds, have combined feminism's mandate for equality in every area of human endeavor with an explicit commitment to Jewish identification and the Jewish community. Pamela Nadell and Sylvia Barack Fishman analyze the impact of this second wave of North American feminism on American Judaism and Jewish life and the ways in which the ordination of women as rabbis and cantors, as well as the spiritual and intellectual empowerment of Jewish lay women through enhanced Jewish education, have significantly altered the contemporary landscape. As Nadell and Fishman detail, changes in liturgical language that render the language of prayer both gender neutral and inclusive of all worshippers, as well as the development of new religious symbols and rituals focused on events in women's lives, are among a number of innovations that have transformed Jewish life and worship at the beginning of the 21st century.

This introductory chapter will focus on four overarching themes that inform all of these areas. The first of these is the repercussions of the inherently androcentric characteristics of biblical religion and rabbinic Judaism for Jewish women and their religious and social options throughout the centuries; the second is the equally important influence of host environments, whose norms and customs have also played a vital part in the ways Jewish women's social and spiritual lives have developed and diverged from place to place. Third, I discuss the role of economic resources in determining women's roles and status in various Jewish communities of the past and present. My final focus is the impact of technological innovations on the personal, educational, vocational, and communal opportunities open to Jewish women in the 21st century. Technological advances have transformed and improved women's lives in numerous ways; at the same time they have brought about broadly accepted cultural changes in attitudes about women and their appropriate roles and activities that will inevitably determine the future contours of Judaism and Jewish life.

The Lasting Impact of Rabbinic Judaism

While originating in the practices and literature of Israelite religion, rabbinic Judaism, which recorded its distinctive legal and literary traditions in the first six centuries of the Common Era, is the foundation of all contemporary forms of Jewish religious life. The earliest written documents of rabbinic Judaism are the Mishnah (henceforth *m.*), a compilation of legal rulings based on biblical law, actual practice, and spiritual vision, organized by subject matter, and edited in the land of Israel in the early 3rd century C.E., and the Tosefta, a contemporaneous collection of legal rulings, which follows the order of the Mishnah. In the centuries following the completion of these two works, rabbinic communities in the land of Israel and in Babylonia (the ancient Jewish communities in the Tigris and Euphrates river valleys) produced extensive commentaries on the Mishnah, known as *gemara*. The *gemara* produced in the rabbinic academies of Babylon was far more complete than that produced in the land of Israel, and when the Mishnah and this more extensive *gemara* were combined to form the Babylonian Talmud sometime in the 6th century C.E., the definitive compilation of Jewish law and tradition for the next millennium had been completed. The Talmud of the Land of Israel, completed in the 5th century C.E., although less comprehensive and considered less authoritative than the Babylonian Talmud (henceforth *b.*), also became a part of the larger body of rabbinic literature together with a number of exegetical (midrashic) compilations. These documents were all produced by rabbis, men who believed that their view of the world reflected a divinely ordained pattern of life for the Jewish people.[1]

As Dvora Weisberg and Judith Hauptman indicate in their chapters, rabbinic Judaism was essentially androcentric. Building on biblical legislation and the variety of women who populate the pages of the Hebrew Bible, described in this volume by Esther Fuchs, the rabbis developed a distinctive view of women as essentially different from men. While rabbinic views about women are as diverse as rabbinic opinions on other subjects, they rest on the talmudic statement that "women are a separate people" (*b. Shabbat* 62a), which conveys the basic rabbinic conviction that females are human entities created by God with physical characteristics, innate capacities, and social functions inherently dissimilar from those of males. Moreover, the ways in which women are perceived to be essentially different are not only ineradicable but problematic for men. In particular, these include woman's sexual attractiveness to men and the biological functions of the female body, especially those related to fertility.[2]

The certainty that women take a secondary place in the scheme of things permeates rabbinic thinking. The sages who produced rabbinic literature apportioned separate spheres and separate responsibilities to women and men, making every effort to confine women and their activities to the private realms of the family and its particular concerns. These obligations included economic activities that would benefit the household, since undertaking business transactions with other private individuals was an expected part of a woman's domestic role.[3] This template was already well established by late biblical times, as indicated by Proverbs 31:10-31, which describes the domestic, philanthropic, and entrepreneurial activities of the ideal wife. In rabbinic times, too, women participated in the economic life of the marketplace, worked in a number of productive enterprises, trades, and crafts, brought claims to the courtroom, met in gatherings with other women, and attended social events.[4] But whatever women did in public, they did as private individuals. The rabbis were determined to exclude women from significant participation in most of their society's communal and power-conferring public activities, not only by custom but as a result of detailed legislation. Since these public endeavors had mostly to do with participation in collective worship, communal study of religious texts, and the execution of judgments according to Jewish law, women were simultaneously isolated from access to authority and leadership and from the spiritual and intellectual sustenance available to men.[5]

As long as women satisfied male expectations in their domestic roles, they were revered and honored for enhancing the lives of their families and particularly for enabling their male relatives to fulfill their religious obligations. The Talmud relates that women earn merit "by sending their children to learn [Torah] in the synagogue and their husbands to study in the schools of the rabbis, and by waiting for their husbands until they return from the schools of the rabbis" (b. Berakhot 17a). Judith Hauptman demonstrates in her chapter that rabbinic jurisprudence often goes beyond biblical precedents in its efforts to ameliorate some of the difficulties women faced as a consequence of biblical legislation. Particular attention was devoted to extending special new protections to women in such areas as the formulation of marriage contracts, which provided financial support in the event of divorce or widowhood, and in allowing a woman to petition a rabbinic tribunal to compel her husband to divorce her in specific circumstances.[6] Nevertheless, in this religious system, men expound the divine rulings that affect women's lives; women, the objects of these directives, have no standing to legislate for themselves or others.

This is not to say, however, that rabbinic Judaism did not grant women spiritual status. Women, like men, were responsible not only for obeying all of Judaism's negative commandments but also for observing the Sabbath and all of the festivals and holidays of the Jewish calendar (although male and female obligations on these days sometimes differed). Although women are exempt from participation in communal prayers that must be recited at specific times, they were not free from the obligation to pray, which is incumbent on each individual (*b. Berakhot* 20a-b). Later Jewish tradition understood that women were to make a personal address to God as they started their day and that the content of women's prayers might be spontaneous and could be voiced in a vernacular language, rather than according to an established liturgy.[7] However, Chava Weissler reminds us that we do not find extant versions of specific formulations of prayers for women until the end of the medieval period.[8]

Women also observed a number of ritual regulations within the domestic sphere. These included preparation and serving of food according to the rabbinic dietary laws (*kashrut*) and the observance of limitations on marital contact during the wife's menstrual period (*niddah*). Similarly, women were expected to separate and burn a piece of the dough used in making Sabbath bread (*ḥallah*), a reminder of Temple sacrifice, and to kindle Sabbath lights (*hadlaqah*). Doubtless, these rituals provided satisfying spiritual avenues for sanctification of aspects of daily life for many women. Yet, it is also the case that at least some strands of rabbinic tradition regard women's performance of these ordinances not as *mitzvot*, that is, as divine commandments whose observance enhances the religious life of the observer and ensures divine favor, but rather as eternal punishments brought upon woman to remind her of Eve's responsibility in the death of Adam and therefore in all human mortality (*Genesis Rabbah* 17:8). According to the Mishnah, "For three transgressions do women die in childbirth: for heedlessness of the laws concerning their menstruation, the dough offering, and the lighting of the Sabbath lamp" (*m. Shabbat* 2:6).[9]

The rabbis believed that to be female was less desirable than to be male and several times listed the physical and social disadvantages to which a woman was subjected.[10] One of the most trenchant statements of the difference in the status of men and women in rabbinic Judaism is found in a discussion of the various ritual obligations incumbent on the adult male Jew. According to this text, one of the three blessings a man is obligated to say daily thanks God "who has not made me a woman" (b. Menaḥot 43b). This blessing ultimately became part of the daily liturgy for morning prayers in traditional Jewish practice, enshrining the difference in the status of men and women in rabbinic Judaism for centuries to come. It remains part of the traditional liturgy to the present day; in its place, women thank God "for making me according to Your will."[11]

The negative ways in which woman were constructed as "other" and as morally inferior to men in the foundation texts of rabbinic Judaism had a long-lasting impact on men's perceptions of women and on women's images of themselves; they play a major role, as well, in the negative images of women found in Jewish folk literature and mystical teachings. Yet, different as they were imagined to be, women were also acknowledged as essential to men as the indispensable social mortar that sustained rabbinic society. Women as wives, mothers, and economic partners were praised as "bolsters to their husbands," eminently worthy of recognition and appreciation.[12] Still, in virtually no time or place prior to the contemporary era did any Jewish man ever imagine that a woman could be his equal.

The Influence of the Majority Culture

Since the Babylonian conquest in biblical times (586 B.C.E.), the majority of Jews have lived outside the land of Israel. Jewish societies, living in a variety of host cultures, have consistently struggled to maintain a balance between the guidance and demands of Jewish law and the social practices of their gentile neighbors. Often this has meant that Jews have adopted the language and dress of the majority society and many of its dominant cultural attitudes, as well. Degrees of Jewish adaptation and acculturation, as well as instances of Jewish uniqueness in any specific instance, can be discerned only through comparisons with the larger cultural context within which any particular Jewish subculture has functioned. Culture is closely entwined with social class. While Jews in both medieval Muslim and Christian societies, for example, were under a number of personal and political constraints as members of a minority community, many nevertheless maintained a higher standard of living than the majority of the gentile population. It is important, therefore, that comparisons of Jews and non-Jews in any given time and place take into account the social norms and practices of groups with similar economic resources.

Although the patriarchal culture of rabbinic Judaism conformed in great part to wider Near Eastern norms that also tended to restrict women to domestic tasks, at least one Jewish social setting in late antiquity allowed independent women significant communal participation. From the 3rd century B.C.E. on, large numbers of Jews lived in the Greek-speaking Diaspora of the Hellenistic and Roman worlds. Evidence suggests that a number of aspects of Jewish life in these communities, including possibilities available for women, diverged significantly from the norms and prescriptions found in rabbinic Judaism, which was centered in the land of Israel and in Sassanian Iraq. While it seems likely that most Jewish women in the Greek-speaking parts of the Roman Empire lived their lives in the relative seclusion of the home, examinations of funerary and other inscriptions demonstrate that some Jewish women acted as autonomous entities in the social, economic, and religious spheres.[13]

On the basis of a number of inscriptions in Greek and Latin, dating from the 1st century B.C.E. to the 6th century C.E. and ranging from Italy to Asia Minor, Egypt, and Phoenicia, in which women bear such titles as "head of the synagogue," "leader," "elder," "mother of the synagogue," and "priestess," Bernadette Brooten has suggested that, contrary to previous scholarly consensus informed by rabbinic texts, Jewish women assumed positions of leadership in the very public sphere of the ancient synagogue in these Diaspora communities.[14] Although it is not clear if these synagogue titles were simply honorific in recognition of significant philanthropy or if they imply that women had meaningful leadership and/or ritual obligations, Ross S. Kraemer has suggested that Jewish communities in the Greco-Roman Diaspora may have been particularly accepting of women's leadership in areas of public affairs where "civic responsibility and religion intersected," as in synagogue activities. She has written "that women's leadership was particularly likely in Jewish synagogues with relatively high numbers of proselytes (both male and female) for whom the participation of women in public life, including religious *collegia*, was familiar and acceptable."[15] It is quite possible that many of these women were widows or otherwise independent women in control of substantial financial resources, since they are almost never mentioned in terms of a relationship to a husband, father, or son.

A few Jewish women of this milieu may also have possessed significant Jewish learning. The 1st-century C.E. writer Philo of Alexandria relates that a small number of upper-class, well-educated Jewish women joined the contemplative monastic Therapeutic community that was located outside Alexandria, Egypt. Apparently, most of those women were older virgins, who, like their male counterparts, spent their days reading Jewish scriptures and allegorical commentaries and living a life of rigorous asceticism, broken only by Sabbath and festival observances. When men and women prayed together on the Sabbath, they were separated by a partial wall that prevented visual contact but allowed women to participate equally with men in prayer and song.[16] Clearly, there were non-Jewish models of female autonomy, religious leadership, and political and economic power in these Greek-speaking Roman communities that sanctioned this kind of independent female activity, and a small number of women who identified themselves with the Jewish community were able to take advantage of them.

Jewish communities have generally conformed to the patterns of the majority culture in terms of the status of women. In her chapter, Renée Levine Melammed discusses roles of Jewish women in the Muslim world and demonstrates how expectations for Jewish women and Jewish marriage practices were strongly influenced by Islamic norms. Although Jewish women of prosperous families were not literally isolated in women's quarters as were Muslim women of comparable social status, religious and community ideals dictated that women should remain at home as much as possible.[17] Polygamy was a feature not only of biblical and rabbinic social policy but of Muslim life; thus, it is not surprising that many Jewish men in Muslim environments appear to have had more than one wife. Documents from this milieu frequently contain agreements to grant equal rights to wives in a polygamous family, the husband generally undertaking to spend alternate nights with each spouse. Wealthy families often insisted on the insertion of clauses in their daughters' marriage contracts that forbade the husband to take a second wife.[18] Polygamy remained a feature of Jewish life in the Muslim world well into the 20th century.

In medieval and early modern Christian Europe, on the other hand, monogamy was the rule, and women generally had significantly more freedom of movement than women in the Muslim world. These cultural patterns had a significant impact on Jewish women. In this social setting, the position of Jewish women, who were active participants in the family economy, was significantly higher than that of Jewish women in the Islamic milieu. This is indicated, in part, by their large dowries, which might constitute 10 percent of their parents' worth.[19] A further recognition of women's high standing, as well as the strong influence of the larger environment, is the 11th-century *takkanah* (rabbinic ruling) forbidding polygamy for Jews in Christian countries. This change in traditional Jewish law is attributed to Rabbi Gershom ben Judah (c. 960–1028), the first great rabbinic authority of Western European (Ashkenazic) Jewry. R. Gershom is also credited with the even more significant pronouncement that no woman could be divorced against her will, a positive enhancement of women's legal status in Judaism.[20] In fact, divorce appears to have been less common among Jews in medieval Christian Europe than in the Muslim milieu, perhaps because it was not sanctioned by Christianity.

Another example of significant social influence on women's lives from the majority culture is found in the period of *Haskalah*, the Jewish Enlightenment movement that began in late-18th-century Germany and brought enormous changes to Jewish religious, political, and social life in Central and Western Europe. Receptive to modernity and European culture, *Haskalah* insisted that Jewish acculturation to the mainstream mores and customs of the public sphere was not incompatible with adherence to traditional Jewish practice. Adoption of the language and values of the non-Jewish world tended to occur first among the wealthiest Jews, who had frequent financial dealings with non-Jews. As Harriet Pass Freidenreich points out, many daughters of the wealthy Jewish elite became highly educated in European languages and culture. Exposure to a world of secular novels, poetry, and plays, together with instruction in music and modern languages, distanced young women from brothers and husbands whose lives were restricted narrowly to commerce and finance. In the late 18th and early 19th centuries, a number of these prosperous and accomplished women found success in a salon society where gentiles and Jews mixed socially, and a few of them ultimately moved entirely into the gentile world through conversion.[21]

Some of the supporters of *Haskalah* championed social changes within the Jewish community that had an impact on less privileged women. Moses Mendelssohn (d. 1786), the founder of *Haskalah* in Central Europe, and others of his circle, for example, expressed opposition to arranged marriages and advocated love matches.[22] *Haskalah* also led to religious transformations that enhanced women's position and status. Indeed, many contemporary forms of Jewish religious practice, including Reform Judaism,

Conservative Judaism, and Modern Orthodoxy, were shaped in this milieu. Reform Judaism, in particular, which offered 19th-century Jews a modernized and acculturated form of Jewish belief and practice, proclaimed that women were entitled to the same religious rights and subject to the same religious duties as men in both home and synagogue. Emphasis on equal religious education for girls and boys, including the introduction of a confirmation ceremony for young people of both sexes and the shaping of an accessible worship service in the vernacular, made the new movement attractive to many women. Similarly, the introduction of family seating in North American Reform synagogues, permitting men and women to sit together during worship, was also appealing to acculturated Jews. Pressure from young women may have prompted the Reform rabbinate to adopt the Christian model of double-ring wedding ceremonies in which not only men but women made a statement of marital commitment.[23]

Nevertheless, Freidenreich reminds us that the process of acculturation to the larger society was generally quite different for women and men in Central and Western Europe. Confined to the domestic scene, restricted in their educational opportunities, and prevented from participating in the public realms of economic and civic life, most Jewish women had few contacts with the non-Jewish world. Rather, women were encouraged to cultivate a home-based Judaism in which spirituality was expressed in domestic activities; in secularized homes they were usually the last to preserve elements of Jewish tradition. This 19th-century domestic Judaism not only reflected traditional Judaism's preferred positioning of women in the private realm of husband and family but also was a form of Jewish conformity to the Christian bourgeois model of female domesticity that put religion in the female sphere.[24]

Similarly, emulation of Christian models of female philanthropy and religious activism inspired middle-class Jewish women to establish service and social welfare organizations in Germany, England, and North America in the late nineteenth and early twentieth centuries. These organizations, some of which were connected with synagogues, advocated greater recognition of women within their respective Jewish communities as "sustainers of Jewish communal life and guardians against defection from Judaism."[25] In her chapter, Freidenreich demonstrates the extent of female activism in Germany in this era and discusses Jewish women's support of social welfare services, feminist trade unionism, women's suffrage, and religious change. She also documents Jewish women's prominence among university graduates in German-speaking Europe prior to the Nazi period.[26]

The ordination of women as rabbis is another innovation that was very much affected by larger cultural attitudes. As Pamela Nadell has chronicled, female rabbinical ordination was first seriously considered in late-19th-century Germany and the United States as a natural result of Reform Judaism's insistence on the equality of men and women. The discussion about female ordination within the Jewish community was actually part of a larger social debate as women began to gain access to higher education and the learned professions. Women were now able to become doctors, lawyers, and ministers; why should Jewish women not also aspire to the rabbinate? However, the ambivalence of Reform Jewish leaders, who struggled to balance their long-stated commitment to the religious emancipation of Jewish women with their own engrained prejudices about women's proper sphere and their perceptions of the receptivity of their congregations to female rabbis, delayed a positive commitment to women's ordination for nearly a century, despite a series of challengers. It took the collision between second-wave feminism and American Judaism to propel women into the rabbinate in a sustained and institutionalized way.[27]

At the beginning of the 21st century, much of the creativity in contemporary Jewish spirituality, liturgy formation, scholarship, and artistic life is coming from women. This phenomenon raises many questions about continuing male roles in liberal forms of Jewish practice, learning, and institutional life. As Sylvia Barack Fishman has cautioned, the stakes for American Jews are significant, since "The American Jewish community not only shares in all the human consequences of feminism but also carries with it the additional responsibility of preserving three thousand years of Jewish history and culture and confronting the problems of a numerically challenged population as well."[28] However, if the past is any indication, forces from outside the Jewish community will be as influential as any from within in determining the roles of women in American Judaism and American Jewish life in the decades to come.

Economic Resources

In eras of opportunity, Jewish women who controlled significant economic resources frequently assumed prominent roles in their households and in their communities. Widows and other independent women of means, such as divorcées, were particularly likely to become influential. In her chapter, Dvora Weisberg discusses the wealthy and politically well-connected Yalta in rabbinic Babylon,[29] while Renée Levine Melammed talks about the independent Cairo businesswoman Wuhsha. Clearly, the women in the Greek-speaking Diaspora discussed earlier, who were leaders in their synagogues or who devoted their lives to study, were also individuals of means.

One region where the phenomenon of women and economic success is particularly striking is northern France and Germany, known to medieval Jews as Ashkenaz. Avraham Grossman has shown that Jewish women's position here markedly improved between 1100 and 1300, relative both to the talmudic era and to the situation of Jewish women in Muslim countries. He suggests that this was a result of the economic success that transformed relatively small Jewish communities into a bourgeois society. As Jews prospered in trade and money lending, Jewish women played an increasingly vital and often autonomous part in their family's economic lives, both as merchants and as financial brokers. Indeed, Jewish women's influential position and activities during the High Middle Ages paralleled those of Christian women within the upper bourgeoisie, as both groups of women achieved literacy and financial skills and ran their households and economic affairs effectively during their husbands' absences, whether on mercantile or military endeavors.[30]

As I noted earlier, one indication of the high status of Jewish women in this medieval milieu was the large dowries they brought into marriage. Since the capital with which a young couple started life had its origin mainly in the bride's portion, parents demanded strong guarantees in the ketubah (marriage contract) that the bride would be treated with respect, that her marriage would have some permanence, and that she would be financially secure. Jewish women's economic activities generally supplied a part or even the whole of the family income, sometimes allowing their husbands to devote themselves to study. Medieval Jewish literature is full of references to women's business undertakings and to their frequent meetings and travels with Jewish and gentile men for business purposes; no objections are cited anywhere to women's wide-ranging freedom of action. In fact, rabbinic authorities allowed Jewish businesswomen traveling alone to disguise themselves as men or as nuns for self-protection.[31]

Women engaged in all kinds of commercial operations and occupations, but money lending was especially common. Jewish matrimonial and property laws permitted women to manage capital they acquired through dowry, inheritance and, in case of divorce or widowhood, their ketubah.

Surviving records indicate that women were responsible for one-third to one-half of all loans in Northern France in the 13th and 14th centuries and in German and Austrian communities between 1350 and 1500. These figures represent loans granted by women who were acting alone or as the head of a business consortium. A small group of women, mostly widows, were active in top-level business with the nobility or rulers.[32] Because of their high tax contributions, some of these businesswomen gained administrative power as tax collectors. Others, such as Kändlein of Regensburg in 1354 and Josephine of Regensburg in 1374, were elected officers in their Jewish community administrative council (*kehillah*), a most unusual honor for a woman and evidence of the power these individuals had attained through their economic success.[33]

Another indication of women's high economic status in Ashkenaz was their voluntary assumption of religious practices from which they were exempt in rabbinic Judaism. Thus, in 12th-century Germany and northern France, at least some women of means insisted on assuming time-bound positive precepts, such as putting on *tefillin* (phylacteries), even though they were not obligated to do so by *halakhah*, and contemporary sages felt compelled to acquiesce. The 12th-century scholar R. Simcha of Speyer included women among the quorum of ten people required to recite the grace over meals.[34] A fascinating example of women's assumption of ritual roles in the public domain was the prominent women who served as godmother (*sandeqa'it*) at the circumcision of a son or grandson. R. Meir of Rothenburg, a major rabbinic leader of the 14th century, attempted to abolish this practice, since he believed the presence of perfumed and well-dressed women in the synagogue among men was immodest. He was unsuccessful, and this custom continued until the beginning of the 15th century, an indication of Jewish women's high status and financial clout in the communal realm of Ashkenaz.[35] However, as the political and economic situation of European Jewish communities gradually worsened, beginning in the 13th century, and as traditional practice and laws were reasserted, most of the nonhalakhic privileges Jewish women had achieved in this and other areas of daily life were firmly curtailed.[36]

Following the expulsion from Spain in 1492, the experience of immigration and the encounter with non-Iberian communities offered some female refugees with significant financial resources a similar empowerment and independence. Powerful and wealthy widows, such as Benvenida Abravanel and Doña Gracia Nasi, both of the 16th century, continued their deceased husbands' business ventures successfully, intervened with rulers on behalf of threatened Jewish communities, and were renowned for their philanthropy and their support of Jewish culture and learning.[37]

Several wives and widows of the early "Court Jews" of German-speaking Europe were also active entrepreneurs. One example is Esther Schulhoff Aaron Liebmann (c. 1645–1714), who was married first to Israel Aaron (d. 1673), a supplier of goods to the Brandenburg court and founder of the Berlin Jewish community. She subsequently married Jost Leibmann; she and her husband were the court jewelers to Frederick I of Prussia and the leading family in the Berlin Jewish community. Esther worked actively alongside her husband and successfully carried on their business after her husband's death. Like many Jews who served the courts of local and regional rulers, Liebmann's fortunes depended on personal favor. After the death of Frederick I and the accession of Frederick William I, in 1713, Esther Liebmann was put under house arrest and released only after she had paid the king a substantial fine.[38]

Control of economic resources provided women with other kinds of communal and spiritual options. One woman who crossed gender boundaries to achieve independent religious leadership in a Hasidic sect was Hannah Rochel Werbermacher (1815–1888?), a woman of independent means. Well-educated and pious, Webermacher, known as the Holy Maid of Ludmir, acquired a reputation for saintliness and miracle-working in her Polish town. Her wealthy father died when she was nineteen, leaving her a sufficiently large inheritance to support herself without a husband or community aid, and she built her own prayer house and held gatherings like a Hasidic rebbe. Werbermacher attracted both men and women to her "court," where she delivered lectures from behind a closed door. Not surprisingly, reaction from the male Hasidic leaders of her region was uniformly negative, and Hannah was pressured to resume her rightful female role in marriage. Although her marriages were unsuccessful, they had the intended result of ending her career as a religious leader, at least in Poland. Around 1860, Werbermacher used her financial resources to relocate to Jerusalem where she reestablished herself as a holy woman. Here, too, she attracted a following of Hasidic women and men, as well as Sephardi and possibly some Muslim Arab women, and led gatherings at the Western Wall, the Tomb of Rachel, and her own study house.[39]

In the contemporary era, too, Jewish women of substantial financial resources frequently play important roles in the Jewish community, particularly in North America. It is the case, however, as Sylvia Barack Fishman and others have documented, that women remain poorly represented in the upper echelons of Jewish philanthropic leadership. During the late 1990s, concluding that issues important to women and girls were not being appropriately funded by community allocations, female philanthropists established Jewish women's foundations in a number of North American cities. In their first ten years, more than twenty such funds have raised more than $35 million to support services that are specifically directed to the needs of girls and women. In addition to drawing attention and resources to Jewish women's issues, the new philanthropies are also attracting more women to the Jewish organizational world.[40]

Technological Changes and Jewish Women

Advances in technology over the centuries have profoundly affected many aspects of human society, including the lives of women. The invention of printing in the 15th century, which made the dissemination of popular literature practicable and inexpensive, played an important role in expanding Jewish women's religious lives and piety in the early modern period. In her essay in this volume, Chava Weissler discusses *tkhines*, supplicatory prayers for women written in the vernacular, and notes the significance of this new technology in making these liturgical texts easily available. Access to reading matter in the vernacular had a transformative effect for many women, deepening their knowledge of Judaism and Jewish traditions and even empowering a few women to become writers.[41] Rabbinic injunctions against women's learning were believed to apply to Talmud study but not to the Bible or legal rulings necessary for women's everyday activities. While Jewish women were generally ignorant of Hebrew, most were literate in Jewish vernaculars (Judeo-German [Western Yiddish] in Central Europe and Yiddish in Eastern Europe, written in Hebrew characters), which had long been essential to women's economic activities. Translations of the Hebrew Bible, the first books to be printed in the Jewish vernacular, gave women access to Judaism's holy texts. Particularly popular were the *Taytsh-khumesh*, first published by Sheftl Hurwitz in Prague in 1608 or 1610, and the *Tsenerene*, by Yankev ben Itzkhok Ashkenazy (c. 1590–1618), both of which included homilies on the weekly biblical readings from the Torah and Prophets, as well as stories, legends, and parables drawn from rabbinic literature, the Zohar and other mystical texts, and histories and travel accounts. Ethical treatises that discussed proper conduct, woman's religious obligations, and a woman's relations with her husband, such as the *Brantshpigl* (Burning Mirror) by Moses ben Henoch Altschuler (1596) and the *Meneket Rivkah* of Rebecca bas Meir Tiktiner of Prague (d. 1550; posthumously published in the early 17th century), were also available to female readers. These vernacular books, which were also read by Jewish men, many of whom were not possessed of significant Jewish scholarship, were printed in a special typeface, *vayber taytsh* ("women's vernacular"), based on the cursive Hebrew hand women were taught for business contracts, marriage agreements, and correspondence. With the publication of these works, the new technology of printing provided a vehicle of education and expression for nonelite Jews, including literate women.[42]

A similar phenomenon of female literary empowerment was also present in Italy, where Deborah Ascarelli translated Hebrew liturgical poetry into rhymed Italian, presumably for use by female worshippers. Her book, containing translations of liturgical selections into Italian, as well as her own poetry in Italian, is the only source of information about her. According to the book's dedication, Deborah and her husband, Joseph Ascarelli, lived in Rome; the family is associated with exiles from Spain and the leadership of the Catalan community of Rome. Her *Abitacolo degli oranti*, completed in 1537 and published in Venice in 1601, is probably the earliest published work in Jewish literature written by a woman.[43]

One early modern woman who was strongly influenced by printed vernacular literature was Glikl bas Judah Leib (also Glückel of Hameln) (1646–1724).[44] Born into the prosperous Court Jew milieu of Central Europe, Glikl was well read in Judaeo-German literature and had some knowledge of Hebrew and German, as well; her memorial notice characterizes her as "a learned woman" (*melumedet*), unusual praise in her time and place.[45] Betrothed at twelve, married at fourteen, and the mother of fourteen children, Glikl was active in business and pious in religious observance, including regular synagogue attendance. Her autobiography, written to drive away the melancholy that followed her husband's death and to let her children know their ancestry, is an engrossing document that interweaves and juxtaposes pious tales and moralizing from her extensive reading with Glickl's accounts of events in her own life and those of her loved ones. At the threshold of modernity, both as a woman and as a Jew, Glikl undertook business activities that reflect the growing economic participation of Jews in the non-Jewish world, while her religious and secular educations speak to the broader horizons and new educational and intellectual opportunities available to some 17th-century Jewish women thanks to the proliferation of printed books. Her journey from reader to writer would be experienced by a growing number of Jewish women in the centuries to come, as Sara Horowitz and Nehama Aschkenasy have demonstrated in their scholarship and in their chapters.[46]

Over the past two hundred years, the domestic, religious, and communal roles of Jewish women in the Western world have undergone significant expansions as a result of the technological transformations associated with modernity. By the end of the 19th century, the industrial production of textiles and ready-to-wear clothing and the commercial milling of flour and baking of bread liberated women from what were historically their most time-consuming activities. Similarly, growing industrialization and urbanization in Europe and North America led to the separation of economic activities from the domestic realm. These social changes wrought by technological advances played a significant part in the contemporaneous growth of women's service organizations discussed earlier, as middle-class women found that they could care for their families and also play a role beyond their domestic responsibilities.

By the second half of the 20th century, the widespread availability and affordability of refrigerators, washing machines and dryers, vacuum cleaners, modern cooking equipment, and dishwashers reduced the time that women were required to devote to household maintenance.[47] These new appliances, together with ongoing innovations in communication devices, allowed many women to consider undertaking paid employment and broader communal responsibilities outside the home to assist in the economic support of their families and to expand their personal, intellectual, and spiritual horizons. None of the phenomena that Nadell and Fishman describe would have been possible without these technological leaps forward.

Concurrently, the development of a range of effective birth control options in the 1960s and 1970s enabled Jewish women to plan their families. At the beginning of the 21st century, medical fertility technology is also playing an increasingly important role for a Jewish population in demographic decline, given the late ages at which Jewish couples tend to marry, a rate of reproduction below that of other ethnic groups, and the growing incidence of marriage outside the Jewish community.[48]

And, just as the invention of the telephone transformed human interactions one hundred years ago and the invention of the typewriter opened office employment to women in the first decades of the 20th century, so, too, the development of computer technology, particularly the Internet, has also given Jewish women unimagined new options for learning, organizing, and communicating with each other in every sector of the Jewish female community.

Conclusion

In the first decade of the 21st century, Jewish women have encountered new challenges in the areas of family formation; unprecedented opportunities in higher education and vocational choice; increased communal acceptance of homosexuality and other alternative lifestyles; and a wide range of options in religious and spiritual expression and political and civic activism. However, many of the battles for female integrity and equality within Judaism remain to be fought within traditional forms of Judaism, Jewish communities with roots in the Muslim world, and Israel, where Jewish women's rights in marriage and divorce remain circumscribed by halakhic regulation.

The chapters of this volume make clear that whatever the future holds for the Jewish people, there can be no doubt that these four factors—Judaism's traditional androcentric views of women, the impact of the larger societies in which Jews live, Jewish women's increasing economic clout, and future technological advances—will continue to play central roles in determining the contours of Jewish women's lives.

NOTES

1. On rabbinic literature and its development, see H. L. Strack and G. Stemberger, *Introduction to the Talmud and Midrash* (Minneapolis: Fortress Press, 1996). It is important to remember that rabbinic texts are prescriptive, not descriptive. They tell us very little about the actualities of Jewish women's lives in any particular time and place of late antiquity. For an analysis of the attitudes toward women expressed in rabbinic writings, see Judith R. Baskin, *Midrashic Women: Formations of the Feminine in Rabbinic Literature* (Hanover, NH: University Press of New England, 2002).

2. On feminist approaches to representations of women in the Hebrew Bible, see Esther Fuchs's chapter, "Jewish Feminist Approaches to the Bible," in this volume. For rabbinic discourses on women as sources of both pollution and temptation, see J. Baskin, *Midrashic Women*, pp. 22–36.

3. J. Baskin, *Midrashic Women*, pp. 76–79; on the elasticity of women's domestic responsibilities in late antique Palestine, see Cynthia Baker, *Rebuilding the House of Israel: Architectures of Gender in Jewish Antiquity* (Stanford: Stanford University Press, 2002).

4. On Jewish women's various activities in late antiquity, see Miriam Peskowitz, *Spinning Fantasies: Rabbis, Gender and History* (Berkeley: University of

California Press 1997); and Shulamit Valler, "Business Women in the Mishnaic and Talmudic Period," *Women in Judaism: A Multidisciplinary Journal* 2:2 (2001).

5. On women's exclusion from communal study, prayer, and leadership in rabbinic Judaism, see J. Baskin, *Midrashic Women*, pp. 79–87.

6. See also Judith Hauptman, *Rereading the Rabbis: A Woman's Voice* (Boulder, CO: Westview Press, 1998), and Rachel Biale, *Women and Jewish Law: An Exploration of Women's Issues in Halakhic Sources* (New York: Schocken Books, 1984).

7. On women and prayer, see J. Baskin, *Midrashic Women*, pp. 79–83, and Dvora Weisberg, "Men Imagining Women Imagining God: Gender Issues in Classic Midrash," in *Agendas for the Study of Midrash in the Twenty-First Century*, ed. Marc Raphael (Williamsburg, VA: Department of Religion, College of William and Mary, 1999), pp. 63–83.

8. See also Chava Weissler, *Voices of the Matriarchs: Listening to the Prayers of Early Modern Women* (Boston: Beacon Press, 1998).

9. On these texts, see J. Baskin, *Midrashic Women*, pp. 71–73, and idem, "'She Extinguished the Light of the World': Justifications for Women's Disabilities in *Abot de-Rabbi Nathan B.*," in *Current Trends in the Study of Midrash*, ed. C. Bakhos (Leiden: E. J. Brill, 2005), pp. 277–97.

10. For discussion of enumerations of women's disabilities in rabbinic texts, including *Genesis Rabbah* 17:8 and *b. 'Erubin* 100b, see J. Baskin, *Midrashic Women*, pp. 65–87.

11. See, for example, Philip Birnbaum, trans., *Ha-Siddur Ha-Shalem: Daily Prayer Book* (New York: Hebrew Publishing Co., 1949), pp. 15–17. J. Hauptman suggests that "the real reason a man should thank God for not being a woman is not his higher status but his greater level of ritual obligation. . . . A Jewish man's superiority flows from his being commanded by his Creator" (*Rereading the Rabbis*, p. 237).

12. For rabbinic praise of women, see J. Baskin, *Midrashic Women*, pp. 17–18, 68, 95–99, and 113. *B. 'Erubin* 100b counts "serving as a bolster to her husband" as one of the disadvantages to which women are subject.

13. Ross S. Kraemer, *Her Share of the Blessings: Women's Religions Among Pagans, Jews, and Christians in the Greco-Roman World* (New York: Oxford University Press, 1992), pp. 93–94, 99, and 192.

14. Bernadette Brooten, *Women Leaders in the Ancient Synagogue* (Atlanta: Scholars Press, 1982).

15. R. Kraemer, *Her Share of the Blessings*, p. 123.

16. Philo, *On the Contemplative Life*, §27–29, 30, 34–39; quoted in R. Kraemer, *Her Share of the Blessings*, pp. 113–15.

17. On medieval Jewish women in the Muslim world, see Shlomo Dov Goitein, *A Mediterranean Society: The Jewish Communities of the Arab World as Portrayed in the Documents of the Cairo Geniza*, 5 vols. (Berkeley: University of California Press, 1967–1988), particularly vol. 3, *The Family* (1978) and vol. 4, *Daily Life* (1983).

18. S. Goitein, *Mediterranean Society*, vol. 3, p. 263.

19. Irving Agus, *The Heroic Age of Franco-German Jewry* (New York: Yeshiva University Press, 1969), p. 278; Avraham Grossman, *Pious and Rebellious: Jewish Women in Medieval Europe*, trans. J. Chipman (Hanover, NH: University Press of New England, 2004), pp. 148–52.

20. On the *takkanot* of R. Gershom, see Ze'ev W. Falk, *Jewish Matrimonial Law in the Middle Ages* (London: Oxford University Press, 1966), pp. 1–15, and A. Grossman, *Pious and Rebellious*, pp. 68–77.

21. On the "salon Jewesses," see H. Freidenreich, "How Central European Jewish Women Confronted Modernity," in this volume and Deborah Hertz, *Jewish High Society in Old Regime Berlin* (New Haven: Yale University Press, 1988) and idem, "Emancipation Through Intermarriage? Wealthy Jewish Salon Women in Old Berlin," in *Jewish Women in Historical Perspective*, ed. J. R. Baskin (2nd ed., Detroit: Wayne State University Press, 1998), pp. 193–207. Similarly, Iris Parush has described the contributions of middle-class Jewish women toward the end of the 19th century in furthering the ideals of *Haskalah* in Eastern Europe, through their reading of secular literature in German, Yiddish, Polish, and Russian (*Reading Jewish Women: Marginality and Modernization in Nineteenth-Century Eastern European Jewish Society* [Hanover, NH: University Press of New England, 2004]).

22. For *Haskalah* attitudes about women and gender relations, see David Biale, *Eros and the Jews: From Biblical Israel to Contemporary America* (New York: Basic Books, 1992), pp. 153–58.

23. Marion A. Kaplan, *The Making of the Jewish Middle Class: Women, Family, and Identity in Imperial Germany* (New York: Oxford University Press, 1991), pp. 66–68.

24. Paula E. Hyman, *Gender and Assimilation in Modern Jewish History: The Roles and Representations of Women* (Seattle: University of Washington Press, 1995), pp. 25–30, and M. Kaplan, *Making of the Jewish Middle Class*, pp. 64 and 69–72.

25. P. Hyman, *Gender and Assimilation*, p. 41.

26. On Jewish women's organizations, see P. Hyman, *Gender and Assimilation*, pp. 36-44, M. Kaplan, *Making of the Jewish Middle Class*, pp. 211–19, and Linda Gordon Kuzmack, *Women's Cause: The Jewish Woman's Movement in England and the United States, 1881–1933* (Columbus: Ohio State University Press, 1990). On women and university education, see Harriet Pass Freidenreich, *Female, Jewish and Educated: The Lives of Central European University Women* (Bloomington: Indiana University Press, 2002).

27. Pamela S. Nadell, *Women Who Would Be Rabbis: A History of Women's Ordination 1889–1985* (Boston: Beacon Press, 1998), and her chapter in this volume.

28. Sylvia Barack Fishman, *A Breath of Life: Feminism in the American Jewish Community* (New York: Free Press, 1993) p. 247 and her chapter in this book.

29. On Yalta, see also J. Baskin, *Midrashic Women*, pp. 83–87.

30. A. Grossman, *Pious and Rebellious*, pp. xiii, 2–3, and 114–22.

31. *Sefer Ḥasidim* (Book of the Pious) [Bologna version], ed. Reuven Margoliot (Jerusalem: Mosad Harav Kook, 1964), par. 702. On medieval Jewish women's economic activities, see A. Grossman, *Pious and Rebellious*, pp. 114–22, and Judith R. Baskin, "Jewish Women in the Middle Ages," in *Jewish Women in Historical Perspective*, ed. J. Baskin, pp. 114–15.

32. On Jewish women's moneylending activity, see A. Grossman, *Pious and Rebellious*, p. 122, Martha Keil, "She Supplied Provisions for Her Household: Jewish Business Women in Late Medieval Ashkenaz," in *The Jews of Europe in the Middle Ages* (Ostfildern: Hatje Cantz, 2004), and William C. Jordan, "Women and Credit in the Middle Ages," *Journal of European Economic History* 17/1 (1988): 33–62.

33. Martha Keil, "Public Roles of Jewish Women in Fourteenth- and Fifteenth-Centuries Ashkenaz: Business, Community, and Ritual," in *The Jews of Europe in the Middle Ages (Tenth to Fifteenth Centuries)*, ed. C. Cluse (Turnhout, Belgium: Brepols, 2004), pp. 317–30.

34. A. Grossman, *Pious and Rebellious*, pp. 186–87 and n. 20, p. 300.

35. Ibid., p. 185.

36. Ibid., pp. 7, 250.

37. On Benvenida Abravanel, see David Malkiel, "Jews and Wills in Renaissance Italy: A Case Study in the Jewish-Christian Cultural Encounter," *Italia* 12 (1996): 7–69, and Renata Segre, "Sephardic Refugees in Ferrara: Two Notable Families," in *Crisis and Creativity in the Sephardic World, 1391–1649*, ed. B. R. Gampel (New York: Columbia University Press, 1997), pp. 164–85 and 327–36. On Doña Gracia Nasi, see Renée Levine Melammed, "Sephardi Women in the Medieval and Early Modern Periods," in *Jewish Women in Historical Perspective*, ed. J. Baskin, pp. 137–39.

38. Deborah Hertz, "The Despised Queen of Berlin Jewry, or the Life and Times of Esther Liebmann," in *From Court Jews to the Rothschilds, Art, Patronage and Power 1600–1800*, ed. V. B. Mann and R. I. Cohen (Munich and New York: Prestel Verlag, 1996), pp. 67–77.

39. On Werbermacher, see Nathaniel Deutsch, *The Maiden of Ludmir: A Jewish Holy Woman and Her World* (Berkeley: University of California Press, 2003), and Ada Rapoport-Albert, "On Women in Hasidism: S. A. Horodesky and the Maid of Ludmir Tradition," in *Jewish History: Essays in Honour of Chimen Abramsky*, ed. A. Rapoport-Albert and S. J. Zipperstein (London: Peter Halban, 1988), pp. 495–525.

40. See Fishman's chapter in this volume and Susan Chambré, "Parallel Power Structures, Invisible Careers and the Changing Nature of American Jewish Philanthropy," *Journal of Jewish Communal Service* 76:3 (2000); idem, "Philanthropy" in *Jewish Women in America*, 2 vols., ed. P. E. Hyman and D. D. Moore (New York: Routledge, 1998), vol. 2, pp. 1049–54.

41. On this topic, see Judith R. Baskin, "Jewish Women's Piety and the Impact of Printing in Early Modern Europe," in *Culture and Change: Attending to Early Modern Women*, ed. M. Mikesell and A. Seeff (Newark: University of Delaware Press, 2003), pp. 221–40.

42. For a survey of vernacular printed material available to Jewish women in the early modern period, see Shmuel Niger, "Yiddish Literature and the Female Writer," trans. and abridged by Sheva Zucker in *Women of the Word: Jewish Women and Jewish Writing*, ed. J. R. Baskin (Detroit: Wayne State University Press, 1994), pp. 76–77 and 83–86. On the *vayber taytsh* typeface, see Natalie Zemon Davis, *Women on the Margins: Three Seventeenth-Century Lives* (Cambridge, MA: Harvard University Press, 1995), p. 24.

43. Howard Tzvi Adelman, "Italian Jewish Women," in *Jewish Women in Historical Perspective*, ed. J. Baskin, p. 154. Modern translations of Ascarelli's poems by Vladimir Rus appear in *Written Out of History: A Hidden Legacy of Jewish Women Revealed Through Their Writing and Lett*ers, ed. S. Henry and E. Taitz (New York: Bloch, 1978), pp. 130–31.

44. Glikl's autobiography was not published until the late 19th century. A standard English translation is Marvin Lowenthal, trans., *The Memoirs of Glückel of Hameln* (New York: Schocken Books, 1977), although it should be noted that this version is significantly abridged. See N. Z. Davis, *Women on the Margins*, p. 220, n. 1, on the histories of the various Yiddish, German, and English versions and translations of this autobiography, and p. 230 n. 53 on the manuscript versions; on Glikl's name, see N. Z. Davis, *Women on the Margins*, pp. 8–9. See also H. Freidenreich, "How Central European Jewish Women Confronted Modernity," in this volume.

45. N. Z. Davis, *Women on the Margins*, p. 25.

46. See Nehama Aschkenasy, *Eve's Journey: Feminist Images in Hebraic Literary Tradition* (Detroit: Wayne State University Press, 1994).

47. On American Jews and consumer culture, see Andrew Heinze, *Adapting to Abundance: Jewish Immigrants, Mass Consumption, and the Search for American Identity* (New York: Columbia University Press, 1990), and Jenna Weissman Joselit, *The Wonders of America: Reinventing Jewish Culture, 1880–1950* (New York: Hill and Wang, 1994); idem and Susan Braunstein, *Getting Comfortable in New York: The American-Jewish Home, 1880–1950* (New York: The Jewish Museum, 1991).

48. On Jewish attitudes toward fertility technologies, see Susan M. Kahn, *Reproducing Jews: A Cultural Account of Assisted Conception in Israel* (Durham, NC: Duke University Press, 2000).

Part I

||||||||||||||||||||||||||||||||||||||||||||||||||||||||||||||||

Classical Tradition

II

Jewish Feminist Approaches to the Bible

Esther Fuchs

Jewish feminists have been studying the Bible since the late 1970s. Most of this study has been from a theological perspective because of the Bible's role as the bedrock of Jewish norms and attitudes. It continues to be a focus of theological debate to this day, as feminist thinkers from various denominations attempt to establish its meaning for Jewish women.

Unlike feminist theology, feminist biblical scholarship is interested not in an ethical, normative, prescriptive, or denominational agenda but rather in the literary, historical, ideological, and philosophical configurations of gender. In this regard, it is part of the ongoing project of both feminist biblical studies and Jewish feminist scholarship. Having previously outlined a theoretical approach to the field as a whole,[1] in this chapter I provide an overview of specifically Jewish feminist approaches to the Bible, including work that has already been done, as well as a map of trajectories for future research.

In an essay on Jewish feminist scholarship, I suggested that two theoretical trends structure the field of Jewish women's studies: critique and reconstruction.[2] Critique is the classic approach that was pioneered in the 1970s by theologians like Rachel Adler and Judith Plaskow, while reconstruction has dominated the field since its emergence in the late 1980s, to some extent as a response to the previous stage.[3]

As its label suggests, critique is concerned with feminist critical perspectives on Jewish texts, traditions, and practices. What it criticizes are usually the omissions, erasures, and misrepresentations of Jewish women's historical experiences and literary expressions. While the disciplines most relevant to such critiques are history and literature, other related disciplines in the social sciences and the humanities, from sociology to philosophy and from anthropology to film studies, became contexts for critical reflection. Reconstruction involves elaborating the minimal references to women in classical texts by shifting the focus to female lives and voices so as to expand the traces of memory in authoritative histories that took place in the late 1980s, as attention shifted to women as subjects, cultural producers, and agents of social change.

The earliest critiques in Biblical Studies were published throughout the 1980s. They were mostly written in response to Christian feminist interpretations of biblical literature that tried to "depatriarchalize" the Hebrew Bible by reconstructing it as an egalitarian text.[4] They did this by highlighting the contributions of women to the biblical tradition and their crucial roles in the lives of male leaders and heroes and in Israel's history as a people. Texts that described the oppression of women by men in both domestic and public spheres were framed as deviations from biblical social norms, indeed as "texts of terror" meant to evoke empathy and identification in the modern woman reader for the woman victim.[5] Contemporary readers were encouraged to condemn oppressive behaviors and to reconstruct their stories of female victims for collective ritual purposes.

Method

In the early 1980s I began to challenge both the method and the conclusions of this early phase of Christian theological interpretation. My earliest article challenged the rhetorical and archetypal criticism in feminist biblical interpretations, suggesting instead a critical reading.[6] Shifting that frame of reference reconfigured female biblical characters that had previously been taken for granted as representative of either female authenticity or historical reality as problems or subjects for feminist critical inquiry. Everything about them became problematic: their actions, their speech acts and motivations, their geographic and chronological placement, their names or namelessness, their appearance, to the extent that any details were offered, their relationships with others, their biographical trajectories, their relations with their families, communities, and nation. This approach made it possible to question the terms and conditions of the literary representation of the ways in which both heroic and villainous women were presented. Focusing on "heroines" like Esther and Ruth, I raised the question "who benefits?" (*cui bono*) from attributing to them the survival of the group, be it familial or national. I questioned the strategies attributed to these heroines, such as politeness and obedience, and characteristics such as youth and sexual attractiveness.

A second article sought to focus on villainous women, many of whom were characterized as deceptive.[7] Though I conceded that male characters also stood in some problematic relationship to language, their deceptions are both "motivated" and resolved; as a result, their deceptions are seen as temporary and accidental, rather than inherent in their gender.[8]

In my article "The Literary Characterization of Mothers and Sexual Politics in the Hebrew Bible," I suggested that we examine the positive and negative categories that characterized Christian treatments of this subject since the publication of Elizabeth Cady Stanton's *The Woman's Bible* in 1895.[9] Cady Stanton and her committee of interpreters distinguished between "positive" texts that had the potential to empower women and "negative" texts that presented them as unworthy of trust or public office. I noted that we should question what the biblical narrative presents as "positive," rather than accept it willy-nilly. In other words, I argued that biblical women reflect a patriarchal ideology that promotes the self-interest of the elite, including the scribes and editors who were responsible for the final literary product. A case in point is the characterization of mothers as producers and protectors of sons; they are secondary characters who disappear from the text as soon as their function is completed. I defined these literary dynamics as "sexual politics," suggesting that we read the Bible not merely as a reflection of an ultimate truth or historical reality but as a political text with gendered interests.[10]

As I was exploring the potential of a deconstructive approach to the Bible, other scholars, notably Carol Meyers, promoted a reconstructive approach. Though Meyers agreed that the Bible is the product of a small select group of male scribes, she saw its text not as political but rather as a (partial) reflection of historical reality. In order to fully appreciate the roles women played in ancient Israel, we needed a historical reconstruction of their daily lives, including their economic activities and their contributions to the subsistence and survival of the basic social unit, the extended family (*bet av*). Meyers's reconstruction of ancient Israelite women's lives went beyond the available reconstructions that were based for the most part on biblical evidence. Her basic argument was that, as an agrarian society, Israel depended on both the labor and the fecundity of women. Their productive and reproductive activities were therefore crucial to the survival of the economy of ancient Israel, where there was no absolute separation of private and public spheres.

Meyers reads the Genesis creation story in light of the economic pre-scription for women to increase their productivity and procreativity. In addition to her economic roles, "Eve" (the ancient Israelite woman) was also charged with producing the future labor force. Besides caring for and raising infants, women had distinct religious duties and privileges. Most significant, Meyers argues that, in premonarchic times, as described for the most part in the book of Judges, women had leadership roles in the political and religious life of the nation. She summarizes her analysis as follows: "The Eve of the premonarchic era has become visible: the peasant woman now seen is hardly the exploited, subservient creature imagined by those who have been influenced by the androcentricity of the bibli-cal canon and by the misogyny of much of the postbiblical tradition."[11] Meyers sees the ascent of male authority and dominance as a historical accident that is the result of the urbanization of Israelite society and the centralization of religious life. In the prophetic period, the monarchy was the focus of criticism, and the vision of social justice and equality that emerged during this time harks back to Israel's origins when women were autonomous, powerful, and equal to men.

Though few scholars elaborated or extended Meyers's method, the re-constructive approach emerged as the dominant interpretive theory in the 1990s. Using a feminist literary critical method known as gynocriticism that had been applied mostly for reading modern female-authored texts, Ilana Pardes sought to reconstruct the authentic voices and experiences of biblical women from speeches and discourses attributed to them in the text. Pardes's reconstruction suggested that biblical women's speeches reveal a protofeminist countertradition, one that asserts women's power over their male counterparts.[12] Women's voices are interpreted as isolated instanciations of a prebiblical, antipatriarchal tradition that can somehow be reconstructed through an astute application of the right interpretive methodology. Thus, for example, Pardes focuses on Eve's naming speeches as expressions of maternal power and authority. Pardes associates female naming speeches with earlier mythological phases in which mother god-desses were described as the creators of life on earth. She interprets Eve's naming speech as transgressive and insurrectionary, nothing less than a critique of monotheism's underlying patriarchal presuppositions. Pardes reconstructs the passages that scholars attribute to the J source as an an-tipatriarchal countertradition, much as Harold Bloom conceived J as au-thored by a woman.[13] Pardes then applies her gynocritic method to the story of Rachel's rebellion against her father, Laban, and reconstructs a story analogous to Jacob's dream, with Rachel dreaming of liberation from hierarchy. In a similar light, Pardes reads Zipporah, Moses' wife, as exemplifying a female struggle for deliverance through association with the mythological figure of the goddess Isis.

The reconstructive approach was adopted as well by Tikva Frymer-Kensky, who is best known for her important book on ancient Near Eastern goddesses.[14] In much of her work Frymer-Kensky follows the "de-patriarchalizing" methodology articulated by Phyllis Trible in the late 1970s. Her reading of biblical women ignores the patriarchal frame and context, while focusing on female characters' motivation, resourcefulness, autonomy, wisdom, and devotion to God.[15] Frymer-Kensky reconstructs what she calls "women-stories" as egalitarian and diverse: some women are presented as heroes and some as victims. Her theological reading pushes beyond Trible's more individualistic reading, focusing on women's contributions to Israel's national life. She divides the "women-stories" into four categories: women as victors, victims, virgins, and voices. Among the victors, Frymer-Kensky names Rebekah and the saviors of Exodus, as well as "evil" women like Delilah and Athaliah. She reconstructs the stories of Jephthah's daughter, the concubine of Gibeah (Judges 19), Bathsheba, and David's daughter Tamar as victim stories, while Dinah, Jacob's daughter, Queen Jezebel, Hagar, and Ruth are reconstructed as virgin stories. These categories reflect various phases and aspects of Israel's collective life, its general ascent and strength or its chaos and political disintegration. Women-stories are reconstructed as symbolizing the collective national life, signifying the historical evolution of the people's relationship with its deity. While Pardes sees women's speeches as countertraditional and counterpatriarchal, Frymer-Kensky reconstructs them as expressing the identification of Israel's national collective consciousness as feminine. Frymer-Kensky's reconstructive reading, then, suggests that, despite its patriarchal history and social organization, the stories Israel told and recorded in the Bible were refracted through a female perspective.

Although these reconstructive interpretations were eloquent and influential, critical approaches to the Bible continued to assert themselves. A particularly articulate critique was generated by Alicia Ostriker, who suggests that the stories of the covenant and of monotheism are a coverup, obsessively told and retold stories of erased female power. Making use of psychoanalytic theory, she suggests that the numerous stories about the murder of women reflect the repression of the primal mother of all living, the Goddess, who in the Hebrew Bible is replaced by an asexual male

God. Ostriker reads the story of the binding of Isaac (*Akedah*) as a symbolic validation of the notion that the father, rather than the mother, is the author of birth and the producer of life. She goes on to argue that the recounting of Sarah's death so soon afterward is the literal trace of the elimination of the mother in this critical moment of transition to patriarchy. She also reads the silencing and subsequent death and burial of Miriam in psychoanalytic terms as the trace of the repression of the woman as the potential leader of the people. Miriam's punishment, death, and burial point to the repression of the great mother as the people's prophet, poet, and leader. Ostriker asks: "Is it possible that the whole story of canonicity, the whole story of authority in our culture, is intimately bound up with the repressed Mother, shimmering and struggling at the luminal threshold of consciousness, against whom the Father must anxiously defend himself?"[16] She sees the insistence on obedience to detailed rules and regulations, the tenor and style of biblical laws, as yet another symptom of the mother's repression and the father's obsessive attempt to assert his authority.

While Ostriker takes a psychoanalytic approach, Athalya Brenner uses linguistic and philological methodologies in her book *The Intercourse of Knowledge*, where she argues forcefully that biblical language as such reveals patriarchal assumptions. Brenner highlights the ways in which biblical language constructs men as subjects and agents and women as passive sexual objects. She reads the very terms for man and woman (*zakar* and *neqevah*) as indicating the male cultural function (*zkr* means "remembrance, memory") and the female biological function (*nqv* meaning "hole, orifice"). Verbs denoting love and sexual desire are rarely attributed to women, who usually appear as objects of male sexual desire. The language of procreation and birth confirms a patriarchal ideology that attributes to women a natural desire for offspring and motherhood (as I argued in my article "The Literary Characterization of Mothers and Sexual Politics in the Biblical Narrative"), thus portraying motherhood as a natural and biological state of being, rather than a literary strategy. Brenner concludes that the language of incest taboos and other sexual transgression laws reflect a patriarchal social order. Men are by and large described as autonomous sexual agents, while women are presented as dependent on male owners, who are to be legally compensated in case of any sexual violence aimed at the female victim.[17] Biblical language presents female sexuality as dangerous and in need of strict male control.

Postbiblical Scholarship

Since the early 1990s, Jewish feminist scholarship has challenged the tendency to present Christianity as representing the social liberation of women from the oppression of Jewish social norms. Several essays in an anthology edited by Amy-Jill Levine question the common characterization of Jewish women as more restricted than and generally inferior in social status to pagan and Christian women. Adele Reinhartz, for example, argues that most of the women mentioned in the Gospels are Jewish. She notes that women like Mary and Martha were neither exceptional nor revolutionary in light of commonly held Pharisaic teachings.[18] Using a similar reconstructive method, Ross S. Kraemer suggests that Jewish women in the Greco-Roman period were likely to have benefited from both religious and classical education and that such educated Hellenistic women may have authored books focusing on Jewish heroines.[19] Kraemer goes on to argue that Jewish women's works did not survive because Christian monks controlled the copying and dissemination of literary compositions in early antiquity. Jewish women's literature survived only when it was preserved under the cloaks of pseudonymity and anonymity. Using a different reconstructive method that centers on interpretation, Amy-Jill Levine calls attention to apocryphal works, focusing on Jewish heroines like Judith, whose name means "Jewess."[20] Not only was the heroine depicted in the loftiest terms as courageous, pious and attractive, but she was also associated with the people of Israel. Levine sees the characterization of Judith as a symbolic self-presentation of national identity. Judith represents not only the nation's loftiest cultural ideals as a fearless and independent woman acting on her own initiative and confronting the redoubtable Holofernes, but feminist ideals, as well. The feminization of the people suggests a high degree of identification with and acceptance of women in leadership roles. In Levine's reconstructive approach, Jewish Hellenistic culture was no more patriarchal than the pagan or Christian cultures of the time.

Less sanguine about the social status of Jewish women and less certain about the national iconicity of literary heroines like Susannah, Judith, and Esther is Tal Ilan, whose method is critical rather than reconstructive. She argues that, despite the remarkable heroines' autonomy and power, none of them was shown to usurp a man's position in the biblically endorsed social hierarchy, nor did any one of them threaten the implied patriarchal order that is already embedded in the story of

Genesis.[21] While she agrees that these fictional narratives challenge the blatantly misogynous philosophy that was prevalent in the Greco-Roman period, they nevertheless conform to patriarchal norms. Susannah embodies the modest, pious, and faithful wife who prefers death to adultery. The book of Judith is the story of a woman who comes forward to save her people in an ad hoc capacity and then returns to her pious solitude as soon as she has accomplished her goal. To the extent that the book of Judith recommends female leadership, it does so cautiously, presenting it as a possibility *in extremis*, prompted by national crisis and the failure of traditional leadership. As for the book of Esther, which is the only one to mention female royal authority, the Jewish heroine is promoted to this position by virtue of her association with a king. Esther's leadership is also described as a promotion for a particular purpose, under extreme circumstances. Ilan's critical approach suggests that Esther, Judith, and Susannah serve as propaganda pieces to validate the reign of Salome Alexandra (Shelomzion) in Jerusalem toward the end of the first century B.C.E. Her critical reconstruction of women's status during the Second Temple period paints a complex picture, where class as well as gender determines the social status, privilege, opportunity, and advantage of being a woman in Jewish communities of the Greco-Roman period. In this sense, it far transcends simplistic Christian binary oppositions between Judaic and Christian communities during both religions' formative eras. Both reconstructive and critical approaches to postbiblical literature agree that any clear-cut distinction between the Jewish and Christian Bibles is apologetic and religiously biased.

Feminist Midrash

Feminist midrash, the creative and fictional reconstruction of biblical stories—though still in its infancy—holds out the promise of producing a contemporary response to the elaboration of classical rabbinic retellings of biblical stories.[22] Feminist midrashim usually seek to provide intention, motivation, psychological depth, and political relevance to the female characters. In this sense, all feminist midrashim are reconstructive. Yet, it is possible already at this early stage to distinguish between a reconstructive genre that elaborates the story line already sketched out by the biblical text and a critical genre that questions the biblical perspective on the female characters involved.

Within the reconstructive genre, Norma Rosen, for example, writes Sarah into the story of the binding of Isaac (*Akedah*) in such a way as to complete rather than challenge the original account.[23] According to Rosen, Sarah accompanied Abraham and Isaac on their way to the top of the mountain, rebuking and questioning God about his decision to sacrifice Isaac. In response to the determined mother, God finally relented and agreed to substitute a ram for her son. Rosen implies that Abraham misunderstood God's command and did not challenge it on either moral or theological grounds. In her telling, Sarah emerges as the true heroine of the *Akedah*, the one who has been put to the ultimate test of human endurance and who interpreted God's intentions correctly.

More recent reconstructive midrash focuses on marginal female characters whose presentation is cursory. Thus, for example, Jill Hammer imagines Elisheva, Aaron's wife, whose name and genealogy are fleetingly mentioned (Exod 6:23-25), as a principled and morally enlightened midwife.[24] Hammer describes Elisheva's moral struggles during the fateful night of the tenth plague. As the entire population of firstborn Egyptian sons is decimated, Elisheva is caught in a conflict of identities—as an Israelite she is reluctant to assist an Egyptian woman in labor who is crying out for her help; as a midwife, she owes allegiance to any and all women who need her. Finally, Elisheva decides in favor of her professional identity and saves the Egyptian woman's life. Hammer attributes to the imaginary Egyptian woman the name Putiel, which appears fleetingly in conjunction with Aaron's genealogy (Exod 6:25) and is therefore appropriately linked to Elisheva, who is also mentioned in the Aaronic genealogy. Hammer's midrash thus explains why these two women were mentioned in this context at all. They are mentioned because they acted in accordance with God's desires and Israel's highest principles. Elisheva risks her life for an Egyptian woman; in response to this self-sacrifice, Putiel decides to join the Israelites and flee from her own country. Like Rosen, Hammer does not question God's moral authority as the final arbiter of truth and justice, nor does she question the national ideology that represents the Egyptians as the Israelites' mortal enemies.

This kind of questioning, typical of the critical midrash, is nicely exemplified by Athalya Brenner's creative retellings of biblical women's stories.[25] In her midrashic recreations of foreign women, Brenner is especially careful not to suggest that they merely join the Israelites' struggle against their oppressors. Sensitive to contemporary feminist theory, she invents for foreign women a biography of their own, rooted in their own culture and land. Thus, Rahab, the Canaanite, is imagined as a Canaanite noble-woman who was forced into prostitution by the foreign occupation of her country and as a Palestinian contemporary woman who has been reduced to poverty as a result of the Israeli occupation of Jericho. Rahab both witnesses and experiences the invasion of the Israelites/Israelis as an unstoppable historical storm that leaves her and her family destitute and helpless. The national conflict in its ancient and contemporary dimensions is construed as a territorial dispute between male warriors on both sides. As a Canaanite, the biblical Rahab is the victim of both Jews and Muslims, who rejected the ancient Near Eastern pagan goddess. On the other hand, the contemporary Rahab is clearly victimized as a woman and as a colonized native by Israeli male aggression.

In a similar manner, Brenner challenges the rabbinic midrash that depicts Orpah, the Moabite, as the mother of Goliath. Rather than denigrate Orpah as the ancestress of Israel's prototypical Philistine enemy, Brenner's midrash recreates Orpah as a sympathetic and vulnerable character, with a biography, a perspective, and a voice of her own. Orpah's story suggests that she stayed in Moab not because she did not care for Ruth and Naomi but because she was forced to stay behind for economic reasons. The Moabite who did not leave her country during the great famine outshines Ruth, who did give up her family and her country to follow her mother-in-law to Judah and a better fate. Brenner's midrash is critical of both the original biblical marginalization of Orpah and subsequent rabbinic derogations of her national otherness.

Modern Hebrew Literature

The retelling of biblical stories by Hebrew authors since the 18th century that has been defined as modern midrash played an important role in the emergence of Israeli secular culture.[26] Hebrew women poets, secular socialist pioneers in the early 1920s like Rachel (Bluwstein), adopted the names and personas of biblical women in an act of radical self-invention in the newly regained land of Israel. Yocheved bat Miriam, whose very name, "the daughter of Miriam," denotes an imaginary direct line from the biblical prophet, is perhaps best known among a whole generation of women poets for her midrashic recreations of biblical women. Her poems about Eve, Hagar, and Miriam modernize their subjects in such a way as to represent their struggles in intellectual and sexual terms familiar to and shared by modern secular women. As a Zionist pioneer woman, Bat Miriam, like other women poets of the 1920s, sought to validate her connection to the land by feminizing its landscape and by inventing the persona of a daughter addressing her old/new land in terms that indicate a relationship equal to that of the returning sons. Bat Miriam's midrashic poems reinvent the land, which was already feminized in the Bible, in terms that enable women to participate equally in the national rebirth.[27] Reconstructive poetic midrash repeatedly alludes to biblical female leaders, prophets, and poets in an attempt to legitimize the revolutionary use of Hebrew as a secular literary language by women who were traditionally denied access to the Holy Tongue and who were only reluctantly admitted into the coterie of intellectuals at the turn of the century.[28]

Contemporary women poets who emerged in the 1960s and 1970s as part of the "New Wave" tend to use a critical idiom in their poetic midrash. Not only are the references to the Bible more allusive and oblique, but they tend to focus on ambiguous female characters like Potiphar's wife and Jezebel.[29] The critical idiom in the work of Dalia Ravikovitch and Ona Wallach targets biblical typologies, models, and concepts—including the land of Israel—in ways that question rather than elaborate their original representation in the biblical text.[30] The critical midrash of contemporary women poets—and authors—challenges the Zionist representations of biblical prototypes of previous generations. The contemporary midrash seeks to understand rather than reject the "enemy" (in both biblical and contemporary terms), using biblical texts to reinvent rather than to repeat literary configurations of national identity.[31]

History

While feminist biblical scholarship is often studied in relation to Elizabeth Cady Stanton's protofeminist interpretation, little has so far been done on Grace Aguilar's interpretation, which preceded it by several decades. As suggested earlier, Cady Stanton's approach to the Bible rejected "negative" portrayals of women as historically inaccurate, ancient or primitive, and Oriental or Semitic, thus reproducing the anti-Semitic canard regarding Judaism's inferior treatment of women.[32] It is precisely this stereotyping of the Hebrew Bible as the less enlightened and more antiquated testament that Grace Aguilar sought to debunk in her massive *Women of Israel.* Aguilar's two-volume book focuses on biblical law as protective of rather than oppressive to women. She highlights the crucial contribution biblical women made to their societies and culture in their capacity as educators, poets, and mothers. Her reading of Deborah emphasizes that public and private activities need not be in conflict with one another and that the women of Israel performed well in both domains. Aguilar raises the position of mothers like Jochebed and Leah to the level of their famous sons. Throughout her treatise, she is equally adamant about the privileged position women held and about God's abiding love for and protection of the Jewish people in general and women in particular. Aguilar presents women as conduits for God's special love for His chosen people. Her repeated emphasis on God's love is clearly intended as a challenge to anti-Semitic stereotyping of the "Old Testament" God as an angry and violent deity in contrast to the Christian God of love.

Aguilar points up the high status women enjoyed in ancient Israel as prophetesses. In her commentary on Deborah, she highlights the prophet's reference to herself as a "mother in Israel" (Judg 5:7), rather than as a prophet.[33] Aguilar explains that Deborah clearly valued her maternal role as much as her public role. In addition, she claims that the prophet chose to emphasize the more private domestic role out of humility, which she interprets as the sign of a truly chosen (wo)man of God. In her commentary on Huldah, Aguilar argues that during the period of the monarchy all women were entitled to a high level of education and were free to engage in intellectual pursuits.[34] It is clear that Aguilar seeks not only to substantiate her repudiation of the anti-Judaic singling out of Jewish women as the more oppressed class but also to legitimize her own career as a woman of letters. Aguilar concludes that modern women, both gentile and Jewish, seem to be less privileged than their biblical predecessors. She explains that Jewish women's inferior status is not the result of any moral flaw in Judaism as a religion but rather a symptom of a nation in exile. Aguilar's interpretation of Deborah and Huldah implies that modern Jewish women's demand for education is grounded in Judaism's foundational texts and as such should not be dismissed by the current male leadership. As a leading figure of the Jewish European Enlightenment, Aguilar sought through her biblical interpretations to legitimize the modernization of Judaism, while at the same time rejecting assimilation and missionary pressures.[35] Her interpretation of female prophecy and prayer as manifestations of poetic creativity and intellectual sophistication suggests that women's modern avocation and vocation as writers is grounded in biblical literature. She thus speaks not only on behalf of Jewish women but for all women who aspired to write in Victorian England. The Romantic model of antischolastic, personal, and emotional poetic expression—which Aguilar uses in her own poetry—is naturalized and universalized in her creative interpretation of Hannah's and Esther's prayers.[36]

Aguilar's focus on women's religious experience as the true locus of Jewish practice anticipates contemporary Orthodox and Reform reconstructions of feminist theology.[37] While *Women of Israel* is clearly a product of 19th-century Anglo-Jewish Enlightenment and Victorian ideologies of female authenticity and propriety, it anticipates recent reinterpretations of the Bible in particular and Judaism in general as female-centered. Her sensitive responses to anti-Judaic charges regarding biblical women can be helpful even today to feminist Bible scholars, who continue to be scandalized by similar attitudes in contemporary feminist biblical scholarship.[38]

Conclusion

While Jewish feminist readings of the Bible are diverse and often indistinguishable from non-Jewish readings, I have tried to show that they have a unique interpretive philosophy. Most apparent is the understanding that the Hebrew Bible is not merely the first act in a two act play but rather the full drama. The text is both endorsed and rejected by feminist readers, but in either case it is not considered to be inferior to a sequel or second set of scriptures. In this chapter, I have outlined the ways in which recuperation and resistance feed each other as major trends in Jewish feminist interpretation. Neither of these approaches is more or less authentically Jewish. Both can be discerned in biblical and postbiblical scholarship and emerge in creative readings, in feminist midrash, and in modern Hebrew literature. As such, they testify to the ongoing dialogue within Jewish feminist studies in general. Historically, the recuperative or reconstructive approach has its roots in the 19th century, while the critical approach is inspired by contemporary reading methods. Both the historical and the theoretical origins of these approaches deserve closer attention than I could possibly offer here, and much remains to be done by way of defining and evaluating Jewish feminist interpretation of the Bible.

The multilayered perspective that includes several historical and geographical foci will probably emerge as one of the most consistent characteristics of a specifically Jewish feminist interpretation. The ability to read any given text from several locations and several angles all at the same time reflects not only the complexity of the original text but also the ability to appreciate the multilayered nature of Judaism. Though this area has grown remarkably in the past two decades, much remains to be done. What I have offered here is a first step toward a broader and deeper appreciation of this important area of study.

NOTES

1. Esther Fuchs, "Feminist Approaches to the Hebrew Bible," in *The Hebrew Bible: New Insights and Scholarship*, ed. Frederick E. Greenspahn (New York: New York University Press, 2008), pp. 76–98.

2. Esther Fuchs, "Female and Jewish: Critique and Reconstruction," *Shofar* 17:2 (Spring 1999): 1–7.

3. For examples, see the selections in Susannah Heschel, *On Being a Jewish Feminist* (New York: Schocken Books, 1983).

4. Phyllis Trible, *God and the Rhetoric of Sexuality* (Minneapolis: Fortress Press, 1978).

5. Phyllis Trible, *Texts of Terror: Literary-Feminist Readings of Biblical Narratives* (Minneapolis: Fortress Press, 1984).

6. Esther Fuchs, "Status and Role of Female Heroines in the Biblical Narrative," *Mankind Quarterly* 23:2 (1982): 149–60, reprinted in *Women in the Hebrew Bible*, ed. Alice Bach (New York and London: Routledge, 1999), pp. 77–84. On the rabbinic or distinctly Jewish sources of deconstruction as a theory of reading, see Susan A. Handelman, *The Slayers of Moses: The Emergence of Rabbinic Interpretation in Modern Literary Theory* (Albany: State University of New York Press, 1982).

7. Esther Fuchs, "Who Is Hiding the Truth? Deceptive Women and Biblical Androcentrism," in *Feminist Perspectives on Biblical Scholarship*, ed. Adela Yarbro Collins (Missoula: Society of Biblical Literature and Scholars Press, 1985), pp. 137–44.

8. See also Esther Fuchs, "'For I Have the Way of Women:' Deception, Gender and Ideology in the Biblical Narrative," in *Reasoning With the Foxes: Female Wit in a World of Male Power*, ed. J. Cheryl Exum and Joanna W.H. Van Wijk-Bos (*Semeia* 42 [1988]), pp. 68–83.

9. In *Feminist Perspectives on Biblical Scholarship*, ed. Adela Y. Collins, pp. 117–36; reprinted in *Narrative Research on the Hebrew Bible* (*Semeia* 46), ed. Miri Amihai, George Coats, and Anne M. Solomon (Atlanta: Society of Biblical Literature, 1989), pp. 151–68.

10. See Esther Fuchs, *Sexual Politics in the Biblical Narrative: Reading the Hebrew Bible as a Woman* (Sheffield: Sheffield Academic Press, 2000).

11. Carol Meyers, *Discovering Eve: Ancient Israelite Women in Context* (Oxford: Oxford University Press, 1988), p. 189.

12. Ilana Pardes, *Countertraditions in the Bible: A Feminist Approach* (Cambridge, MA: Harvard University Press, 1992).

13. Harold Bloom, *The Book of J*, translated by David Rosenberg and interpreted by Harold Bloom (New York: Grove Weidenfeld, 1990).

14. Tikva Frymer-Kensky, *In the Wake of the Goddesses: Women, Culture and the Transformation of Pagan Myth* (New York: Free Press, 1992).

15. Tikva Frymer-Kensky, *Reading the Women of the Bible* (New York: Schocken Books, 2002).

16. Alicia Ostriker, *Feminist Revision and the Bible* (Oxford and Cambridge: Blackwell, 1992), p. 50.

17. Athalya Brenner, *The Intercourse of Knowledge: On Gendering Desire and 'Sexuality' in the Hebrew Bible* (Leiden: E. J. Brill, 1997), pp. 136–37.

18. Adele Reinhartz, "From Narrative to History: The Resurrection of Mary and Martha," in *"Women Like This": New Perspectives on Jewish Women in the Greco-Roman World*, ed. Amy-Jill Levine (Atlanta: Scholars Press, 1991), pp. 161–84.

19. Ross S. Kraemer, "Women's Authorship of Jewish and Christian Literature in the Greco-Roman Period," in *Women Like This*, ed. A.-J. Levine, pp. 221–42.

20. Amy-Jill Levine, "Sacrifice and Salvation: Otherness and Domestication in the Book of Judith," in *Women in the Hebrew Bible*, ed. Alice Bach, pp. 367–76.

21. Tal Ilan, *Integrating Women into Second Temple History* (Tübingen: Mohr Siebeck, 1999), pp. 127–54.

22. For a critique of rabbinic midrash, see Leila Leah Bronner, *From Eve to Esther: Rabbinic Reconstructions of Biblical Women* (Louisville: Westminster John Knox Press, 1994), and Judith R. Baskin, *Midrashic Women: Formations of the Feminine in Rabbinic Literature* (Hanover, NH: University Press of New England and Brandeis University Press, 2002).

23. Norma Rosen, *Biblical Women Unbound: Counter-Tales* (Philadelphia: Jewish Publication Society, 1996), pp. 46–60.

24. Jill Hammer, *Sisters at Sinai: New Tales of Biblical Women* (Philadelphia: Jewish Publication Society, 2001), pp. 107–13.

25. Athalya Brenner, *I Am . . . , Biblical Women Tell Their Own Stories* (Minneapolis: Fortress Press, 2005).

26. David C. Jacobson, *Modern Midrash: The Retelling of Traditional Jewish Narratives by Twentieth Century Hebrew Writers* (Albany: State University of New York Press, 1987).

27. Wendy I. Zierler, *And Rachel Stole the Idols: The Emergence of Modern Hebrew Women's Writing* (Detroit: Wayne State University Press, 2004), pp. 169–86.

28. See Iris Parush, *Reading Jewish Women: Marginality and Modernization in Nineteenth Century Eastern European Jewish Society*, trans. Saadya Sternberg

(Hanover, NH: University Press of New England and Brandeis University Press, 2004).

29. E.g., Shirley Kaufman, Galit Hasan-Rokem, and Tamar S. Hess, eds. *Hebrew Feminist Poems From Antiquity to the Present: A Bilingual Anthology* (New York: The Feminist Press, 1999), p. 91.

30. Ruth Kartun-Blum, *Profane Scriptures: Reflections on the Dialogue With the Bible in Modern Hebrew Poetry* (Cincinnati: Hebrew Union College Press, 1999).

31. Miriyam Glazer, *Dreaming the Actual: Contemporary Fiction and Poetry by Israeli Women Writers* (Albany: State University of New York Press, 2000), e.g., pp. 3 and 13.

32. See Judith Plaskow, "Anti-Judaism in Feminist Christian Interpretation," in *Searching the Scriptures: A Feminist Introduction*, ed. Elizabeth S. Fiorenza (New York: Crossroad, 1993), pp. 117–29.

33. Grace Aguilar, *Women of Israel* (New York: D. Appleton, 1845), vol. 1, pp. 218–26.

34. Ibid., vol. 2, pp. 71–79.

35. Cf. Michael Galchinsky, *The Origin of the Modern Jewish Woman Writer: Romance and Reform in Victorian England* (Detroit: Wayne State University Press, 1996), pp. 135–89.

36. Cynthia Scheinberg, *Women's Poetry and Religion in Victorian England: Jewish Identity and Christian Culture* (Cambridge: Cambridge University Press, 2002), pp. 179–83.

37. Rochelle L. Millen, "Her Mouth Is Full of Wisdom: Reflections on Jewish Feminist Theology," in *Women Remaking American Feminism*, ed. Riv-Ellen Prell (Detroit: Wayne State University Press, 2007), pp. 27–50.

38. Amy-Jill Levine, "Discharging Responsibility in Matthean Jesus: Biblical Law and the Hammorrhaging Woman," in *A Feminist Companion to Matthew*, ed. Amy-Jill Levine and Marianne Blickenstaff (Sheffield: Sheffield Academic Press, 2001), pp. 70–87.

2

Women and Torah Study in *Aggadah*

Dvora E. Weisberg

The rabbi and his wife retired for the evening. Unbeknownst to them, one of the rabbi's students was hiding under their bed. When the student was discovered, his teacher angrily questioned him: "What do you think you are doing?" The student replied, "This too is Torah, and I need to learn."[1]

This story, found in the Babylonian Talmud, offers several lessons. The most obvious one is that the behavior of rabbis, including their sexual habits, is viewed by their disciples—and by the editorial voice of the Babylonian Talmud—as Torah, just like the teachings they convey in the house of study. A good student, a student who wants to immerse himself in his teacher's Torah, absorbs not only the teacher's formal lessons but also the lessons conveyed through the teacher's behavior, even if it means following the teacher into the bedroom.

A second, more subtle message is taught through this story. Rabbis and their students are engaged in an intimate relationship, the object of their mutual desire being Torah. This relationship trumps the intimate relationship between the rabbi and his wife. When the rabbi in question confronts his student, he indicates that the student's presence is intrusive. At that moment, the three actors in the drama are triangled; the rabbi's reaction suggests that the student is the outsider, while the rabbi and his wife are paired. Through his reply, "This too is Torah, and I need to learn," the student proposes a different way of seeing the relationship. He and his teacher are now allied, for together they are engaged in the study of Torah; the rabbi's wife is now the outsider. The sexual act, which is too private to be shared with a third party, is transformed; the proper behavior of a sage during the sexual act is Torah, something meant to be analyzed by student and teacher. The wife, by virtue of her gender, is not a suitable study partner for her husband; she is displaced by both Torah and her husband's student. She is now the intruder, the unwanted, unnecessary outsider.

This story supports the argument that, in excluding women from the study of Torah,[2] rabbinic culture marked women as Other. While this is not the only way in which rabbinic Judaism differentiates between men and women,[3] it is one of the most powerful. Rabbinic culture idealizes the study of Torah, naming it the highest calling and most rewarding endeavor open to Jews. In doing so, it dismisses, to a greater or lesser degree, those who do not engage in the study of Torah.[4] Every male Jew is a potential student of Torah, but study by women is ignored or discouraged.

Even a woman who learns Torah has no place in rabbinic circles. Nowhere is this more evident than in the stories told of Beruriah, the only woman described in classic rabbinic documents as a Torah "scholar." Beruriah is said to have learned "three hundred laws from three hundred teachers."[5] In one source, her legal ruling is said to have been preferable to that of her brother.[6] At the same time, Beruriah is never shown learning Torah from or with a rabbi. Nor does she teach, except through dismissive comments.

Moreover, women's knowledge of Torah is viewed by the Babylonian Talmud (Bavli) as problematic and even dangerous. In the Mishnah, one sage counsels that women should not be taught Torah, for, even when taught, women transform Torah into frivolity (*tiflut*) or worse.[7] In various talmudic stories, women are portrayed using Torah for their own purposes, often at odds with rabbis and rabbinic law.

In this chapter, we consider the relation of women and Torah as portrayed in nonlegal material in classical rabbinic texts (*aggadah*).[8] We analyze aggadic texts about women and Torah and discuss contemporary scholarship on *aggadah* and gender issues. We conclude with a brief consideration of the future of gender studies in relation to aggadah.

Stories About Women Studying Torah: Interpreting From Silence

Rabbinic literature is replete with stories about rabbis and Torah study. There are stories about rabbis' first exposure to Torah study, including stories about how individuals overcame serious disadvantages—illiteracy, poverty, parental opposition—to become great sages. Scholars are frequently portrayed in discussion with their teachers, students, and colleagues. Many of these stories contain valuable lessons about the centrality of Torah study and warnings about proper and improper ways to interact with one's colleagues.

Women are almost uniformly absent from these stories. Legal discussions about women and Torah study do not segue into stories that illustrate the danger of teaching women Torah or highlight individual women who did study Torah. Instead, legal statements about women and Torah study end abruptly, moving to other issues. Commenting on the obligation of a father to teach his son Torah, the Babylonian Talmud offers interpretations that contend that women are not required to teach their sons or to learn on their own and that men are not obligated to teach women. Rather than offering any stories or incidents to elaborate on these issues, it then proceeds to explore the problem that arises when both a man and his son need to study Torah but there are funds to finance only one education.[9] Similarly, women's exemption from the study of Torah is used as support for their exemption from other commandments without any discussion of women actually studying Torah.[10]

In *Mishnah Sotah* 3:4, we learn that a woman may drink from the waters of jealousy (Numbers 5:11ff.) and not feel the effects immediately "if she has some merit." This unspecified merit may delay the impact of the waters as long as three years, according to the Mishnah. In response to this teaching, Ben Azzai asserts that "a man must teach his daughter Torah, so that if she drinks [the waters of jealousy and experiences no adverse effects] she will know that her merit is the source of the delay." The Mishnah continues, "Rabbi Eliezer says, 'Anyone who teaches his daughter Torah teaches her frivolity.'" The ensuing talmudic discussion focuses on the length of the delay caused by merit and then asks "what type of merit" the Mishnah imagines a woman might have.[11] It quickly dismisses the possibility that the merit could be for studying Torah, since a woman would be in the category of "one who is not commanded but performs," implying that the merit involved would be inadequate to counteract the waters of jealousy. The Talmud concludes that a woman might be protected by the merit of the commandments she has performed and then goes on to compare the merit afforded by Torah study to that afforded by the performance of other commandments. There is no discussion of a woman's studying Torah—even though the possibility has been raised—and no elaboration of Ben Azzai's exhortation that fathers teach their daughters Torah. While there is a brief discussion of Rabbi Eliezer's statement, it offers no textual support for his contention that teaching women Torah leads to frivolity.

Classical rabbinic literature shows no interest in the subject of women as students of Torah. While women occasionally cite Torah, we are rarely given any sense of how these women came to their knowledge of Torah. The "exceptional" women cited in contemporary feminist discussions of women in rabbinic literature have no "paper trail"; we never learn how they came to possess the information they offer. We can assume that some women learned some Torah at home, as a result of proximity to learned male relatives. Imma Shalom, explaining to her husband, Rabbi Eliezer, how she knew that his prostration and prayer had led to her brother's death, says, "I received this tradition from the house of my father's father—all the gates are locked except the gate of oppression."[12] There is no reason to read this statement as an indication that Imma Shalom studied formally at home; she may have learned a number of traditions by virtue of growing up in a rabbinic household. Similarly, when some women are taken captive and appear before Rabbi Hanina to testify regarding their captivity, he remarks, "They are obviously the daughters of a scholar."[13] The women, who are in fact the daughters of a prominent Babylonian rabbi (Samuel), are "learned" enough to stage their appearance and testimony in a way that benefits them by protecting their status as marriageable virgins. Neither the rabbis in the story nor the Talmud speculate on the manner in which Samuel's daughters learned the law that allowed them to maintain their status. There is no way to know whether the observation "They are obviously the daughters of a scholar" indicates that rabbis' daughters were formally educated by their fathers or simply suggests that proximity to rabbis might afford a woman some informal access to Torah.[14] Similarly, rabbis' daughters are sometimes mentioned as women knowledgeable in matters of law concerning food preparation, and this knowledge is attributed to the fact that the woman in question had a rabbi-father who was meticulous.[15] We are left to assume that women raised in rabbinic households somehow acquired knowledge, but, again, the Talmud displays no interest in how that acquisition occurred or what part rabbis played in educating their daughters.

Rabbinic literature displays a similar lack of interest in the scholarly beginnings of Beruriah, the woman most often cited in the quest for learned women in early rabbinic circles. The most impressive testimony to Beruriah's erudition is found in *b. Pesaḥim* 62b, where she is described by Rabbi Yohanan to Rabbi Simlai as a person who "learned three hundred laws in one day from three hundred teachers" and as someone who devoted years to the study of a particularly challenging work, *Sefer Yuḥasin.* The Talmud records this impressive feat without comment, offering it primarily as a snub to the ambitious and overconfident Rabbi Simlai. There is no discussion of Beruriah's Torah study; the passage offers no hint as to why she chose to study Torah or why so many rabbis were willing to teach her, beyond identifying her as the daughter of one rabbi and the wife of another.[16] It is fair to assert that the Talmud displays no interest whatsoever in the study of Torah by women, which the Talmud views as anomalous at best and problematic at worst.

Aggadah *and Gender: Thirty Years of Scholarship*

In considering the relationship of women to Torah study, we turn to recent scholarship on *aggadah* and gender. In the 1970s and 1980s, there was a surge of interest in discussions about women in classical Jewish texts. Early studies[17] that mined rabbinic literature for insights into the status of women in Judaism focused on *halakhah*, attempting to describe the legal status of women in Judaism.[18] At the same time, there was some interest in *aggadah*, since *aggadah* could be cited to support competing views of Jewish attitudes toward women. Rabbinic stories were also cited as evidence for the existence of extraordinary Jewish women, women whose actions did not conform to gender stereotypes. For those who argued for a broader role for women in Jewish life, these stories were inspirational. For those who defended the status quo or those who condemned Judaism as patriarchal or antiwoman, these stories were exceptions that proved the rule.

What these articles and books had in common was a tendency to read rabbinic stories as if they were historical sources.[19] This approach was adopted by both academics[20] and nonacademics.[21] There was also a willingness to read stories out of their literary context and to read stories uncritically, using *aggadah* to create "biography." In fairness, this approach had been used by important scholars of rabbinics, including Louis Finkelstein and, in his early work, Jacob Neusner, and was not called into question until the early 1980s.[22] At the same time, it rendered early forays into the topic somewhat questionable as serious scholarship.

Explorations of the feminine in *aggadah* in a critical, scholarly context are a more recent development. These studies offer a varied approach to rabbinic *aggadah*. In *Mine and Yours Are Hers*, Tal Ilan considers the possibility of using *aggadah* as a source for recovering women's history. Ilan begins by discussing the attempts of other scholars to "recover" specific women—Beruriah (identified at times as the wife of Rabbi Meir and/ or the daughter of Rabbi Hananiah ben Teradion, Palestinian rabbis in the 2nd century C.E.) and Rachel, the wife of Rabbi Akiba. Ilan's discussion of the work of other scholars focuses on the importance of reading rabbinic *aggadah* critically, recognizing that the literary goals of redactors are paramount and that these stories are often "a-historical."[23]

Despite her critique of her colleagues' work, Ilan believes that rabbinic literature can be a valuable resource for scholars of women's history.[24] While most of her book focuses on legal traditions, she titles one chapter "Extracting Women's History from *Aggadah*." Ilan acknowledges that *aggadah* consists mainly of stories and that these stories are first and foremost literary compositions that should be read utilizing tools developed for literary analysis. Nevertheless, Ilan argues, "Having discredited *aggadah* as worthless for historical investigation, I now wish to suggest that it can nonetheless be used as a reliable historical tool for the study of Jewish women's history."[25] Ilan suggests that rabbinic stories primarily employ "free, male, adult Jews" as characters, employing slaves, women, and gentiles only when those personal traits are "necessary" for the story. On the basis of this argument, Ilan claims that

> since in purely fictional literature a women [*sic*] would be mentioned only if she has a specific feminine function, one mentioned in a midrashic tradition, is probably historical if she appears within an episode or story to which she is not inherently critical or where her role could just as well have been played by a male.[26]

Ilan's thesis is an intriguing one and allows her to make historical claims about some female characters in individual *aggadot*. However, even if one were to accept Ilan's criteria, her method offers extremely limited results. One cannot dispute Ilan's conclusion that even if she could collect all the *aggadot* that meet her criteria for containing historical information, they would "not yield a vast amount of information about real Jewish women of the rabbinic period."[27] Whatever promise *aggadah* holds for those interested in Jewish women, that promise is not of great significance for those concerned with women's history.

Few scholars share Ilan's optimism on recovering history from *aggadah*. A more common approach focuses on literary analysis of rabbinic stories and seeks to draw insights into rabbinic culture from these sto-ries. This approach is used by Daniel Boyarin and Jeffrey Rubenstein,[28] and elicits valuable observations about the centrality of Torah in rabbinic culture and the apparent conflict between the study of Torah and mar-riage and family. Boyarin's *Carnal Israel: Reading Sex in Talmudic Culture* focuses on rabbinic culture's understanding of sexuality and the body. In his analysis, Boyarin considers many *aggadot* about marriage, female ori-gins, and desire.

Boyarin argues that rabbinic literature adopts a positive attitude toward female desire and sexuality within marriage.[29] At the same time, he also acknowledges that the Babylonian Talmud highlights the tension between a life devoted to the study of Torah and family life. In particular, a set of stories in *b. Ketubot* 62b-63a offer ample evidence that the redactors of the Babylonian Talmud realized that devotion to Torah often required that a man abandon his wife and children for long periods of time, sometimes resulting in poverty, infertility, and emotional distress for wives.[30]

In his acknowledgments, Boyarin explains that his book had its origins in a discussion about "Beruria [*sic*] and the study of Torah for women in the Talmudic period."[31] The chapter of the book that resulted from that conversation, chapter 6, begins with the statement that "classical Talmudic Judaism denies women access to the most valued practice of the culture, the study of Torah."[32] Boyarin argues that opposition to women studying Torah was particularly strong and univocal in Babylonia. Boyarin reads the Babylonian Talmud's stories about Beruriah in light of Rabbi Eliezer's dictum "A man who teaches his daughter Torah teaches her lascivious-ness," for, despite Beruriah's learning, she comes to a bad end.[33]

Boyarin's work offers readers a nuanced view of sexuality and gender in rabbinic culture. It also reinforces our sense of a sharp dichotomy be-tween men and women in rabbinic culture, particularly in the area of To-rah study. Women are not potential students and teachers of Torah—the only woman named as a student of Torah is eventually revealed as just another frivolous woman—and marriage and family are described in op-position to devotion to Torah.

Jeffrey Rubenstein's work offers a model for reading Talmudic stories, insisting that these stories or *aggadot* should be read in the broader con-text of the often halakhic passages (*sugyot*) into which they are embed-ded. Reading stories in context, Rubenstein argues, allows us to under-stand the ways in which stories in the Babylonian Talmud were reworked from earlier narrative sources. Furthermore, reading in context allows us to appreciate the insights these stories offer about the rabbinic culture that produced them.[34]

The stories that Rubenstein analyzes focus on Torah and rabbinic authority. Women occasionally make appearances in these stories as the wives, sisters, and daughters of rabbis. Rubenstein considers the actions and words of these women as important elements in the literary units he analyzes,[35] but his work makes it clear that women are marginal figures in rabbinic stories. This marginalization of women is evident in another of Rubenstein's books, *The Culture of the Babylonian Talmud*. In that book, Rubenstein explores that culture through analysis of stories about rabbis that consider the study of Torah, the rabbinic academy, lineage, and relations between rabbis and nonrabbis. One chapter focuses on rabbis and wives. Rubenstein argues that

> Torah study, an activity pursued exclusively by men, inevitably created tensions for the sages in relation to their wives and families. Because women did not participate in the dominant aspects of rabbinic life—study, collegiality, master-disciple relationships—they could not share in the concerns most important to the sages.[36]

Not only were women excluded from the study of Torah, they were seen—as wives and as symbols of family life—as distractions from the study of Torah.[37]

Rubenstein's analysis of *b. Ketubot* 62b-63a underscores the tension between marriage and Torah study. Rabbis are portrayed first and foremost as lovers of Torah, not of their wives. Sometimes the intense devotion of a rabbi to his studies has disastrous consequences for the sage,[38] but often the consequences of a rabbi's prolonged absence from his family have the greatest and most problematic impact on his family.[39] What also emerges from Talmudic stories is the powerful desire of rabbis for the Torah, which is presented as an alternative to the eroticism of marital relations.[40] As we saw in the story of the student who hid under his teacher's bed, the study of Torah displaces the wife as the focus of the rabbi's energy. In a similar way, the strong bond between two sages, study partners, or teacher and student can displace the bond between husband and wife.[41]

Rubenstein's work offers both a model for and a challenge to those interested in studying women in rabbinic *aggadah*. Rubenstein rightly notes that removing a story from its broader context in a Talmudic *sugya* skews the story and impairs our ability to "read" it as a cultural artifact. At the same time, it is difficult to "read" women in context, because there is no place in the Babylonian Talmud in which women are the subject of a sustained discussion. This is true even in halakhic discourse, because, for the rabbis, women are always the Other, the object of men's control and desires. It is even more the case in *aggadah*, where women are occasional characters flitting on and off the stage of the rabbis' drama. If the culture of the Babylonian Talmud is, as Rubenstein asserts, the culture of the rabbis, of Torah study, of the *beit midrash*, then studying women requires that we read in the margins and not in the center, at times sacrificing context in order to consider marginalized figures.[42]

While Boyarin and Rubenstein view *aggadah* as a window into elite culture, the culture of the rabbinic academy, other scholars see *aggadah* as equally informative about folk culture. Galit Hasan-Rokem, an Israeli scholar of folklore, argues that rabbinic *midrash* shows the influence of many institutions, that "the academy and the synagogue . . . were also open to other socializing institutions, above all, the family, rural and urban public spaces, and the political, commercial, and artistic discourse of the time."[43] Hasan-Rokem presents *aggadot* as multivocal texts that "represent both the elite and the broader layers of society."[44]

Hasan-Rokem's work offers a venue for recovering women's voices in midrashic texts. While she acknowledges that one cannot hope to recover the narrative context of folk literature through study of stories committed to writing fifteen hundred years ago, she does believe it is possible to find within these texts "clear marks of the social context within in which they were created."[45] In a chapter entitled "Social Context of Folk Narratives in the Aggadic Midrash: The Feminine Power of Laments, Tales and Love," Hasan-Rokem "highlights the perspective of women, both as characters in the stories and as part of the society creating folk literature."[46] The chapter goes on to highlight stories in *Lamentations Rabbah* that portray women as mourners, martyrs, and intercessors. Hasan-Rokem's analysis focuses on themes of birth and death, strength and compassion, and violence and love, underscoring themes of masculinity and femininity.

One of the stories Hasan-Rokem cites deals with God's response to the destruction of the Jerusalem temple. While God, according to *Lamentations Rabbah*, allows the Romans to destroy the temple, God is also overcome by grief. The prophet Jeremiah is sent to summon first the patriarchs and then Moses to comfort God and to intercede with God on behalf of Israel. They come and offer counsel, but God is unmoved. "At that moment, Rachel leapt before the Holy One"; unbidden, she pleads the case of the Jewish people. She does so by reminding God of Jacob's love for her, love that was thwarted when Laban decided to replace Rachel with her sister, Leah. Rachel claims to have warned Jacob of her father's plan and to have provided Jacob with a way to see through the ruse. However, in the end, Rachel became a party to her father's and sister's deception of Jacob. "Later, I repented and suppressed my desire, and took pity on my sister so that she would not be shamed." Rachel not only teaches Leah the sign she had given Jacob; she lies under the bed and speaks for her, so that Jacob will not recognize that he is making love to Leah, not Rachel. Given her compassion, Rachel argues, surely God should show compassion for Israel. We are told, "Immediately, the mercy of the Holy One . . . was stirred, and God said, 'For your sake, Rachel, I will restore Israel to their place.'"[47]

As Hasan-Rokem points out, Rachel's presentation differs on several levels from those of the patriarchs and Moses. They are summoned; she comes of her own accord. They speak of momentous events in the history of the Jewish people; she speaks of her personal struggle. They speak of justice; she speaks of love, loyalty, and empathy.[48] This story highlights a woman speaking with a woman's voice about women's concerns, and it is that voice that impels God, frequently portrayed as an angry, violent father-figure, to relent and show compassion to Israel.[49]

Another avenue of research focuses on *aggadot* that offer rabbinic expansion of the stories of biblical women. This type of work allows scholars to explore the ways in which the classical rabbis dealt with women whose behavior challenged rabbinic views about women's roles in society. How did rabbinic exegesis grapple with God's command to Abraham to "listen to the voice [of Sarah]" or Deborah's leadership of the Israelites during the period of the judges? Was Michal, the daughter of Saul, a "bad" daughter because she deceived her father to save David? How is Esther's marriage to a non-Jewish king read by rabbis who saw intermarriage as a threat to Jewish continuity?

Research on *aggadot* about biblical women also challenges feminist arguments about the patriarchal nature of various Jewish texts. There is a school of thought that presents the Hebrew Bible as a text with "a remarkably unified vision of humankind" in which women have "the same inherent characteristics as men."[50] For Tikva Frymer-Kensky, the "Otherness" of women in Judaism is a legacy of Israel's encounter with Greek thought and culture.[51] Analysis of rabbinic *aggadot* about biblical women may serve to test Frymer-Kensky's thesis.

One analysis of such stories is offered by Leila Leah Bronner in *From Eve to Esther*.[52] Bronner explores rabbinic traditions about a variety of biblical women. Her work suggests that there was no single rabbinic approach to biblical women. Serach bat Asher, a woman mentioned only in passing in biblical genealogies, becomes, in Bronner's words, a "heroine" in rabbinic *aggadah* and is credited with informing the aged Jacob that Joseph is still living and with identifying the burial place of Joseph when Moses and the Israelites are ready to depart from Egypt.[53] Deborah, portrayed in an unabashedly positive light in Judges 4-5, is criticized in rabbinic literature for her haughtiness.[54]

Biblical women, whether praised or criticized, are never portrayed in *aggadah* as students or teachers of Torah. While the patriarchs are said to have studied Torah, the same is not true of the matriarchs. Women described as prophetesses in the biblical text or accounted as prophetesses by the rabbis are never portrayed teaching Torah in aggadic discussions. While *aggadot* about biblical women may attribute positive virtues and character traits to them, they also underscore the rabbinic assumption that Torah study is and has always been the province of men.

Perhaps the most fruitful work done on women in *aggadah* is scholarship that acknowledges that *aggadah*, like *halakhah*, is androcentric and that all of classical rabbinic literature represents a male point of view. Studies that begin with this acknowledgment nonetheless see the value in exploring images of women in *aggadah*. The most comprehensive of these studies is Judith Baskin's *Midrashic Women*. Baskin recognizes that rabbinic literature "preserves a variety of competing interpretations and opinions" in diverse documents that were composed over several time periods.[55] At the same time, Baskin argues, "the shapers and expositors of rabbinic Judaism were men and the ideal human society they imagined was decidedly oriented towards their own sex."[56] Baskin reads rabbinic texts aware that even women's "voices" in these texts are mediated through male sensibilities and assumptions about women.

Baskin's work focuses on *midrash*, which she sees as the "basic literary method of the rabbinic enterprise,"[57] and her focus is on *midrash aggadah*. Baskin, like Rubenstein, acknowledges the importance of context in reading *aggadah*.[58] This acknowledgment is reflected in her decision to restrict her primary analysis in each chapter to "one or two lengthy and contextualized aggadic passages."[59] If Baskin goes beyond the "context" of a given text, relating one passage to other *aggadot* on the same theme, it is because she believes that "one cannot work with *aggadah* and aspire to a high degree of systematic exposition."[60] She may also agree with other feminist scholars that the absence of women's voices and unmediated women's experience in the rabbinic corpus necessitates going beyond the confines of individual talmudic *sugyot* or midrashic musings on a biblical verse.

Baskin's work explores a number of issues that are important to our understanding of rabbinic ideas about the nature of women. The first and last chapters of her book focus on the "Otherness" of women in rabbinic literature. Analyzing a passage from *b. Niddah* 31b, Baskin notes that the distinction between males and females begins for the classical rabbis at birth, when a male "comes into the world with his provisions" but a female comes into the world "with nothing." Of course, all children are born "emptyhanded"; the passage's editors see men as equipped to make their way in the world, whereas women must depend on others (presumably male relatives) for sustenance.[61] While women are seen in this passage as more in need of men than men are of women, the passage goes on to claim that it is the way of the world that men "go in search of women [i.e., wives] and women do not go in search of men [i.e. husbands]." This, too, reflects women's nature; created from the rib of man, woman is compared to a lost object that is sought by its "owner" and cannot actively seek restoration to that owner but must wait passively to be (re)claimed. The creation story in Genesis 2 and the story of Adam and Eve's expulsion from the Garden of Eden in Genesis 3 are used by the rabbis to assert gender differences and to explain and justify the subordinate position of women.

In a chapter entitled "Why Were the Matriarchs Barren? Resolving the Anomaly of Female Infertility," Baskin argues that aggadic texts on female infertility "convey important insights into the dilemma of suffering and the efficacy of prayer."[62] Because female infertility is a recurring motif in the Bible, which describes three of the four matriarchs as barren, these *aggadot* also provide "examples of the ways in which biblical models could become paradigms and symbols of empowerment in women's lives."[63]

The matriarchs' responses to their barrenness, as imagined in rabbinic literature, portray biblical women as women of faith and compassion. Sarah affirms that God controls fertility, rejecting the folk remedies offered to her, amulets and spells.[64] While the Torah describes Isaac praying on behalf of his barren wife,[65] at least one *midrash* claims that Rebecca, too, prayed on her own behalf.[66] The Torah portrays the relationship between Leah and Rachel, sisters who became the wives of Jacob, as highly competitive and antagonistic; nonetheless, *midrashim* imagine Leah praying on behalf of her barren sister.[67]

Baskin's presentation of *aggadot* that portray women as active agents on their own behalf is reinforced in my own work. In "Men Imagining Women Imagining God: Gender Issues in Classical Midrash," I argue that, in classical *midrashim*, women are portrayed as "confident supplicants before God."[68] These *aggadot* involve biblical women addressing prayers to God in response to a number of situations, including barrenness, imprisonment, and threats to the Jewish people. In these stories, women do not hesitate to hold God to account. Beseeching God to free her from the house of Pharaoh, Sarah reminds God that, although her husband "Abraham went forth [from Haran] on [the basis of God's] assurances, I went forth because of [my] faith."[69] Sarah's claim for divine protection is rooted in her willingness to leave her home for destinations unknown on the strength of faith in God, despite receiving none of the promises God directed toward Abraham.

Dangerous Knowledge: Women and the Manipulation of Torah

At least one woman's prayer to God includes a barely veiled threat based on her knowledge of Torah. In a lengthy analysis of Hannah's prayer for a child (1 Samuel 1), the Talmud considers the significance of the words "If You will look" (1 Sam 1:11). Playing on the repetition of the Hebrew verb "to look," the Talmud suggests that Hannah said to God:

> Master of the Universe, if you look [favorably upon my request], all will be well. If you do not look [favorably upon my request], I will go and conceal myself [as if I were committing adultery] against Elkanah my husband. When I do this, they will administer the waters of jealousy to me. [This will result in pregnancy], for You will not allow Your Torah to be regarded as false, and it is written, "[But if the woman has not defiled herself and is pure], she shall be unharmed and she shall become pregnant" (Num 5:28) . . . this teaches that if she was previously barren, she will now conceive.[70]

Hannah is presented here as a woman who knows the law and is willing to use it to her own advantage. A virtuous woman, she is nonetheless prepared to feign adultery to force God to give her a child. The Talmud's discomfort with this strategy is displayed in the comment of Rabbi Akiba, who says, "If so, all barren women will conceal themselves [in order to conceive]." Using the test of the bitter waters as a fertility treatment is a dangerous ruse, threatening the confidence of husbands in their wives' chastity and raising the possibility that a virtuous yet barren woman might come to question the truth of the Torah upon which Hannah is relying.

This story is only one of several in which women use the Torah or their knowledge of Jewish law to manipulate the legal system, challenging the decisions of God and man. In *b. Giṭṭin* 35a, there is a legal discussion about a widow's right to collect her marriage settlement in court. The Mishnah requires a widow to take an oath that she has not already received all or part of the settlement, but a later authority preferred to have the woman make a vow, a milder form of declaration. According to the Talmud, some sages were reluctant to administer oaths or vows to widows, creating a situation in which widows were unable to collect the monies they had been promised in their marriage contracts. The Talmud continues with a story.

> A certain woman came before Rav Huna [and demanded her marriage settlement]. He said to her, "How can I help you? [My teacher] Rav did not allow a widow to collect her marriage settlement." [Rav would not administer an oath or a vow to the widow and therefore had no legal mechanism to extract the monies from the estate of the deceased husband.] She said, "Is the concern here that I might have collected part of my settlement already? I swear by the Living God of Hosts that I have collected nothing!" Rav Huna said, "Rav acknowledges that if a woman jumps in [and takes an oath without being asked, then we may give her the settlement].

This story features a woman who successfully manipulates the law to her advantage. It is unclear whether she is knowingly manipulating the law or whether she is simply lucky enough to inadvertently use language that forces Rav Huna to collect her marriage settlement. If we assume the former, then this unnamed widow is what Rachel Adler refers to as a "rabbinic trickster" or "legal guerrilla," a woman who "incarnates and unmasks what is arbitrary, chaotic, or unjust in our universe."[71]

Adler analyzes another rabbinic *aggadah* that features a female legal guerrilla, a story about Yalta. Yalta appears as the wife of R. Nahman and a member of the family of the exilarch.[72] In this story, R. Nahman asks his guest and colleague Ulla to lead Grace after Meals. Ulla does so and passes the "cup of blessing,"[73] the cup of wine over which the Grace was recited, to his host. R. Nahman then asks Ulla to "Please pass the cup of blessing to Yalta, sir." Ulla instead initiates a discussion in which he argues that the blessing that accrues to women through fertility accrues only because of their husbands. For this reason, we are to assume, Ulla sees no need to pass Yalta the cup of blessing; any blessing she receives—and fertility seems to be the only one Ulla can imagine a woman receiving—she will receive through God's blessing of her husband. Yalta is furious and breaks four hundred jars of wine in the storeroom. R. Nahman asks Ulla to pacify Yalta by sending her "another cup," which he does, insisting that "All of this is a goblet of blessing." Yalta is not pacified; she responds, "From travelers come tall tales and from ragpickers lice."

Adler sees Ulla's discourse and his refusal to send the cup to Yalta as a reworking of the rule earlier in the passage that directs a man to "send around [the cup over which Grace is recited] to the members of his household . . . so that his household will be blessed]." Ulla reinterprets the nature of the blessing bestowed by the cup, restricting it to a blessing of fertility.[74] He also excludes women from this blessing, justifying his choice to deny Yalta the cup of blessing. Yalta's words and actions can be read as a rejection of Ulla's interpretation. While she is powerless to shape the law, she can "challenge law-as-meaning" and destabilize the law.[75] Denied access to Torah and a voice in the interpretation of Torah, women, even wealthy, well-connected women like Yalta, can sometimes do nothing more than break crockery.

In another story, Yalta displays a willingness to challenge legal rulings that she dislikes. This story involves the determination of the ritual purity/impurity of uterine blood. A determination that such blood was impure rendered a woman sexually unavailable for twelve to fourteen days and necessitated her immersion in a ritual bath.

Yalta brought blood to Rabbah bar Hana, and he ruled that it was impure. She then turned around and brought it to R. Yitzhak b. R. Yehuda, and he ruled that it was pure. How could he do such a thing when a *baraita* teaches: "If a sage ruled it impure, his colleague is not permitted to rule it pure [and vice versa]?" At first, [R. Yitzhak] ruled that it was impure. When [Yalta] told him, "Every other time [Rabbah] has ruled for me that [blood] just like this was pure, and today he has a pain in his eye," R. Yitzhak then ruled it pure.[76]

In this story, Yalta succeeds in getting the ruling she wants. She does so in an unusual and somewhat improper way. First, she seeks a second opinion, something the rabbis regard as questionable. Then she convinces R. Yitzhak that he should reverse his ruling, claiming that Rabbah usually declares such a stain pure and implying that his failure to do so that day was due to physical infirmity.

Adler observes that there are two ways to read this story. The milder reading portrays Yalta as someone who simply wants an accurate assessment of her situation; she seeks a second opinion only because of Rabbah's illness. The stronger and, according to Adler, more problematic reading from the tradition's point of view imagines Yalta as a woman who proceeds in a calculated way to manipulate the law.[77]

Adler's suggestion that the story of Yalta and the bloodstain can be read two ways underscores one of the difficulties facing scholars of *aggadah*, particularly when they deal with marginalized figures such as women. The ambiguity inherent in many of these stories—the absence of editorial comment on the stories and the terseness of the stories themselves—lends itself to a variety of readings. As reader-response criticism insists, what we get out of these stories or what we see in them depends on what we bring to them.[78] For some, Yalta's smashing of the wine jars and her insistence on a second opinion (not to mention her insistence that the second opinion be to her liking) and the unnamed widow's rush to take an oath are models for female resistance and a response to a male-dominated legal system. Are the women who defy attempts to declare them ritually impure or deny them their marriage settlement to be viewed as heroes, irritants, or sources of danger? The answer to this question seems to me to be determined by the stance of the reader; the texts themselves leave all possibilities open.

Comparing the Models: Beruriah

How do the various academic approaches to *aggadah* further our understanding of the relationship between women and Torah? The following discussion offers a comparison of several scholars' work on a single rabbinic story or group of stories. This comparison offers a glimpse into the end results of different methods and may offer us some idea of what future studies can hope to accomplish.

One name that is mentioned in nearly all discussions of women in rabbinic literature is that of Beruriah. Beruriah is often mentioned as the only woman portrayed in rabbinic literature as a student or a teacher. Because she is mentioned in the work of many of the scholars who analyze gender issues in *aggadah*, a consideration of scholarly treatments of Beruriah offers us a window into the methods of various scholars.

Some of the early explorations of women in rabbinic literature discussed Beruriah, describing her as "an example of dedication and knowledge"[79] and an "exception that proves the rule."[80] These discussions, as I indicated earlier, tended to be uncritical readings of rabbinic traditions that treated all stories about or statements attributed to Beruriah as historically accurate. In 1975, David Goodblatt published an article entitled "The Beruriah Traditions."[81] Goodblatt's article explored the characterization of Beruriah as the daughter of Rabbi Hanania ben Teradion and the wife of Rabbi Meir. He noted that Beruriah is mentioned seven times in early rabbinic literature.[82] Beruriah is twice described as both the daughter of Rabbi Hanania ben Teradion and the wife of Rabbi Meir and once only as the wife of Rabbi Meir. The remaining four traditions refer to Beruriah without mentioning any family connections. Six of the traditions are found in the Bavli in Babylonian Aramaic; one is found in the Tosefta and is in Hebrew. There are also several traditions that refer to an unnamed daughter of Hanania ben Teradion, all of which are in Hebrew and several of which present Hanania's daughter as a learned and/or pious woman.[83]

Goodblatt concludes that we are dealing with a merging of identities. Early sources mention an unnamed daughter of Hanania ben Teradion; at least one other early source mentions a learned woman named Beruriah. Goodblatt proposes that the two were merged into one and that at some later date, this woman was also identified as the wife of Rabbi Meir.[84]

Like scholars and writers before him, Goodblatt ascribes historic significance to the Beruriah traditions. Arguing that "all of the anecdotes which portray Beruriah as possessing an advanced education are of Babylonian Amoraic origin," Goodblatt concludes that the "historic situation they reflect is not second century Palestine, i.e., the time and place of the historical Beruriah, but Sassanian Babylonia. . . . It was in Sassanian Babylonia that the existence of a woman learned in rabbinic tradition was a possibility, however uncommon."[85] Thus, Goodblatt accepts both the historicity (although not the family connections) of Beruriah and the idea that educated women were not considered beyond the realm of the possible at some point in the rabbinic period.

Like Goodblatt, Tal Ilan focuses on the search for the "historical Beruriah." Ilan builds on Goodblatt's work, suggesting that "[i]f we can demonstrate that a Beruriah tradition is a literary framework into which

Beruriah was incorporated at a later stage, the compilation in which the parallel is found is not essential to the model."[86] Ilan dismisses the historicity of the Beruriah story in *b. Berakhot* 10a on the basis of its similarities to *b. Ta'anit* 23b; she argues that the existence of a literary theme undermines the historicity of individual stories in which it occurs.

Ilan notes that, while Goodblatt argues that an educated woman was imaginable in sixth-century Babylonia but not in second-century Palestine, he fails to offer proof for his assertion beyond his understanding of the Beruriah traditions. Furthermore, she notes that Daniel Boyarin makes the opposite claim.[87] For Ilan, both claims are suspect; she finds the claim of Rachel Adler that "Beruriah is a fantasy and nightmare" rather than a historic figure "more historically correct."[88]

Adler's analysis of the Beruriah traditions is a literary rather than a historical one.[89] She acknowledges that she is interested in the "legend of Beruriah" and how it has been read and understood by generations of posttalmudic Jews. Adler notes that, through the various stories told about her, Beruriah becomes a "rounded character rather than a flat or stylized one."[90] Adler sees Beruriah as the receptacle for the "mixed feelings" rabbis would have had about a "woman like them." For Adler, the answer is powerful and painful. Noting that the "discrediting of Beruriah . . . is accomplished only by means of a betrayal" by her husband, a teacher of Torah, and a student of Torah, Adler argues that, for the rabbis, a woman who was "rabbinic" in character and inclination would be destroyed by "the institutionalized denigration, subordination, and exclusion of women."[91]

Conclusions: Beyond Otherness

In his work on gender and Talmud, Boyarin seeks to "recover alternate points of view and so chang[e] our understanding of the past."[92] Feminist scholars must now ask whether changing our understanding of the past is a viable or appropriate goal. There is no question that the work of the past thirty years has deepened and broadened our understanding of rabbinic Judaism and Jewish antiquity. The question is: what now? While Baskin rightly points out that rabbinic texts require "continuous reading and constant reinterpretation,"[93] surely we have reached the point at which we must acknowledge that the Judaism of these texts is clearly androcentric and that no interpretive gymnastics can change that.[94] What we can do is pursue scholarship even when the results are disheartening and/or painful and/or infuriating to us. Feminist scholarship will not "correct" the androcentricity of rabbinic Judaism; it does, however, enrich the study of rabbinics. There are certainly areas of inquiry worth pursuing that will expand our understanding of gender in rabbinic culture.[95] *Aggadah*, on its own and studied together with halakhic material, still has much to add to our understanding of the feminine in Judaism.

Clearly, gender has become an acceptable tool with which to explore rabbinic texts; the task of scholars is to wield that tool as they do all others, with precision, for the sake of deepening our understanding and appreciation of classical texts.

NOTES

1. *B. Berakhot* 62a.

2. While women are exempt from the study of Torah rather than categorically forbidden to study, the end result is largely the same. There were no institutions for teaching women Torah, and those women who may have been taught by male relatives had no outlet to share their learning.

3. See Judith Baskin, *Midrashic Women* (Hanover, NH: Brandeis University Press/University Press of New England, 2002), chapter 1.

4. The invocation recited upon completion of the study of a tractate of the Talmud thanks God for "granting our portion in the house of study, and not among those who hang out on the corner. For we rise and they rise; we rise to words of Torah, while they rise to idle matters. We toil and they toil; we toil and receive a reward, while they toil and do not receive a reward. We run and they run; we run toward life eternal, while they run toward a pit of destruction." The disdain of the rabbis for nonrabbinic Jews is particularly noticeable in Babylonian sources but is present in Palestinian traditions, as well. See Richard Kalmin, *The Sage in Jewish Society of Late Antiquity* (London: Routledge, 1999), chapter 1.

5. *B. Pesaḥim* 62b.

6. *T. Kelim Baba Qamma* 4:17.

7. *M. Sotah* 3:4.

8. Ideally, such a study should differentiate among different documents; the view presented in the Babylonian Talmud could differ from that in Genesis Rabbah. In fact, most of the stories I mention in this chapter appear in the Babylonian Talmud. As I argue, few stories about women and Torah exist in ancient rabbinic texts; much of my argument is an argument from silence.

9. *B. Qiddushin* 29b.

10. *B. Qiddushin* 34a.

11. *B. Sotah* 21a-b.

12. *B. Baba Metsia* 59b.

13. *B. Ketubot* 23a.

14. See Dvora Weisberg, "Desirable but Dangerous: Rabbis' Daughters in the Bavli," *Hebrew Union College Annual* 75 (2004): 142–47.

15. *B. Betsa* 29b, *b. H.ullin* 110a.

16. In fact, the description of Beruriah's credentials is so impressive that it probably should be read as an exaggeration intended to make a point (*guzma b'alma*), not about Beruriah but about Rabbi Simlai.

17. Much of the early feminist work on women and Judaism was not, strictly speaking, scholarly work; it was directed at a general rather than a scholarly audience and did not employ scholarly methodology. Tal Ilan dismisses much of this work (*Mine and Yours Are Hers: Retrieving Women's History From Rabbinic Literature* [Leiden: Brill, 1997], pp. 16–25), and her critique is a valid one, particularly from a historical perspective. It should be noted, however, that such work, whatever its limitations, was an important first step in that it highlighted the absence of women and issues related to women in modern scholarship of Judaism.

18. See Elizabeth Koltun, ed. *The Jewish Woman: New Perspectives* (New York: Schocken Books, 1976); Blu Greenberg, *On Women and Judaism* (Philadelphia: Jewish Publication Society, 1981); Susannah Heschel, ed., *On Being a Jewish Feminist* (New York: Schocken Books, 1981); and Rachel Biale, *Women and Jewish Law: An Exploration of Women's Issues in Halakhic Sources* (New York: Schocken Books, 1984). Although both Koltun's and Heschel's anthologies include pieces on *aggadah*, the primary focus of both works is the status of women in Jewish law and ritual. Apologetic works from the same period also focus on *halakhah*, arguing that women are treated favorably by Jewish law. See, for instance, Moshe Meiselman, *Jewish Woman in Jewish Law* (New York: Ktav, 1979).

19. See Tal Ilan, *Mine and Yours Are Hers*, pp. 16–25.

20. Paula Hyman, "The Other Half," in *The Jewish Woman*, ed. Elizabeth Koltun (New York: Schocken Books, 1976), pp. 107–8, and Leonard Swidler, *Women in Judaism* (Metuchen, NJ: Scarecrow Press, 1976), pp. 97–104.

21. Anne Goldfeld, "Women as Sources of Torah in the Rabbinic Tradition," in *The Jewish Woman*, ed. E. Koltun, pp. 257ff., and Sondra Henry and Emily Taitz, *Written Out of History* (New York: Bloch Publishing, 1978), pp. 47–48 and 54.

22. T. Ilan, *Mine and Yours Are Hers*, pp. 9–16.

23. Ibid., pp. 28–31 and 38–48.

24. Tal Ilan herself relies heavily on early rabbinic literature in her book *Jewish Women in Greco-Roman Palestine* (Peabody, MA: Hendrickson, 1996).

25. T. Ilan, *Mine and Yours Are Hers*, p. 237.

26. Ibid., pp. 238–39.

27. Ibid., p. 277.

28. Another scholar who uses *aggadah* to consider cultural issues is Aryeh Cohen, *Rereading Talmud: Gender, Law and the Poetics of Sugyot* (Atlanta: Scholars Press, 1998).

29. Daniel Boyarin, *Carnal Israel: Reading Sex in Talmudic Culture* (Berkeley, Los Angeles, and London: University of California Press, 1993), chapter 4.

30. Ibid., pp. 146–58.

31. Ibid., p. ix.

32. Ibid., p. 168.

33. Ibid., pp. 183ff.

34. Jeffrey Rubenstein, *Talmudic Stories* (Baltimore and London: Johns Hopkins University Press, 1999), pp. 2–3.

35. Ibid., pp. 45, 78, 111–12, 153–55.

36. Jeffrey Rubenstein, *The Culture of the Babylonian Talmud* (Baltimore: Johns Hopkins University Press, 2003), 102.

37. Ibid.

38. Ibid., p. 106.

39. Ibid., pp. 108–9.

40. Ibid., pp. 118–20.

41. D. Boyarin, *Carnal Israel*, pp. 215–19.

42. Dvora Weisberg, "Desirable but Dangerous," pp. 4–5.

43. Galit Hasan-Rokem, *Web of Life: Folklore and Midrash in Rabbinic Literature* (Stanford: Stanford University Press, 2000), pp. xi–xii.

44. Ibid.

45. G. Hasan-Rokem, *Web of Life*, p. 108.

46. Ibid.

47. *Lamentations Rabbah*, proem 24.

48. G. Hasan-Rokem, *Web of Life*, pp. 127–28. For another analysis of this story, see my article "Men Imagining Women Imagining God: Gender Issues in Classical Midrash," in *Agendas for the Study of Midrash in the 21st Century* (Williamsburg, VA: College of William and Mary, 1999), pp. 74–77.

49. This story supports Jacob Neusner's argument that in this world, Israel is called upon to "embody traits defined as feminine." The paradigm Israel must embrace in order to awaken God's compassion and ensure its own redemption is that offered by Rachel, who succeeds where the patriarchs and Moses fail (see Jacob Neusner, *Androgynous Judaism* [Macon, GA: Mercer University Press, 1993]).

50. Tikva Frymer-Kensky, *In the Wake of the Goddesses* (New York: Fawcett Columbine, 1992), p. 120.

51 Ibid., pp. 203–12.

52. Leila Leah Bronner, *From Eve to Esther* (Louisville, KY: Westminster John Knox, 1994).

53. Ibid., pp. 45–51.

54. Ibid., pp. 172–73.

55. Judith Baskin, *Midrashic Women*, p. 2.

56. Ibid., p. 3.

57. Ibid.

58. Ibid., p. 5.

59. Ibid.

60. Ibid.

61. Ibid., pp. 14–15.

62. Ibid., p. 119.

63. Ibid.

64. Ibid., p. 133.

65. Genesis 25:21.

66. *Midrash Eliyahu Rabbah* 18, cited in J. Baskin, *Midrashic Women*, p. 135.

67. *B. Berakhot* 60a and *Genesis Rabbah* 72:6.

68. D. Weisberg, "Men Imagining Women Imagining God," p. 80.

69. *Genesis Rabbah* 41:2, cited in D. Weisberg, "Men Imagining Women Imagining God," pp. 72–73.

70. *B. Berakhot* 31b, cited in D. Weisberg, "Men Imagining Women Imagining God," p. 69.

71. Rachel Adler, *Engendering Judaism* (Philadelphia: Jewish Publication Society, 1998), p. 57.

72. Adler refers to Yalta as the daughter of the exilarch R. Huna, citing a short biographical sketch in the Steinsaltz edition of the Talmud, *b. Berakhot* 51b.

73. I am following R. Adler's translation of *b. Berakhot* 51b in *Engendering Judaism*, p. 53.

74. R. Adler, *Engendering Judaism*, p. 54.

75. Ibid., p. 56.

76. *B. Niddah* 20b, as translated by R. Adler in *Engendering Judaism*, p. 56.

77. This story is also discussed by Charlotte Fonrobert in *Menstrual Purity* (Stanford: Stanford University Press, 2000), pp. 118–22. Fonrobert argues that menstrual blood, a powerful source of ritual impurity in biblical and rabbinic law, marks an area in which the rabbis' desire for control clashed with female autonomy. The rabbis present themselves as "experts" in determining the status of blood; however, Fonrobert notes that women may have resisted such control, maneuvering the system for their own ends.

78. For discussions of reader-response criticism and the role of the reader in "making meaning" in texts, see Stanley Fish, *Is There a Text in This Class?* (Cambridge, MA: Harvard University Press, 1980), pp. 1–17, and *Reader-Response Criticism*, ed. Jane Tompkins (Baltimore: Johns Hopkins University Press, 1980), pp. ix–xxvi.

79. S. Henry and E. Taitz, *Written Out of History*, p. 54.

80. Leonard Swidler, *Women in Judaism*, p. 97.

81. David Goodblatt, "The Beruriah Traditions," in *Journal of Jewish Studies* 26 (1975): 68–80.

82. I am omitting a posttalmudic mention of "the matter of Beruriah" found in the commentary of Rashi to *b. Avodah Zarah* 18b, s.v. *d'Beruriah*.

83. For a discussion of each of the sources and a chart, see D. Goodblatt, "The Beruriah Traditions," pp. 68–80.

84. As Goodblatt notes, the "assimilation of an unnamed character with a named one is not unprecedented in folklore" ("The Beruriah Traditions," p. 81). It is also known in rabbinic literature, which often assigns a name to an unnamed biblical figure or attributes acts previously assigned to an unnamed figure with a known character.

85. D. Goodblatt, "The Beruriah Traditions," p. 84.

86. T. Ilan, "The Quest for the Historical Beruriah, Rachel and Imma Shalom," in *AJS Review* 22:1 (1997): 3.

87. T. Ilan, "The Quest for the Historical Beruriah, Rachel and Imma Shalom," p. 8.

88. Ibid.

89. Adler's article "The Virgin in the Brothel," cited here from *Vox Benedictina* 7:1 (1990): 7–29, first appeared in *Tikkun* 3:6 (November–December 1988).

90. Ibid., p. 8.

91. Ibid., pp. 28–29.

92. D. Boyarin, *Carnal Israel*, p. 227.

93. J. Baskin, *Midrashic Women*, p. 164.

94. See Jacob Neusner, Review of *Midrashic Women* by Judith Baskin in *The Review of Rabbinic Judaism* 6:1 (2003): 130–34.

95. Ibid.

||||||||||||||||||||||||||||||||||||||||||||||||||||

3

Women and Jewish Law

Judith Hauptman

Supreme Court Justice Oliver Wendell Holmes famously said that law is not "a brooding omnipresence in the sky."[1] The constitutional scholar Ronald Dworkin later added, "it is rather a historical fact."[2] Holmes's point was that the law is not a platonic ideal but something to be developed as different situations arise. Dworkin notes that law is specific to time and place. By implication, as time passes and places change, the law, too, must be altered.

These statements set the stage for a discussion of Jewish law over time. Were *halakhah* regarded as divine and hence immutable, there would be no need for endless, ongoing discussions about its fine points. We would not find ourselves with code after code of Jewish law, each trying to modify and expand the previous one. We would also not be deciding Jewish law on our own but turning to God for a resolution of problems, much as Moses did several times in the Torah.[3] However, the practitioners of Jewish law did not view Jewish law as "a brooding omnipresence in the sky." Rather, the many self-reflective texts of rabbinic sages make it clear that they saw themselves as active participants in an unfolding process. They were adducing answers to new questions.

This chapter surveys literature on the subject of women and Jewish law from the Talmud through the Middle Ages. A number of recently published volumes examine this subject. I present the highlights of the authors' findings and then evaluate them. Most important, I examine these developments from a feminist perspective. To state my conclusions at the outset: in the first wave of feminist writing, in the 1980s and 1990s, large studies were produced that reviewed entire systems of marital and ritual law. These studies exposed the patriarchal bias of Jewish jurisprudence. A second wave is now emerging, characterized by more localized studies of particular time periods or individual series of rabbinic enactments. It is studies like these that will verify the general theories of the first wave.

Before looking at these works, let me provide a feminist framework for the discussion. Gerda Lerner, in her influential volume *The Creation of Patriarchy*, lays the basis for much of the feminist writing about texts and culture that followed. She begins by thinking through gender relations in the Bible. The patriarchal family, she notes, is the dominant biblical form. In such a family, a man has authority over the members of his household. Focusing on the Genesis narratives, she argues that Lot's offering his daughters to the mob (Gen 19:7) shows that men could do with women as they pleased.

Lerner further observes that there were very few women leaders in the Bible. Men served as priests, filling a key religious role, but women did not. In other, earlier ancient societies, women played a role in public religious ritual. In biblical religion, they did not. God created woman from man's rib, thus giving rise to the notion that women are inferior to men. God blessed Abraham and his seed, entering into a covenant with him, with its sign of circumcision. The penis was likely chosen as the site for inscribing the covenant because it emits the seed that God will bless. Lerner does note that women's position improved over time, as Israelites moved from family to tribe to nation. Limits were gradually placed on a father's control of his household. Instead of an inheritance, which went to sons only, fathers were required to give daughters a dowry. This wealth gave a wife a measure of power over her husband, who would have to return the dowry if he divorced her.

Going outside biblical society, Lerner broadly claims that biblical women occupied a position inferior to that of their Mesopotamian counterparts. Babylonian women could own property, sign contracts, take legal action, and claim a share of their deceased husband's estate. Not so biblical women. She concludes, trenchantly, "For females, the Book of Genesis represented their definition as creatures essentially different from males; a redefinition of their sexuality as beneficial and redemptive only within the boundaries of patriarchal dominance; and finally the recognition that they were excluded from being directly able to represent the divine principle."[4]

Is Lerner right about all of these claims, or is she reading sexism into the text? She is surely on target when she says that women were under men's authority in the Bible. Society was patriarchal, as she asserts, with men at the top of the pyramid, in control of those beneath them—wives, children, and slaves. It seems to me, however, that Lerner does not distinguish sufficiently between women as slaves, owned by their masters and disposed of at will, and women as second-class citizens, subordinate to men. The stories in Genesis portray the wives of the forefathers as personalities in their own right, far from slaves, not under their husbands' thumbs but nonetheless not in control of themselves.[5] I have no quarrel with Lerner or anyone else who wants to expose patriarchy. It is right there in the words. But the description needs to be more nuanced. Neither the laws nor the narratives portray women as men's sexual playthings and little more. Subordination is not slavery. There aren't just two points on the continuum of freedom but a whole range of possibilities.

Lerner also suggests that the covenant is described as being made with Abraham alone, which certainly seems to be the case, even though, when his name is changed as a sign of the covenant between him and God (Gen 17:5), Sarah's name is also changed (v. 15). It would be very hard to separate these two name changes. I am not saying that Sarah's role is equal to that of Abraham but only that one cannot see her as excluded from the covenant. I would make the same claim for the revelation at Sinai. It is clear, according to the Torah, that the entire people stands at the foot of the mountain. The text makes repeated references to *kol ha'am*, the whole nation (Exod 19:8,11,16; 20:18). Of course, the men fill roles that the women may not fill, such as that of elders (*ziqnei ha'am*). And it is the men, not the women, who are told to avoid sex with women for three days so that the men will be ritually pure.[6] These instructions do not exclude women from the revelation; they merely make men's purity—but not women's purity—an issue of importance. There is every reason to think that, according to the Bible, women, along with men, stood at the foot of the mountain and were included in God's promise to take Israel as His special people if they would agree to the terms of His covenant, which included obeying His commandments. The men are addressed by God as heads of household, as first in line; the women are addressed by God as standing behind the men. Even so, the covenant binds them both. This point matters.

As for the claim that women in the Bible were of lower status than women in other ancient Near Eastern cultures, more information is needed to support such an idea. What was the role of female priests in other cultures? Of male priests? Were women in those societies bought and sold in marriage? Were they subordinate to their husbands? Until that information is made available, I cannot accept that women's biblical exclusion from the priesthood necessarily means that they occupied a lower status than did women in other cultures. If one were to claim that Israelite women, who could not divorce their husbands at will, were at a disadvantage when compared to Roman women who could, I would still need to know what else the law said about Roman women. If they were under the control of a head of household (*paterfamilias*) and women in the Bible were not, then one could not use the power of divorce to generalize that Roman women enjoyed a higher overall legal status.

Finally, Lerner seems to be suggesting that the Bible created patriarchy, that it did not exist prior to the biblical period. I am not so sure. Perhaps the Bible did not produce the patriarchal system but rather *reflected* gender relations in ancient society, such as those we find in the Code of Hammurapi.[7] It is likely that the Bible came, after the fact, to explain why ancient Near Eastern society was configured as it was.

I think we are on firmer ground if we point to the extensive influence of the Bible on Western society, to this very day, than if we claim that the Bible shaped society in its own day. Some people try to justify patriarchy today by pointing to biblical patriarchy. That, however, is very different from saying that the Bible created patriarchy. Those who accept the authority of the Bible must grapple with this question: is patriarchy mandated by God, or is it simply an artifact of the ancient world and hence subject to change?

With this feminist framework and these questions in mind, let us now turn to six volumes on women and Jewish law published in the past twenty-five years. The first, chronologically speaking, is Rachel Biale's *Women and Jewish Law*, which surveys key areas of Jewish law from a feminist perspective. By that I mean that the author notes the different treatment of men and women in the Jewish law codes, from the Bible to the present, and suggests that women are inferior to men in economic power, social standing, legal rights, religious role, and importance.[8] On occasion, she advocates for change to make public rituals more open to women.[9]

Here are two samples of Biale's feminist analysis. In discussing women and the study of Torah, Biale notes that women are exempt but then asks if this means that women are forbidden to study Torah or that they may still choose to do so. She brings an array of opinions on the matter. Among them is *Sefer Ḥasidim*, a very influential pietistic work from the 12th or 13th century that advocates broad Torah study for women.[10] It offers the rationale that if a woman does not know the commandments (*mitzvot*), she will not be able to keep them. Biale also cites Joseph Karo, who, in his now-authoritative 16th century code of Jewish law, seems to oppose Torah study for women. But Yeshayahu Leibowitz, a contemporary thinker, advocates equal education for boys and girls.[11]

In a discussion of abortion, Biale cites several verses from Exodus that discuss accidental abortion. They say that if men fight and inadvertently strike a pregnant woman and she miscarries but there is no *ason*, they will have to pay her husband whatever amount the judges determine; if there is an *ason*, they will have to pay with their lives (Exod 21:22-25). *Ason*, a much debated term,[12] apparently refers to the death of the mother. The fetuses are not treated as having the same status as those already born. Their death does not result in the execution of those who killed them. One might deduce from here that elective abortion is permitted because it does not involve the taking of a life. Biale goes on to present both stringent and lenient views of elective abortion, from talmudic and posttalmudic sources.[13]

My critique of Biale is that she moves from Bible to Talmud to present times, citing along the way those whom she wishes to cite but not giving the reader a clear sense of the logic of her choices. Other choices might have led to an altogether different kind of presentation of the issues. Nonetheless, she has provided an important, popular, nontendentious introduction to the subject of women and Jewish law. Biale arms the reader with options. Since she includes, among others, views that tend toward seeing women as capable and deserving of equal status with men, a reader inclined to that view will have a basis in tradition for such a view.[14]

Other recent volumes include Jacob Neusner's *Method and Meaning in Ancient Judaism* and Judith Wegner's *Chattel or Person: The Status of Women in the Mishnah*.[15] Each has made a significant contribution to analyzing women's legal status in rabbinic law. Neusner is the first, I believe, to provide a feminist reading of rabbinic texts that culminates in an overarching theory. He claims that the framers of the Mishnah worked out a division on the subject of women because they viewed women as abnormal, anomalous, dangerous, dirty, and polluting. Since the source of this abnormality was women's sexuality and its potential for disturbing the social order, the framers found it necessary to regularize the transfer of women from one man to another. In a somewhat similar vein, Judith Wegner surveys the Mishnah's laws about women and arrives at the conclusion that men treat women in two different ways, depending on the subject under consideration: when the subject is a woman's sexual and reproductive capacities, she is treated like chattel, but where all other matters are concerned, she is treated like a person.

As incisive as are these two attempts to read rabbinic literature through a feminist lens, I suggested in a critique that each is fine but flawed.[16] Neusner fails to note that men, like women, are viewed by the Mishnah as sources of pollution. An entire tractate, *Zavim*, is devoted to the topic of men's ritual impurity. In addition, Neusner overlooks the fact that in mishnaic society there does not seem to have been a sharp delineation between public and private spheres. Private space was not exactly that. Many tradesmen and salesmen visited women in their homes, thereby making the home into a quasi-public space. If so, one cannot claim that women were relegated to the private sphere and hence had extremely low social status. Finally, a close reading of mishnaic texts suggests that it was men's unruly sexual potential, not women's, that led to the segregation of the sexes.[17] As for Wegner, I think she overstates her case. A woman is not fully chattel with regard to reproduction nor fully person with regard to other areas. The situation is more complex. These critiques notwithstanding, Neusner and Wegner have made weighty contributions to the analysis of rabbinic texts from a feminist perspective.

In 1998, in response to feminist critiques that were unduly harsh and Orthodox defenses that were unnecessarily apologetic, I wrote my own volume on women in rabbinic law, entitled *Rereading the Rabbis: A Woman's Voice.* My method of reading rabbinic passages on a given topic is to trace legal developments over time. Were we to look at laws affecting women at any given moment, the results would invariably show discrimination against women simply because they are women. But, if we trace developments over time, in particular from Torah to Talmud, we still find a bias against women, but we also find developments in the direction of seeing women less as chattel and more as second-class citizens. In order to guard against biases of my own, I did not select texts from here and there but picked individual topics, like marriage or divorce or rape, and then analyzed material in a systematic manner.

My findings, regarding the ten topics of the book, are that the rabbis did not see equality for men and women as the end product of their legislation but did see marriage and divorce and rape and many other issues very differently than did the writers of the Bible. This is not to deny that their thinking was influenced by other cultures or by popular culture. The introduction of consent into marriage may not have been their own invention; it may have already become standard practice. The rabbis may have just been catching up to what the people were already doing, which is an argument made by some about popular practice *(minhag)* in the Middle Ages becoming part of Jewish law, as we will see later. Whatever the case may be, however, one notices, upon reading the texts carefully, that the rabbis made changes in the laws that had been handed down to them, often in the direction of altering women's status for the better.

Let me offer one sustained example. According to the few biblical verses that address the subject, when a man forces himself on an unbetrothed virgin and has sexual relations with her and they are later found out, he must pay fifty silver pieces to her father and accept the woman as his wife for life, with no option for divorce (Deut 22:28-29). This is a very different outcome from that of the immediately preceding case, in which a man who forces himself on a betrothed young woman is considered guilty of a capital crime.

To be very clear: the Torah says "and she will be his wife" (Deut 22:29), which means that there is no choice, that is, that she must be—and already is—his wife and that he must retain her as such. But the Tosefta, a tannaitic compilation from about the same time as the Mishnah, about 225 C.E., says "only with her consent" (*t. Ketubot* 3:7). It is not at all clear how the Tosefta arrived at this derivation. The rabbis of the Babylonian Talmud cite the words of the verse that mean "she will be his wife" (*velo tihe'yeh le'ishah*) and comment, just like the Tosefta, *mida'atah*, which means "only with her consent." They then proceed to deduce that the father, too, may refuse to give his daughter's hand in marriage or may object to the marriage that has already taken place (*b. Ketubot* 39b). What led the rabbis to interpret the words of the Torah in this manner? Surely not the simple and obvious meaning of the words themselves. It is much more likely that it is their own sense that a girl who was raped should not be automatically married off to the rapist that led them to this creative interpretation. Not that this interpretation is very different from so many others found in rabbinic collections. I am merely pointing out that the rabbis of the Talmud often have a social agenda that drives their legislative interpretation, their *midrash halakhah*. Words can be understood in many ways. The rabbis chose to interpret them in ways that led to greater justice and equity, as they saw it in their day. One might guess that in the rabbinic period, but not in the biblical period, a rape victim would be able to find a better husband for herself than the man who assaulted her.

By the end of the twentieth century, feminist approaches in different disciplines had made an impact. First, no one would any longer dream of writing a history of a period of Jewish life by writing only about political developments, which would be a history of male leaders. History now includes social history, and social history requires that the historian tell the story of women's and common people's lives, alongside political lives. Second, researchers must now examine their material through the lens of gender, something they did not used to do. They have to look at how a society is configured and examine a society's assumptions about men and women, how power is understood, where it resides, and how it is used. These approaches have spilled over into rabbinic research, too.

Books on women and Jewish law continue to be written in the twenty-first century. Since the first feminist forays are already on the shelves, the time has arrived for detailed studies of more limited subjects. Avraham Grossman and Elimelech Westreich have both written books about women and Jewish law in the Middle Ages. Their titles reflect that interest: *Pious and Rebellious: Jewish Women in Europe in the Middle Ages* and *Transitions in the Legal Status of the Wife in Jewish Law.*[18] It is an achievement, in and of itself, that two Orthodox men have devoted book-length studies to the subject of women and Jewish law. One might say that the Jewish law that governs the lives of Orthodox Jews has been under such severe attack by feminists in the past two decades that these volumes were written in defense. Alternatively, one might say that feminists have put women high on the historical agenda, with the result that researchers who wish to reach a wider audience choose to write about women. Be that as it may, the question to ask is this: is the scholarship reasonably objective? Let me review some of the findings.

I begin with a chapter on history, not law, in order to provide some background for the legal volumes. In an article on Jewish women in the Middle Ages, Judith Baskin shows that in areas like marriage, divorce, economic activity, education, and martyrdom (*kiddush hashem*), women fared better than we might have guessed they would in a society in which men controlled women.[19] In Muslim society, she writes, the expectations for Jewish women were domestic. Marriages were arranged. Women were wed at about thirteen or fourteen years of age to men who were somewhat older. A *ketubah* was written that listed, in particular, the wife's property brought in as a dowry. Women earned money within marriage, through the needle trades. Divorce was not uncommon. In Christian Europe, by contrast, women were married off very young, at eight or nine. Their fathers gave them large dowries. Some women became literate, and some women were involved in business transactions. There was a high degree of piety among many women, as evidenced by references to their regular times for prayer. When crusaders massacred Jewish communities, women sacrificed themselves and their children, rather than convert to Christianity.

In *Pious and Rebellious,* Avraham Grossman notes that, overall, Jewish women's status in Europe represented an improvement over their status in the Talmud and in Islamic countries.[20] He does point out that there are no women's voices from this period to assist in determining the status of women and that it is hard to generalize from occasional sources. In anticipating criticism of bias, he claims that he does not intend to make things look better than they were, and they were at times rather bad.

Grossman notes, at the outset, that he will consider three major influences on each topic: its biblical and Talmudic legacy; outside social realities; and the economic status of the Jews. Of these, he immediately adds, the general economic improvement of the Jews altered women's status more than any other factor.[21] To give a well-documented example: a great many Jews in 8th-century Babylonia moved off the land and into the cities. There they entered commerce and financial services. This shift led to changes in the law. From that time, a *ketubah*, which previously could be collected from land only, could be collected from movables. Another legal change precipitated by the new lifestyle was that wives in cities no longer needed to perform all of the household chores prescribed by the Mishnah (*m. Ketubot* 5:5), like grinding grain and baking bread, and could not be punished for failing to do so.[22]

Once more anticipating his critics, Grossman notes that the situation of Jewish women worsened at the end of the 15th century. He is thereby saying that, although there were many improvements in women's position in Europe in the late Middle Ages, the difficulties that women face today can be traced back to the period that followed the one he describes. Three key areas he surveys are the education of women, women's religious lives, and wife-beating.[23]

Education of Women

Grossman writes that Jewish women were not given an education in the Middle Ages because of the Talmud's ban,[24] the demands of modesty, and the practices of surrounding society.[25] Like the ancient philosopher Seneca, the medieval sages felt that women should remain innocent, which meant unschooled. The more wisdom they acquired, the greater the temptation to sin.

Rabbenu Nissim of Kairouan (14th century), for example, argued against teaching women Torah, not just because of talmudic dicta but because giving women knowledge would make it possible for them to engage in witchcraft.[26] Other rabbis moved in the opposite direction. Maimonides (12th century) curtailed the talmudic ban, ruling that a woman who studies Torah will receive a reward, although her father should not be the one to teach her. As noted earlier, the mystical pietists (*Ḥasidei Ashkenaz*) withdrew even further from the ban because they felt it necessary for girls to learn the commandments (*mitzvot*).[27] Grossman suggests that it was women's role in educating children and running the family business, and the fact that they martyred themselves, that changed men's attitudes to them.

The question remains, to my mind, whether rabbinic legislators first decided to oppose the education of women and then wove earlier sources together to support that position or whether the sources themselves stated a clear opposing position, thus leaving the rabbinic interpreters no room to maneuver.

Women's Religious Lives

Setting the cultural context for women in France and Germany (Ashkenaz), Grossman notes that Christian women had no role in religious ritual; even nuns could not touch holy objects. Paul set the standard by saying that women should not talk in public (1 Cor 14:34). But, in the 12th century, there developed a cult of Mary and Mary Magdalene, the sinner who repented. These two Marys became symbols of women's faithfulness and self-sacrifice.

Grossman claims that in the Middle Ages in Ashkenaz, changes for the better came about regarding women's performance of the *mitzvot*. In the Bible, he notes, women played no role in public worship. The Talmud exempted women from *mitzvot* such as prayer and Torah study. But, in the Middle Ages, rabbis granted women in Ashkenaz permission to recite a blessing upon performing a ritual act from which they were exempt, such as shaking a palm branch (*lulav*).[28]

Reciting a superfluous blessing was viewed by some rabbis as taking God's name in vain, a violation of the third commandment. But the Tosafists, commentators on the Babylonian Talmud (11th–13th century), did not see it that way. In several long notes on the subject, they say that

substantial numbers of women were already engaging in such a practice and that they therefore uphold it and justify it.[29] It was women's improved economic and social standing, says Grossman, that brought about
a greater partnership in religious life. He goes on to cite a 13th-century
ruling by R. Mordecai b. Hillel that all women must recline at the seder,
because all women fall into the category of aristocratic women (nashim
ḥashuvot). R. Jacob b. Moses Moellin (Maharil, 14th century) required
that women be present at prayer services on Rosh Hashanah from beginning to end. R. Yonah Girondi (13th century) required that women pray—
evening, morning, and afternoon(!).[30] Women attended synagogues in this
time period in greater numbers, but their lack of knowledge of Hebrew
stopped them from active participation in liturgical activity. Grossman
claims that, even as women had a great attraction to the synagogue, they
also had the perception of being distanced from holy things when they
were menstruants.[31]

Other ways in which women's ritual participation increased was
their participation in the circumcision ceremony for a son or grandson
(sandaqit), their being counted in a mixed quorum for the Grace after
meals, and their gathering on their own to form a quorum for Grace.[32]
Women were trusted to remove leavened products from the home before
Passover (biur ḥameṣ), as they were in the Talmud.[33] Some authorities allowed women to serve as circumcisers (mohalot) before the fact, some after the fact, but some not at all.[34] This leniency may have been intended
to help small communities in Franco-Germany that lacked a male mo-
hel. The Talmud allows women to serve as slaughterers, and it seems that
women functioned in this role in the Middle Ages.[35] This practice, too,
was useful for small Jewish communities, where a woman would train her
daughters in how to slaughter.

What do all of these changes suggest? According to Grossman, they
show that women participated more actively in the religious life of the
community than they did in Babylonia in the Geonic period (7th-11th
centuries). He may be right, and the material he cites is impressive, but
it is important to note that the Talmud raises nearly all of these issues.
Since we do not have information on what women were doing in the time
of the Talmud, it is hard to say that in Ashkenaz they were more active
in performing ritual acts. Perhaps women in Ashkenaz were walking in
the footsteps of their progenitresses who had also adopted these practices.
It is not clear that they were breaking new ground.[36] We have very little
evidence from the talmudic period about how people lived. One cannot,

therefore, make claims that women's lives improved or worsened in the Middle Ages vis-à-vis the talmudic period, because we have no basis for comparison.

Violence Against Women

Grossman states clearly that wife-beating occurred in the Middle Ages in all societal classes. The sages fought against it, but with limited success. Grossman attributes this opprobrious behavior of Jewish men to the influence of surrounding cultures. When Jews lived in Israel, he says, there is very little mention of wife-beating.

This, however, is an argument from silence. If one surveys talmudic literature, one finds only a few references to this topic. The Tosefta fines a husband who beats and injures his wife or anyone else who beats her (*t. Baba Qamma* 9:14). There is also a Mishnah on the subject of wife-beating, which shares many phrases with the Tosefta paragraph; it says that the moneys a man pays a woman for having injured her (*pegamah*) belong to her, not to him (*m. Ketubot* 6:1).[37] This reference to wife-beating is often overlooked because its wording is not clear. The Mishnah's mention of injuries inflicted on a woman by a man can refer to an assailant outside the family and to inadvertent assault, but the phrase surely includes a wife-beating husband, too. Even so, the existence of laws about compensation for an assault on a woman (or on a wife) does not justify the conclusion that wife-beating was (or was not) prevalent.

Grossman goes on to say that the main questions about medieval wife-beating are (1) what was the punishment for it, (2) could a husband beat a wife to make her do her household chores, and (3) was wife-beating grounds for divorce? The context in which wife-beating is examined is that of a hierarchical, medieval European society. As already noted, women were under the authority of husbands. People believed that beating was a valid educational tool, and, as a result, wife-beating was standard social behavior.

In tracing Jewish attitudes toward, and laws regarding, wife-beating, Grossman begins with Babylonia. The Qur'an permits wife-beating for immodesty and for failure to fulfill household tasks.[38] Babylonian rabbis living in Muslim society in the posttalmudic period allowed wife-beating for the purpose of pressuring women to perform household tasks, but for no other reason. Maimonides, living in a Muslim society in Egypt in the

12th century, also says that if a woman does not perform her household tasks, she may be forced to comply, even beaten with a whip.[39]

Let me point out that the 16th-century *Shulḥan Arukh*, which often copies Maimonides word for word, does so in this case, too, but deletes the phrase "even with a whip," stopping after "they force her to comply" (*kofin otah*).[40] It appears that Karo, the author of the code, felt that whipping a woman went beyond what was permissible. The Talmud does not prescribe beating a woman with a whip for any reason whatsoever.

Let me also point out that, when commenting on a husband who beats his wife and then must pay her for injury, Maimonides again innovates and says that the money may be kept by the woman and spent as she wishes. He attributes this ruling to the heads of talmudic academies in Babylonia in the posttalmudic period (*geonim*). The money need not be invested in land for her, as some interpret the corresponding Mishnah. The lesson seems to be this: a husband has permission to beat his wife for not doing her job, but if he injures her, he will have to pay her and she will be able to do with the money as she pleases.

Turning to the topic of divorce as a consequence of wife-beating, Grossman cites an anonymous geonic responsum that says that a husband who beats his wife is not forced to write her a divorce decree (*get*).[41] Another gaon, R. Paltoi (842–857, Pumbedita), however, ruled in an opposite manner, saying that the husband must divorce his wife if he beats her. This gives power to the woman, for it serves as a deterrent to corporal punishment.[42]

R. Menahem Hameiri (13th century, Provence), the author of many volumes of Talmud commentary, was asked if a man could beat his wife with a stick when she was a menstruant and answered that her being a menstruant made no difference but that one should not beat a wife. Other Ashkenazi authorities said that a beaten wife is like any other injured person and should collect payment from her husband. R. Peretz of Corbeil spoke out strongly against beating wives. He even suggested that wife-beaters be banned (*ḥerem*). He further said that beating is grounds for divorce, as did R. Isaiah of Trani (13th century, Italy). In Germany, R. Meir of Rothenberg (13th century) and others prescribed divorce for a husband who continued to beat his wife. R. Simhah of Speyer allowed non-Jews to beat a wife-beating husband into granting his wife a divorce(!).[43]

Grossman warns the reader not to confuse the objection of sages to wife-beating with the reality of Jewish life in Ashkenaz in the Middle Ages, when wife-beating was happening. The fact that the sages objected may have helped women who were lodging complaints against husbands but should not be interpreted as ending this behavior.[44] He also talks about the important enactment made by the Geonim in 651 C.E. (*taqqanat hamoredet*) that allowed a woman to divorce her husband for almost any reason. The origins of this precept can be found in the Talmud.[45] This enactment was later repudiated by R. Eliezer b. Natan, Rabbenu Tam, and others (12th century) on the grounds that forcing a divorce was against Jewish law; the divorce decree (*get*) was therefore not valid and the children of any ensuing marriage were bastards (*mamzerim*).[46]

It seems that in the 12th and 13th centuries, many women fell into the category of "rebellious" wives, as the rabbis understood it.[47] R. Meir of Rothenberg, when confronted with such women, said that they were not modest like the women of old and that they should take heed and honor their husbands. R. Asher (beginning of 14th century), a student of R. Meir, wrote that if women were allowed to divorce their husbands, no marriage would remain intact; the women would find some other man to their liking and leave their husbands. Grossman goes on to point out that divorce was common in the Jewish community and was undermining the family. For that reason, leaders had to find a way to stop women from divorcing their husbands. He claims that these remarks of R. Asher are evidence of the breakdown of the patriarchal family and the rise in "women's power and self-confidence" (*kohan uvithonan ha'asmi*).[48] Note that it is women who are being blamed for the breakdown of the family, not men, even though it is men, in many cases, who are the cause of divorce. There is a level of absurdity, to my mind, in talking about a society in which husbands may beat wives and then blaming women for exercising their right to divorce their husbands, thereby undermining the family. These divorces by women are hardly acts of self-confidence, as suggested by Grossman, but are instead acts of self-preservation.

At the end of his volume, Grossman summarizes his findings. He says that women's lives in the Middle Ages improved in ten ways and worsened in three. He puts women's right to divorce men at the top of the list of ten, even though, as he himself notes, this right was withdrawn in the 12th century, which was still very much the Middle Ages. Later in the period, a woman could still ask for a divorce, and her husband was well advised to grant it, but she could no longer force it. Grossman then lists the prohibition of bigamy and of forcible divorce by a husband of his wife, which, I agree, truly benefited women. He goes on to say that women played an important economic role, that more women learned Torah, that women could recite blessings on *mitzvot* from which they were exempt, and that abusive husbands were punished.[49] He even lists the important place women occupied in kabbalistic thinking. On the other hand, women's lives worsened because of changing attitudes: in Muslim countries, women were asked to dress more modestly, attitudes toward menstruants grew more stringent, and many philosophers saw women as intrinsically inferior to men.[50]

I do not see how Grossman's ten positive changes translate into progress over the talmudic period. If wife-beating was widespread, women's status did not improve, even if men were punished for such actions (although punishment surely was a disincentive to beat one's wife). It seems to me that Grossman is trying to put a patina of improvement on women's medieval status in order to defend medieval rabbis. His arguments fall short.

One other volume on medieval Judaism focuses to some degree on the subject of women. Yisrael TaShma has written extensively on medieval, Ashkenazic popular practice (*minhag*). In *Ritual, Custom, and Reality in Franco-Germany, 1000–1350*,[51] he devotes two chapters to women, one about their reciting blessings when performing ritual acts on a voluntary basis, and the other about their wearing jewelry out into the street on the Sabbath. In both chapters, the author makes it clear that when popular practice conflicted with talmudic rulings, practice often triumphed. In these two instances, women's practice forced the hand of the halakhists.

The last volume I consider is Elimelech Westreich's *Transitions in the Legal Status of the Wife in Jewish Law*.[52] This is a detailed study of the enactments of Rabbenu Gershom, the Light of the Exile (11th century, Ashkenaz), which are among the most famous pieces of Jewish legislation. R. Gershom banned both polygamy and forcible divorce. Prior to reading Westreich's research, one might have concluded that, before the 11th century, Jewish men were taking multiple wives and women were being divorced against their will. Westreich shows that the reality was otherwise, that the ban on polygamy had a long prehistory, and that the corresponding ban on forcible divorce became a necessary adjunct to the ban on polygamy. Once a dissatisfied man could no longer take additional wives, he would have to dispose of the first wife in order to take a second. By banning forcible divorce, Rabbenu Gershom gave women protection from divorce without good reason at a time in their lives when they might be less desirable to either a first or second husband than they were when they were younger. One might almost say that these bans shifted the model of marriage from men seeking sexual partners for their own pleasure, which would mean taking second or even third wives as the first ones aged, to companionate marriage. If we assume that most women did not want divorce late in life, married couples would continue living together into old age.

Before reviewing Westreich's research, let me make reference to an earlier study of these enactments. In 1961, Ze'ev Falk, wrote a history of Rabbenu Gershom's enactments.[53] In placing the enactments in a broader context, he notes that, as early as 326 C.E., the Catholic Church banned both polygamy and concubinage.[54] Catholicism saw marriage not just as a covenant between a man and a woman but as the concrete expression of God's actions, for it is God who joins couples. That ban led not only to monogamy but to a ban on divorce.[55] But, in Germany, at the end of the 9th century, it became common practice for Christian men to take a concubine. Church authorities warned men to put an end to this practice but not by divorcing their wives of many years. Falk claims that, even though Jews were no longer practicing polygamy in Ashkenaz, they were witnesses to the debates about concubines. It was these developments that led Rabbenu Gershom to issue his ban on polygamy. As for enforcing it, although there was general voluntary compliance, the rabbis did not force a divorce if a man took a second wife. This left the enactment imperfect, notes Falk. Even so, this radical change in the structuring of the family—not introducing a second wife, who would make life difficult for the first—was one factor that led to "equal rights for husband and wife"— so says Falk.[56]

I don't think the issue is whether the Jewish community at large was monogamous. It seems that there was good reason for men to accept such a marital restriction because of the expenses that a second wife, and a second family, would require. Mordechai Friedman, however, says that the documents in the Cairo Genizah seem to suggest that the phenomenon of polygamy was widespread.[57] But, whatever the numbers, as long as the law did not protect a woman from her husband's taking a second wife against her will, it was treating women very differently from men and allowing them to be "insulted and humiliated," to use Westreich's terms.[58] Such permission speaks volumes about the powerlessness of wives and of their inability to protect themselves from men who had their own interests at heart. It portrays Judaism as a patriarchally configured religion in the fundamental sense of the term "patriarchy"—that men are primary and women secondary.

Upon analyzing several responsa written by Rabbenu Gershom, Westreich finds that they make no reference to the enactment of a ban either on polygamy or on forcible divorce, which might imply that the enactments were made by someone else. He concludes that Rabbenu Gershom did make an enactment against polygamy but that it was limited in scope and covered a limited geographical area. The reason he did not make an enactment against forcible divorce, once he had forbidden the taking of second wives, was that he saw no reason to ban men from forcing a divorce on women, since women at that time could still invoke the enactment of the rebellious wife (mentioned earlier) and force a divorce on their husbands. True, they had to seek the assistance of the local court to pressure the husband into writing a *get* and would not receive their *ketubah* payment upon leaving their husband, but they could still divorce a husband. It was later, when Rabbenu Tam ended women's right to walk out of a marriage with almost no grounds, that it became necessary, for the protection of women, to stop men from forcing a divorce when the husband wanted to marry someone else but could no longer simply bring her into his home. Westreich thus disagrees with Grossman. The enactment forbidding forcible divorce was not made to stop men from divorcing their first wives in order to marry a second, as claims Grossman. Rather, once women lost the right to divorce their husbands rather easily, it was only fair to make an enactment to stop husbands from forcibly divorcing their wives.

In summarizing these developments and others, Westreich says that women in Ashkenaz in the Middle Ages, because they enjoyed extensive protection of their marital standing, approached "equality in legal standing with men."[59] Communities regarded Rabbenu Gershom's enactments as authoritative, as if given at Sinai. In other words, losing the right to divorce one's husband did not harm women because husbands were no longer allowed to take second wives or to divorce their first wives against their will.[60]

I am not convinced. I fail to see how this "equality" helps a woman in a bad marriage whose husband will not divorce her. Husbands beat wives much more than wives beat husbands. Husbands are heads of households, and wives are subordinate to them. Therefore, taking away a woman's right to divorce her husband means that she cannot free herself from an abusive husband. That is a serious disadvantage. As solid as Westreich's analysis is, the desire to defend the rabbis of the past seems to have led him to see things as more rosy than they really were.

Summary and Implications for the Future

The past twenty-five years have brought a sea change in the reading of rabbinic texts. It used to be possible merely to collect some sources on women and say, "Here is what the Talmud says about women: 'Love your wife and honor her more than yourself.'"[61] We have now progressed way beyond that. Once a feminist approach to texts was created by the academy, it became possible and necessary to look at Judaism through a feminist lens. It should surprise no one that Judaism, like all other ancient religions, favored men over women and configured society in a patriarchal manner. One cannot separate religion from society.

Jacob Neusner and Judith Wegner sought to determine to what extent Judaism views women differently from men. Their conclusions, I think, were influenced by the generally negative esteem in which the feminist movement held religion. These two scholars were looking to find in Judaism precisely what others found in other ancient societies. In broad strokes, they were right. But in many details I think they were wrong. Their work led to mine. My findings are that rabbis retained the patriarchy that characterized Judaism but modified it somewhat. Motives are hard to discern. Rather than say that rabbis succumbed to popular practice, which was more liberal than the law, I think it more accurate to posit that rabbis absorbed evolving ethical thinking from the general culture and allowed it to bring them to make legislative changes.

Avraham Grossman's and Elimelech Westreich's volumes on the lives and legal status of Jewish women in the Middle Ages, even if somewhat tendentious, have carried the feminist agenda forward. They paint a complicated picture of pervasive cultural influence, a rabbinic desire to remain loyal to the highly regarded texts of the past, and the pressure placed on rabbis by women who suffered inequality under the law.

That medieval women had an attraction to the life of the spirit does not surprise me. The Talmud already records, in passing, that women sought to bring sacrifices on holidays even when not required to do so, that women extended the period of menstrual impurity (*niddah*) beyond what the rabbis required of them, and that they came often to the rabbis to ask whether a spot of blood made them *niddah*.[62] It does not strike me, therefore, as warranted to say that women in the Middle Ages were more pious than their earlier talmudic sisters. We do not know. We have so little information on the life of Jews in the talmudic period that it is nearly impossible to say with certainty that Jews grew more or less polygamous in the Middle Ages, or more or less pious. Also, the Talmud reflects the lives of the rabbis. The materials of the Middle Ages seem to represent a much wider swath of Jewish society.

There are two ideas that many people today have a hard time accepting. The first is that rabbis did not treat women fairly. Since we now acknowledge the full humanity of women, which implies that they should be treated as equal to men, it is hard for people who venerate rabbis today to accept that the rabbis of the past, who created the system of Jewish observance that many still find meaningful, discriminated against women. But they were not ahead of their time (and neither was the Torah). The second notion that many people have trouble assimilating is that some rabbinic enactments that benefit women came to Judaism from other cultures. To this very day, many enlightened social practices, feminism prominent among them, are derived from the world in which we live and not from Jewish texts. It therefore behooves us to look beyond the source of the practice and judge it on its own merits, moral and otherwise.

The upshot of all of these volumes is that we are shaped by the culture in which we live and, reciprocally, also shape it. It takes time to develop a new way to read texts. Refining the meaning and message of these texts is an ongoing task. But, as we peruse volume after volume, we begin to see that the insights of the academy and of previous authors on the topic of women and Jewish law have affected the way later authors read and analyze their texts. If this trend continues and if more studies emerge on women and Jewish law, we will get ever closer to grasping what women's lives were like, what effect the patriarchal law codes had on them, and what rabbis did or did not do to ameliorate the situation in which women found themselves.

NOTES

1. Oliver Wendell Holmes, Jr., *The Essential Holmes, Selections From the Letters, Speeches, Judicial Opinions and Other Writings of Oliver Wendell Holmes, Jr.,* ed. Richard A. Posner (Chicago: University of Chicago Press, 1992), p. 230.

2. Ronald Dworkin, "Law's Empire and the Sea of the Talmud: Ronald Dworkin on Jewish Law and Interpretation," lecture delivered on December 7, 2005, at the Center for Jewish History, New York, New York.

3. For instance, in Num 27:5 Moses turns to God to decide how to resolve the request of Zelophehad's daughters to receive his parcel of land in Israel.

4. Gerda Lerner, *The Creation of Patriarchy* (New York: Oxford University Press, 1986) p. 198.

5. Lerner does note that mothers and fathers are equally praised and honored in Proverbs, a much later book of the Bible. But she fails to note that this point may be made from the early books, the Pentateuch. Children are required to honor both father and mother, to obey both, to fear both, and to avoid cursing or striking either one (Exod 20:11, 21:15,17; Num 19:3; and Deut 21:18).

6. More precisely, God orders the men to sanctify themselves and to launder their garments (v. 10). Moses then adds that they may not approach women (v. 15). Judith Plaskow derives from this verse that women were not at Sinai (*Standing Again at Sinai* [New York: Harper & Row, 1990], p. 25). I disagree with her interpretation. They were there, it seems to me, but they were secondary, not equal in standing to the men.

7. An examination of the many paragraphs about marital law in the Code of Hammurapi (§§127ff.) reveals that men are primary and women secondary (James B. Pritchard, *Ancient Near Eastern Texts Relating to the Old Testament* [Princeton: Princeton University Press, 1969], pp. 171–74). A wife, it seems, belongs to her husband; a husband does not belong to a wife.

8. Rachel Biale, *Women and Jewish Law* (New York: Schocken Books, 1984), p. 14.

9. She says, for instance, that barring women from reading the Torah in public is a perpetuation of that aspect of Jewish law that makes women second-class members of society (ibid., p. 28).

10. Ibid., pp. 33–35.

11. Ibid., p. 38.

12. David M. Feldman, *Marital Relations, Birth Control, and Abortion in Jewish Law* (New York: Schocken Books, 1974), pp. 257–59.

13. R. Biale, *Women and Jewish Law*, pp. 219–38.

14. The problem when talking about approaches to Jewish law is that personal bias makes objective review of the materials nearly impossible. If someone wishes to find a way to allow a woman to lead Grace for others, he or she will succeed in doing so. If someone wishes to find a way to declare it illegal or against *halakhah* for a woman to lead Grace for others, he or she will also succeed in doing so. Each will say that the *halakhah* leads to his or her conclusion and to no other.

15. Jacob Neusner, *Method and Meaning in Ancient Judaism* (Missoula, MT: Scholars Press, 1979); Judith Wegner, *Chattel or Person, The Status of Women in the Mishnah* (New York: Oxford University Press, 1988).

16. Judith Hauptman, "Feminist Perspectives on Rabbinic Texts" in *Feminist Perspectives on Jewish Studies*, ed. Lynn Davidman and Shelley Tenenbaum (New Haven: Yale University Press, 1994), pp. 40–61.

17. Cf. Judith Hauptman, *Rereading the Rabbis: A Woman's Voice* (Boulder, CO: Westview Press, 1998), chapter 2.

18. Avraham Grossman, *Ḥasidot Umordot: Nashim Yehudiyot Be'airopa*

Biyemei Habeinayim (Jerusalem: The Zalman Shazar Center for Jewish History, 2001; unless stated otherwise, all page references are to the English version, Waltham: Brandeis University Press, 2004); and Elimelech Westreich, *Temurot beMa-amad HaIshah BaMishpat HaIvri, Masa bein Masorot* (Jerusalem: Magnes Press, 2002).

19. Judith Baskin, "Jewish Women in the Middle Ages," in her book *Jewish Women in Historical Perspective* (Detroit: Wayne State University Press, 1991), pp. 94–114.

20. A. Grossman, *Pious and Rebellious*, p. xiii.

21. Ibid., p. 1.

22. Ibid., p. 2.

23. Grossman claims that the halakhic literature is the best source for determining women's status because literary sources were influenced by the fabliaux, which often portrayed women in negative light (*Pious and Rebellious*, p. 4).

24. R. Eliezer says that a father who teaches his daughter Torah teaches her licentiousness (*m. Sotah* 3:4). Ben Azzai, in dissent, says that a father is obligated to teach his daughter Torah lest she one day be forced to drink the bitter waters. She should know that her merit will protect her.

25. A. Grossman, *Pious and Rebellious*, p. 154. Some women in Christian and Muslim society received an education; however, most Muslim women remained illiterate. The women whom Muslims educated were taught at home, not in madrasas (ibid., p. 157).

26. Women are regularly viewed by men as capable of witchcraft, starting with the Bible and continuing in the Talmud; see Exod 22:17 and *b. Sanhedrin* 67a.

27. A. Grossman, *Pious and Rebellious*, p. 161. According to *Sefer Ḥasidim*, one should teach women *aggadah* and midrash and the easy parts of the Talmud. Women heard the sermon (*derashah*) on Shabbat in the *Ḥasidei Ashkenaz* community.

28. A. Grossman, *Pious and Rebellious*, p. 178.

29. Mordecai, in his commentary on *b. Shabbat* (paragraph 286), quotes Rabbenu Tam, an 11th-century Tosafist, who says: women may recite blessings on optional ritual acts because it is their custom to perform these acts (*mishum denahagu laʾasotan ule-qayeman*); see also Tosafot at *b. Eruvin* 96a, s.v. *dilma*.

30. A. Grossman, *Pious and Rebellious*, pp. 182–83.

31. Ibid., p. 183.

32. Meir b. Baruch of Rothenberg (d. 1293) opposed this practice because of the unacceptability of women mingling with men (A. Grossman, *Pious and Rebellious*, p. 185). Grossman claims that the reason women could not count in the quorum of three for Grace (*zimmun*) is that to do so one had to be free, and women were seen as subordinate to husbands. Even so, Grossman notes that in Ashkenaz there were men who counted women in the *zimmun* for ten, implying that their relatively high status led to this exception. Some women gathered

in a *zimmun* by themselves (p. 187). R. Simhah joined a woman to nine men to be able to recite God's name in the *zimmun*. As we will later see, this same R. Simhah was strict with husbands who beat their wives.

33. *B. Pesahim* 4a; A. Grossman, *Pious and Rebellious*, p. 189.

34. A. Grossman, *Pious and Rebellious*, p. 190.

35. *M. Hullin* 1:1, *m. Zevahim* 3:1; A. Grossman, *Pious and Rebellious*, pp. 190–91.

36. That they joined men in *zimmun* seems new, but it does not seem to have been widespread.

37. See my analysis of these texts in *Rereading the Mishnah: A New Approach to Ancient Jewish Texts* (Tübingen: Mohr Siebeck, 2005), pp. 74–86.

38. Qur'an 4:34.

'39. Maimonides, *Hilkhot Ishut* 21:10 (*kofin otah ve'osah, ve-'afilu bashot*). Grossman suggests that R. Hai Gaon may have preceded Maimonides in this ruling (*Pious and Rebellious*, Hebrew edition, p. 380).

40. *Shulhan Arukh, Even Ha'ezer, Hilkhot Ketubot* 80:15. Grossman notes that it is not clear who, according to Maimonides, may whip her—the husband or the court. He says that he used to think it meant the husband but now thinks it means the court; his mind was changed by R. Qapah, R. Zvi Tal and others (A. Grossman, *Pious and Rebellious*, p. 220; see Hebrew edition, p. 380, n. 38). The word *kofin* means "is forced." Who does the forcing? The court? Someone else? It is not clear. This word, used about fifty times in tannaitic literature, never has a subject. In this context, it seems to mean the husband. Grossman further notes that Sefardic commentators, including R. Solomon b. Abraham Adret (Rashba), clearly state that it is the husband who may beat the wife (*kofin otah ve'osah*). R. Abraham b. David of Posquieres (12th century, Provence) writes, in commenting on Maimonides' permission to whip and in direct disagreement with him, that he never heard of disciplining women with whips. His view was influential, says Grossman (*Pious and Rebellious*, p. 220).

41. A. Grossman, *Pious and Rebellious*, Hebrew edition, p. 378.

42. Some *geonim* did not want to force a *get* lest the children of her second marriage be viewed as bastards (*mamzerim*). One responsum, in which it is stated that the husband pulled out his wife's hair, suggested that he add money to the *ketubah* and thereby fulfill his punishment and that she then forgive him.

43. These German attitudes may result from women's higher standing in 11th-13th-century Ashkenaz, claims Grossman. It may also result from the influence of the pietists (*Hasidei Ashkenaz*) on the Sages of Ashkenaz. The pietists objected to any physical attack, even on an animal, and felt that the attacker should be punished physically, a kind of measure-for-measure approach to atone for his behavior. However, Grossman notes that, toward the end of the period, some Ashkenazi rabbis allowed wife beating if the woman misbehaved (i.e. cursed her parents) (*Pious and Rebellious*, p. 229).

44. He thinks that four factors stood in the way of the fight against wife beating: (1) widespread beating in surrounding culture; (2) feudal hierarchy; (3) young age at marriage; (4) the perception that corporal punishment was educational (A. Grossman, *Pious and Rebellious*, p. 230).

45. B. *Ketubot* 64a.

46. A. Grossman, *Pious and Rebellious*, p. 243.

47. Ibid., p. 244.

48. Ibid., Hebrew edition, p. 444. R. Meir of Rothenberg had ruled that a woman who opted for divorce could not get her *ketubah* payment but could walk out with her dowry. According to a student, R. Meir further ruled that she could not even take her dowry. The student says it is not clear that that the later enactment was applied (*Pious and Rebellious*, p. 245; Hebrew edition, p. 445).

49. He even lists the increase in the number of rebellious wives as a positive development, although this right of women to divorce men was withdrawn before the end of the Middle Ages.

50. A. Grossman, *Pious and Rebellious*, pp. 272ff.

51. Yisrael TaShma, *Halakhah, Metziut, Uminhag BeAshkenaz, 1000–1350* (Jerusalem: Magnes Press, 1996).

52. *Temurot beMa-amad HaIshah BaMishpat HaIvri, Masa bein Masorot* (Jerusalem: Magnes Press, 2002).

53. *Marriage and Divorce, Reforms in the Family Law of German-French Jewry* (Jerusalem: Hebrew University Students' Press, 1961). The Jewish community, Falk claims, was for the most part monogamous (p. 8), the Jews of Israel accepting the view of R. Ammi (*b. Yevamot* 65a) that bigamy is against the law and the Jews of Babylonia accepting the view of Rava that bigamy is permitted. Even so, according to Falk, the Jews of Babylonia did not practice bigamy as a rule, only in extraordinary circumstances, like levirate marriage (p. 12). On this matter, Falk is refuted by Westreich; see below.

54. Ibid., p. 22.

55. Ibid., p. 20.

56. Ibid., p. 31.

57. Mordechai Akiva Friedman, *Jewish Polygyny in the Middle Ages* (Jerusalem: Mosad Bialik, 1986), pp. 2ff. For the evidence from the Cairo geniza, see the chapter "Women in Medieval Jewish Societies," by Renée Levine Melammed.

58. See Adiel Shremer, *Male and Female He Created Them: Jewish Marriage in the Late Second Temple, Mishnah and Talmud Periods* (Jerusalem: Merkaz Zalman Shazar Letoldot Yisrael [Hebrew], 2003), chapter 6, "*Ribui Nashim.*" Practices varied in the land of Israel and in Babylonia, and also over time.

59. E. Westreich, *Transitions in the Legal Status of the Wife in Jewish Law*, p. 157.

60. The ban on forcible divorce was lifted in certain cases, such as for women who lose mental capacity, convert to another religion, or transgress *mitzvot*. There were no reciprocal rules for women divorcing men.

61. *B. Yevamot* 62b.

62. *B. Ḥagigah* 16b; *b. Niddah* 66a; *b. Niddah* 20b.

Part II

||||||||||||||||||||||||||||||||||||||||||||||||||||||||||||||||

History

||||||||||||||||||||||||||||||||||||||||||||||||||||

4

Women in Medieval Jewish Societies

Renée Levine Melammed

The past few decades have seen tremendous advances in the study of women's lives in medieval Jewish societies thanks to the discovery of new material and to the feminist technique of asking new questions of old material. The medieval groups that have been researched to date include women in the Mediterranean, in Spain, in Ashkenazi countries, and in the Middle East.

Recent research has uncovered previously unknown documents pertaining to the lives of two groups, namely women in medieval Mediterranean ("Genizah society") and in 15th- and 16th-century crypto-Jewish society.

The story of the discovery of the Cairo Genizah is well known: at the end of the 19th century, a storehouse of documents that had been closed for centuries was located in the ceiling of the Ibn Ezra synagogue in Fustat, or Old Cairo.[1] Traditionally, Jewish communities have buried or stored documents and books that were either written in Hebrew or had the name of God in them, but this particular storehouse included an unusual amount of atypical material. Because the Jews in Arab lands spoke and wrote Judeo-Arabic, a dialect of Arabic written in Hebrew letters, this genizah held a vast and amazing collection of fragments as well as complete documents recorded in this language. The period from 950 to 1250 is known as the classical Genizah period; these documents reveal a medieval Jewish world in the Mediterranean characterized by a surprising amount of movement and mobility.[2] Merchants, pilgrims, indigents, and women were all on the move, along with ideas and merchandise.

How did women make their voices heard in this medieval Mediterranean society, and how do we, in the 21st century, hear about or, better yet, hear from the women? Are they hidden behind a veil, or do their voices appear without accompaniment? Is a male member of the family responsible for them here as well?

Because of the separations created by living in a mobile society, letter writing became a necessity as a means of communication, and women appeared in the letters as recipients and as senders, a surprising discovery unto itself. Sometimes we hear the women's voices indirectly, as in a letter written by a husband to his wife, frequently with references to comments made by the wife in her letters to him. Some express love and nostalgia for their homes, families, and/or mates; despite the fact that these were arranged marriages, love might result, although some letters were far less tender than others in style. By contrast, women's voices can be heard directly in the letters they themselves wrote or dictated.[3]

Generational separations also prompted correspondence, in particular between a parent and a child. No matter what age the child, maintaining contact was of the utmost importance to the parent. Within the nuclear family unit, we also find that siblings needed to communicate with one another when the distance between them offered no other alternative.

In spite of the matchmaking that was responsible for these couples' unions and the need to follow the convention of writing in the third person, expressions of love slip through the lines and with restraint. Thus, a husband in Hebron writes to his wife:

> To her honor, the eminent, superior, pious and righteous [woman]. What I should like her to know is that I have become terribly ill in Hebron. Were it not for her prayers for me, her righteousness and piety, this servant would be utterly despondent. But I know your remarkable piety [and am therefore hopeful]. Don't ask what nostalgia I feel for the little one and for you. May God, blessed be He, bring about our reunion sooner rather than later. . . . I have not extricated myself from suspension of activity and low income. O Wife, let your heart be only satisfied with me. . . . I pray to God to recompense you with well-being. . . . [May God] give you happiness . . . pray for you abundantly. As for me, I have nothing but your prayers and your pure souls. Peace be upon the children of Israel. May God reunite us soon and thousands of times; I shall not, by God, be lonely for you.[4]

Another husband, whose wife might not have been able to read, wrote:

> May Rabbi Elijah be so kind as to read this note to Umm Joseph . . . and not delay it for a moment, for I heard about her illness. . . . From the one

who loves you and is grateful for your affection, Bu-al Faraj, who informs Umm Joseph [the wife] that I have been tormented by this misery I have been in since the day you met me in the synagogue and even before. My heart has not been void of thinking about you and about your situation, and I have always inquired after you. . . . If I could, I would be there in person instead of by means of this note, but [my] situation is not hidden from you. Give my greetings to the children, may God preserve them, and to the young girls, may the Holy One Blessed be He restore her to normal health and lighten her heart. And peace.[5]

Women's voices can also be heard directly, and one cannot overemphasize how rare it is to find women writing and their writings preserved from a period when women, on the whole, were illiterate. Thus, there is the case of the wife whose husband is away and who has no interest in joining him; she composes a letter in which she states, among other things:

I write to sheikh Khalaf, may God prolong his life and perpetuate his honor and favor, and may He reunite us soon in the happiest of circumstances and in good health. I wish to inform you that since I have been alone following your departure, I have had no one to look after [my affairs]. Furthermore, from the time that you left me, you have not seen fit to send me a letter as people ordinarily do. Now if you have spurned [me, God], the exalted, will certainly rescue me. You may suppose that I shall come to Fustat, but I shall never do so. If I were to come, we two would not live happily together. May God never cause dissension between us! Greetings . . . And peace.[6]

At the same time, mothers spoke to their children through letters. For example, one mother wrote to her sons about the predicament of the children of one of them:

My letter is to the two dear and fortunate sons, may God, the exalted, give them success and reunite us soon in well-being and health. Aside from this, I yearn for you two greatly. Do not ask how heavy my heart is because of you. I inform you that Fustat is in great danger. No one can leave or enter [the town] because of the slave soldiers who run rampant everywhere. . . . If I were to begin to tell you what Fustat is suffering, the account would be too long and paper would not suffice. This is just a part of what took place. No report can be compared to seeing for oneself. . . . The young ones are extremely ill and we cannot abandon them. No water skin can be obtained nor is bread available. There are no medications to relieve the shock of the illness. . . . For now we are content that you are safe from this business until the present. By God, God protect yourself and do not leave the place where you are. We are in Fustat. We are unable to go to Cairo. Consider our situation and do not abandon the little ones.[7]

The Genizah contains a letter from a woman living in the Western Galilee to her mother in Cairo; this woman's husband wants to take her further away from her family, to his home in Aleppo, Syria. Thus, she wrote: "I wish to inform you, mother of mine, that I arrived . . . but my heart was still with you. . . . My yearning and loneliness by our separation is something I cannot well describe. . . . I wish to inform you, mother of mine, that from the time of my leaving you my life has not been serene. . . . My spirit has become weary, and by God, try to release me from this situation. . . . I am with him in the fire . . . from her daughter, may she not be bereft of her."[8]

One mother wrote a letter to remind her son of how desperately his sister missed him, and thus her words represented her daughter's voice, as well. She wrote: "In the name of the Merciful One. From the mother of Abu l'Hasan. My letter is to my son, the dearest person to me—may God prolong his honor and favor, and always bestow good fortune upon you. Apart from this, do not ask how much we yearn for you. We sent you a number of letters but have not received your response. You said that you and the little ones were coming to me for the holiday, but you did not come, so that our hearts were very despondent. Your sister misses you greatly, and keeps watching the door, longing for you."[9]

Needless to say, communication was not always indirect, for women wrote to and received letters from their siblings; they appeared to be worried about one another, especially when communication was interrupted or when facing distress. A woman living in Tunisia sent a business letter with the following message: "If my cousin Barhun b. Isma'il happens to be in town, please give him my best regards and tell him that his sister is very much yearning for him. She has not seen any letter from him since he left, nor any package; she knows about him only through the letters of others. Now, if he is on his way home, may God, the exalted, grant him a safe passage. But if he is staying on, he had better send her some cash she could use for her little ones, the girls."[10]

A well-known example relates to Barakat and Rayyisa, siblings whose beloved mother passed away. Comforting his sister after their mother's death, the letterwriter begins:

From her brother Barakat, may he protect her from evil. I wish to express to you, my sister, who is most noble, virtuous and understanding, my consolation for the loss, by God's will, of the precious jewel, our lady, our mother, may God place her in Paradise. This loss has removed our joy, taken away our cheer, and let fall the crown of our head. We always thrived through her merit and prayed to God by virtue of her worthiness. Now, my sister, you know and understand more than anyone that all of creation must partake of this cup [of sorrow]. . . . And you, Rayyisa, be as patient as you can, for if you were to weep for a thousand years, your tears would be totally unavailing. You would instead make yourself ill, and you only would perish. My sister, I implore you in God's name to be forbearing toward Him. . . . Contemplate, my sister, the book of Ecclesiastes. . . . Furthermore, I am sending to you the book *Relief After Distress* [in Arabic] for you to study. And know that I am only writing this note after having refreshed my eyes with tears on account of my losing her and her love. But we have no recourse from God's decree. . . . Whoever has left behind someone like you has not really died. My sister, I implore you in the name of God not to cause yourself to perish for something that is of no avail. . . . Occupy yourself [with study] so that you do not perish. . . . Study Ecclesiastes and Proverbs, and bear stoutly the judgment of your creator, the Truth. Know that the perpetual wish and prayer of the departed was that she die in your arms and in the arms of your brothers. . . . May God in His mercy accompany you and support you by His might. . . Fortify your spirit by means of God. . . . Forgive me for not coming to condole with you. . . . May God support and sustain you and give you success and may He protect you from all harm and give you happiness and guidance and pass on to you and me her merit. . . . May God help you. Peace be with you.[11]

While we have no idea if this mother left a will, we know that other women did. By studying them, we find a second wonderful and unexpected source of information and can see how these women succeeded in expressing their desires and giving specific instructions to be followed after their demise. One case deals with a deathbed statement in 1143 from Sitt al-Ahl, the wife of a merchant. Her family resided on the third floor of her house, and she wanted to be sure they would remain there after her passing and that her wishes would be carried out.

> When my father gave me this large house . . . a year and a half ago, a document about this gift was made out before Muslim authorities. But before this he imposed on me the condition that he, my mother, and my brother . . . should never be forced to leave the upper floor, as long as they lived in this world. My father should stay in that apartment as long as he lives. I wish now that this stipulation should be carried out unchanged, for it was made in the presence of my husband, the elder Abu Nasr. When that which is ordained for me comes to pass, I wish to be buried in this house in which I am now and not carried out [to the cemetery] except when one of my family dies, I mean, my father, mother, or brother. Then I might be carried out together with the one who will die. The maidservant Fuz does not belong to him [her husband]; my mother gave me the money with which I bought her. She has a daughter, who belongs to my mother, not to me. My boy shall stay with my mother as he does not. No one shall separate him from them. . . . I wish to have the daughter of my brother Abu 'l-Surur for my boy Musa.[12]

Then she describes the cost and quality of the funeral attire to be purchased for her and how to deal with the tenant's rent payments, as well as who is to mourn her, in this case, Muslim professional keeners.

Wealthy women were concerned about how their money would be spent, how their children would be raised, and, in particular, how elaborate their funerals would be. There are numerous examples of instructions given by women prior to their demise. For example, in the mid-12th century, Sitt al-Husn, a woman of means who also owned real estate, made a deathbed declaration, in this case, on the Sabbath, which was later recorded by the clerk who was present: "This house belongs to his [R. Nathan b. Samuel, a judge] wife, Sitt al-Husn, the daughter of Sa'ada, known as the 'daughter of the hunchbacked woman.' She was of sound mind, knowing what she said and talked about, and she realized that it was Saturday." At this point, four witnesses entered the room, and, since she already knew two of them because they had been the witnesses who signed her marriage contract, she was introduced to the other two.

> Whereupon she asked us to bear witness that as from now on and after her death she had freed her virgin slaves Dhahab and Sitt al-Sumr and given to

them the quarter of the house . . . which belonged to her. . . . Furthermore she willed one-half of the house, which was her home, to the community, with the proviso that the slave girls will have the right to stay in the part belonging to the community, namely, in the room in which the will was made, for the rest of their lives on the condition that they profess the Jewish faith. Both the gift and the permission to live in the house depended on this condition. . . . She also said that one-eighth of the house behind the mosque, which belonged to her in partnership with the government . . . and the elder Abu A'la b. Tammam . . . should be sold and the money used for all the expenses of her burial, such as the burial garment, the coffin, the cantors, the tomb, the bearers of the [coffin], etc. In case this was not sufficient, a headband, consisting of eleven ornaments . . . should be sold and used for the expenses. . . . If something should remain from the price of one-eighth of the aforementioned house, it shall be given to the slave girls mentioned above; likewise all clothing suitable for women. That which is not suitable for women shall belong to her husband.[13]

Other women likewise provided for their funerals and their families or for those whom they favored, such as the slave girls. Wuhsha al-Dallala was a wealthy broker from an eminent family in Alexandria. She had been married and divorced and had one daughter from this, her only marriage. She was well known in the business world, was involved in major transactions, was recognized immediately when she appeared in court (unlike most other Jewish women), and was a bit of a maverick. She was living with her lover, who was the father of her son. There are more documents in the Cairo Genizah collection pertaining to her than to any other woman.

Because she had many assets, Wuhsha left a very detailed will, which she dictated to her friend, the cantor, at the end of the 11th century. She left money, rings, and a robe to her surviving brother. To one sister she left a smaller sum of money, mourning dress, part of a bridal outfit, and a headcover. Her niece received less money, a cloak, rings, clothes, and her bed, while her other sister, Sibah, was willed only money. Wuhsha provided funds for the cemetery and for the synagogues of Old Cairo; smaller sums were bequeathed to the synagogues of Dammuh and New Cairo. Small amounts of money went to various relatives, as well as to an orphan girl to whom she was related. Her only son, who was born out of wedlock, received the largest portion of her estate: rugs, carpets, and the remaining cash that was in gold. His inheritance was to be saved for him until he attained maturity. A clause was added in case he did not survive: in that case, half of his portion would be given to synagogues and the other half to other heirs in the family, such as her brother, sister, and her uncle's daughter. At this point she added a most unusual demand: "To his father, Hassun of Ashkelon, not one penny shall be given, except that two promissory notes concerning a debt of eighty dinars which he owes me will be handed over to him. But the rest is for the synagogues and the poor in equal shares." The expenses for her funeral are listed in considerable detail: a large sum was allotted for the shroud so that fine linen could be bought for it, plus a cloak, a cap, a hood, a kerchief, a veil, a cover, and, of course, her coffin. She also included appropriate payment for the pallbearers, who would be walking a considerable distance, "and all other expenses for me until I reach my grave and the tomb will be built." Wuhsha did not forget to include payment for "the cantors who will walk behind my coffin, to each according to his rank and excellence."[14] Last, she provided for the education of her young son; this meant that he should have a live-in private teacher from whom he would learn Bible and the prayers. The teacher would be provided with a blanket, a sleeping carpet, and a small stipend.

We also hear women's voices directly when they petitioned for help; these appeals were usually sent to family members, to community leaders such as the *nagid* or head of the Jewish community, or the gaon, the head of the yeshiva, or to rabbinic courts which sometimes turned to eminent rabbis like Maimonides so that they could serve as decisors.[15] Some women felt abandoned and neglected; others had been abused, verbally and physically, and often the echoes of their desperation ring in our ears.

For example, in the following case, a woman turned to her uncle for protection, a logical choice since her father had passed away. The niece had married a cousin and wrote to her uncle:

My letter is to you, my esteemed sir and leader, dearest of men to me, may God extend your life, protect you and have solicitude for you, and constantly give you good fortune and be your patron and guardian in all your affairs. What I should like to inform you of, sir, is that I cannot describe for you the situation I am in. Even if I were only the daughter of a female slave, you would take care of me for my mother's sake. . . . And do not ask what [my husband] does to me. Let us rather ask God to requite him. We had all moved into a single house. Then shortly thereafter my mother-in-law began to act against me and to alienate people from me by implanting enmity to me in her son. . . . I cannot describe to you the [miserable] state I am in until God brings us together, so that I can inform you of what your sister has inflicted upon me this year, both she and her son. You know that I have no one save God and you. So do not neglect me. Do not abandon me, for I am still under your care. And there remains no one to turn to. . . . You do good deeds for strangers, so how much more for your own child. The adversities that were inflicted upon me I cannot take . . . and I am abandoned.[16]

In a different case, a newly married woman requested a bill of repudiation from her husband; she was afraid of him, mainly because he suffered from fits each time he attempted to approach her. Needless to say, she had no prior knowledge of his condition, was no longer residing with him, and was uncertain as to how to proceed in obtaining a divorce. The question states that "the girl declared also that this husband of hers to whom she was married did not have sexual intercourse with her and that she still was a virgin and no man had known her."[17] Thus, we hear from a bride begging to be released from an impossible situation and hoping that the legal channels will help rectify such an unexpected and undesirable dilemma.

In yet another case, a woman appeals to the nagid, namely Abraham, the son of Maimonides, in a letter that Mordechai Akiva Friedman believes was dictated by her.[18] Because the circumstances were complex, the female petitioner actually appeared in court more than once; thus this tax collector's wife wrote in her appeal:

The maidservant, wife of Mansur, the tax farmer of Sunhur, kisses the ground in obedience to God, the exalted, before the court of our lord the Nagid, may his Creator exalt his eminence. She relies upon the Creator of all being and upon our lord and entreats him to attend to her for the sake of Heaven, for she has no tongue with which to speak. She reports that her son had sent a letter saying that her husband had contemplated marriage. The maidservant entreats our lord to act on behalf of her rights for the sake of God, the exalted. For I have a seven year old boy and have taken him with me to Fustat to study the Law. I am afraid that [my husband] will come and take him from me and prevent me from having access to him. I appeal to God and to you. . . . I fear that he will go to Alexandria to marry his wife to whom he is presently engaged, or that he will employ someone with permission of the judge of Alexandria and go out and marry her. Now, our lord, I appeal to God and you, for you are the father of orphans and widows, and I am your maidservant. Write a note for me to the judge of Alexandria ordering him not to perform a marriage ceremony for him save by your command, and not to delegate someone to marry him until he remits to me my delayed payment. May God grant you what I pray for you, for I am wretched and poor. May God double your reward. Peace.[19]

Another woman petitioned the head of the community, Rayyis Mevorach, for she found herself in dire need of help:

I am the wife of Abu Sari, God's mercy upon him. I married my daughter off to Joseph. . . He went on a journey before her seclusion and left her ill. She remained ill after his journey for two years. . . . There is nothing left for her save the mat that I wrap her with because of my care for her, because I have no one aside from her. No one has spoken to us today for a year and a half. When news of him arrived this Friday, that he was killed in Nastaraw, his cousin arrived . . . they sent a messenger to me and said to me: Pay me a dinar. I said to them, by the truth of your head, O my lord the head, I have nothing. . . . I am alone, I have no one. I throw myself upon God, the exalted, and upon you. Do not abandon me to poverty and do not abandon me in the hands of those who do not fear God. . . . Do not leave me. I am with them under great stress. . . . May God, the exalted, protect you before your sultan. And may your great welfare increase and not decrease.[20]

In another petition, the gaon was the recipient, and the petitioner, a working woman with her own income, was suffering from her marriage.

I hereby inform your Excellency, our Gaon—may his Rock preserve him—that I am a lonely orphan girl whom they have married to a man with no means of support. I have been with him for ten years, and he has always taken what I earned. Finally, when I was in shreds, with nothing to cover me properly, I said to him: "I shall not give you a thing anymore. I'll buy myself clothing with what I earn." He is not worth a thing, not even one dinar.

For a year or more he has given me a bad name. I went to the judges and offered to buy myself free with everything due me from him to save my honor. But they did not grant me a divorce. By God, my honor is worth something to me!

I am requesting now that the Torah scroll be taken out and that he who acted in this way and tells lies about me be excommunicated, and that I be given a certificate clearing [my honor] for God's sake. Thus you will save me from a Hell, which no one knows except God. May your welfare increase and never decrease. Amen, in eternity. Sela.[21]

This poor woman was trying to regain a bit of honor; we can hear her voice resounding in this petition.

Last, we turn to rabbinic responsa found among the Genizah fragments. Many of these questions and answers were uncovered mainly because the Jewish court of the Old Cairo community met in the Ibn Ezra synagogue, and consequently their papers were stored there, as well. As will become evident, they too can grant us an entrée into Goitein's "world of women."[22] For example, one brief question presented to Maimonides deals with a blind teacher who vows not to continue teaching a group of girls.[23] The girls had apparently been studying with him privately and, because he was blind, did not have to wear their veils. It is quite possible that the freedom granted to the girls plus the fact that the teacher could not observe any of their antics led to a frustrating classroom situation for the teacher. He must have lost his composure and sworn that he would never teach them again. Once he had calmed down, he realized that he had sworn away his income and had boxed himself into a corner precisely because he had taken an oath. As a result, he went to the court to see if he could rectify the situation. We, on the other hand, can almost hear the noise of these rambunctious schoolgirls in the classroom as they misbehave in his presence.

The best-known responsum from the collection concerns a 12th-century anonymous woman teacher in Cairo. There are actually two questions, recorded in Judeo-Arabic and translated into Hebrew, in the collection of Maimonides' responsa.[24] However, there is no pressing need here to delve into the question presented by the husband, for we do not hear his wife's voice at all when he appeals to the court and tells his tale. His question is streamlined: he is interested in obtaining permission to take a second wife, despite the fact that he is legally prevented from doing so without his first wife's consent. She refuses, and he does not explain why. Considering the nature of the responsa process, this is not surprising, for cases are presented by one side alone; the other side is neither interrogated nor consulted. The husband clearly and understandably has his own interests at heart, so has no need to let his wife's voice be heard. However, in the second responsum that deals with the same couple, we hear her voice loud and clear. Note the lengthy and detailed description of the plight of this petitioner:

Concerning a man who married a nine-year-old and she had a portion in common property with her mother-in-law and her [own] sister, and they all live in one courtyard. The mother of the aforesaid man obligated herself in writing to support the aforesaid woman for ten years, and did support her for seven years. And after those seven years, the aforementioned mother-in-law said to her: "I am unable to support you [plural]."

And the husband does not have enough [to support her] even for an hour, and he supported her for two months. The young girl became pregnant and gave birth to a male child. And when he [the husband] saw that it was difficult for him to support the household, he left the child with its mother when it was nine months old, and he traveled and was absent for three years in the Land of Israel and in Damascus and elsewhere, and he did not even leave her anything to eat for dinner that evening, not for her and not for the baby. And when he returned from his journey, he had nothing of value on his person. The clerk who collects the head tax [entry tax] caught him, for he did not have the half-dirhem to pay it, until his father paid it for him. And his aforementioned wife and his mother had to pay the poll tax for him, for fear he would be taken to jail; and he entered the courtyard and is completely destitute.

He stayed in the city for two years. The wife became pregnant and gave birth to another son. And he [the father] left him with her when he was a year and a half, and returned to traveling a second time, and he did not leave her with even an hour's worth [of support] and disappeared for another three years. The aforesaid woman's age became twenty-five years [old], and she was in utter degradation from poverty, with two sons whose hunger outweighed their satiation. And all the time that she was with him, he did not provide her with oil for light, not during the week or on the Sabbath or on the holidays; and she could never benefit from the light of a lamp unless she entered his mother's home or his brother's home, since she lives with them in the courtyard. And she was "burned out" by the poverty and the terrible situation [in which she found herself].

And she has a brother who teaches children Bible, and the woman has knowledge of the Bible. She asked her brother to let her teach the children Bible with him, so that she would have a means of sustaining herself and her sons, since she was already near to death from the misery in which she was enveloped, and he [the husband] was absent.

And he [the husband] returned from his travels and found her teaching children Bible at her brother's. And she had been teaching the children with her brother for six years. Later, as it happened, her brother went on a journey. She sat in his place and received the children and taught them Bible, and continued doing so for four years. Her firstborn son grew, and when his age was seventeen years, she took him with her to teach Bible for the aforementioned four years in her brother's stead, so as to talk with the men whose sons [were studying] with her, and she was [there] for the women coming to get their children.

And since the day the aforementioned sons were born, their father never paid the poll tax for them or their school fees for the House of Torah study, nor did he clothe them at all, neither clothing nor turban nor a shoe for their feet. And the woman was under his authority twenty-five years, and he never bought a mat to spread out under them but once, and did not buy a bed-covering or pillow or any household goods; even the linseed oil that she lights, if she did not buy it on her own, she would never have been able to light a lamp. Neither she nor the children have had any pleasure from him, not even verbally, except for curses and foul language.

He told her: "Either live in your house like everyone else or give me the right to wed [another woman]." The aforesaid woman said to him: "I am sick and tired of poverty, which I had at first, and my sons and I have only been able to survive since the day I began teaching the children." And she said to him: "If you want a divorce, I will release you and not detain you. But let you marry [another woman]? I shall never do that!"

Despite the fact that he is at his mother's day and night, and if he buys something for a pittance, it is for him and his mother, and his wife knows nothing of it; later he complains to everyone in the city that she [the wife] is not fulfilling his needs and is not sleeping at home.

She told him: "We have no need of such shame; come, I will take you from your mother's. I will not prevent you from sleeping at home. And if you want, come and live with me at the school, rent out the portion that is mine in the partnership with your mother and my sister, and take the rent for yourself, for I am split in two courtyards [i.e., I have property in one courtyard but rent in another] and pay fourteen *dirhem* rent to the school. And I get no profit from the part that is mine in the courtyard, not for the apartment nor for the rent, in that I forfeit my profit from it out of generosity to you and your mother."

He said to her: "I will not rent it, and I will not take the rent, but you will either live in your house like the rest of the daughters of Israel or grant me the right to marry another."

Later he made a pretext and said to her: "I will borrow a *dinar* and buy you wheat, and you will sit [live] at home." She said to him: "My living is not like other professions, so that I can pick it up again tomorrow if I abandon it today. If I abandon my students even for one day, I will not find them when I return and seek them out, for their parents will take them to other schools. And the people do not bring their children to the aforesaid older son, but [come] because of me, for he is but a lad. And the two afore-mentioned sons have no trade in which to work except Torah study. And if I discontinue teaching the children, I shall lose the children and there will be no wheat [bread], and you will travel and go off as is your custom, and I will remain, the boys and I, and we will be lost, for they have no trade."

Holy eminence, may the Lord glorify you: Does she have to leave her profession and return to [what she had] in the beginning? And does she have to fulfill his needs and serve him, when he does not provide her with food or drink or clothes and does not do a thing for her that is said in the Torah? And is she required to give him permission to marry [another woman]? And inform us, what is the legal obligation in all that is written above? Make it clear to us, as we have been accustomed to your mercy. May your compensation be doubled from heaven.[25]

This is, without a doubt, one of the most compelling voices in the en-tire Genizah collection, both because of the length of this woman's ap-peal and because of the detail offered. We hear her voice directly, learn of the suffering to which she and her sons were subjected, of her trials and tribulations, of her inner strength in overcoming insurmountable odds, of her conversations with her good-for-nothing husband, and of the empow-erment that transforms her life. A dependent preadolescent girl develops into a totally self-sufficient woman, running a school, citing her rights and questioning the treatment to which she has been subjected now that she has gained knowledge of what had been the domain of the Jewish male, namely, Torah. With this knowledge, she succeeds in finding the inner strength to appeal to the Jewish court in the hope of clarifying both her husband's and her own rights. The severity of her plight is stunning at first, but, once her voice is raised, it is deafening, for we as well as Maimo-nides hear and understand her and her situation.

So as not to leave the reader in suspense, the decision needs to be men-tioned, even though it is Maimonides' voice that is heard. His original ruling after hearing the husband's rather eschewed presentation is that he may not take a second wife but that, as her husband, he may prevent her from teaching. This was not the ruling the husband desired, and, while he most likely let his wife know that he was empowered to remove her from the school (with the backing of the court), it is doubtful that he did so, since the wife did not mention such a development. After hearing the wife's story, Maimonides realized that he needed to find a way to enable her to continue supporting herself and her children, since her husband had never taken on that responsibility since the couple were wed. Thus, this rabbinic scholar offered her a way to obtain a divorce from her husband that would allow her to be her own person and do as she pleased, including continuing to run her school successfully.[26] He had thus altered his stance after learning the details of the case and did not turn a deaf ear to the woman teacher's plight.

The voices heard here represent only a small percentage of the women who lived in the Genizah society from the 10th to the 13th centuries. While sometimes these voices can be heard indirectly, as through letters written by husbands, women were also writing and dictating their own letters to their husbands from whom they were separated, as well as to their children, parents, and siblings. Letters were an essential means of dealing with separations in this mobile society. At the same time, voices echo resoundingly in the form of wills, often declared at the deathbed, for these women were concerned about the fate of their property, including their slaves, about their children and their education, and about their funeral expenses, which were often considerable. Last, we hear petitions on various levels, made to a family member such as an uncle, to a community leader such as a nagid or gaon, and to the court. We listen to the tales of suffering, bad and horrible marriages, poverty, disgrace, husbands who did not provide for wives and children, and death and illness and witness women's hardships and inability to maneuver because of the limitations placed on them by Jewish law. We can only hope that their voices were heard clearly by the recipients of these letters and petitions and that their prayers and pleas were answered.

While many of the aforementioned women had to overcome separations, illness, losses, and even abuse, most of their troubles pale in comparison to those encountered by women who faced the Spanish Inquisition. For the sake of comparison, we will take a brief look at the lives of crypto-Jewish women in the 15th and 16th centuries now that Inquisition documents have been accessed and analyzed.

Crypto-Judaism was a clandestine religion; because these Jews or their descendants had been baptized, they could no longer officially observe Judaism.[27] Nevertheless, between the time of the forced conversions of 1391 and the expulsion of the Jews from Spain in 1492, the conversos lived their lives in relative freedom. While it was not wise to observe Jewish laws and rituals overtly or ostentatiously, those who wanted could successfully maintain a Jewish lifestyle, albeit in a modest manner. However, once the Jewish community was expelled, there was no longer a living example of Judaism from which to learn. Moral support was not available, nor was there access to functionaries such as ritual slaughterers, rabbis, teachers, and circumcisers.

As a result, the only means by which this clandestine religion could be perpetuated was orally, and for the "People of the Book," this was a difficult task indeed. An additional aspect must be taken into consideration when discussing crypto-Jewish life, namely the perennial threat of the Inquisition. Once this institution was established in 1478 and began to function in 1481, there was no safe place for a judaizer. The crypto-Jew never knew who might decide that it was his or her duty to inform the Holy Tribunal that any given converso was not behaving according to the mandates of the Catholic Church, and, consequently, life was stressful.

Once the Jews were expelled, almost every Jewish institution also disappeared: the synagogues, the houses of study, and the schools. Essentially, the only remaining institution was the family; thus, the majority of judaizing transpired within the home. Although one would hope that the home would be a safe place, this was simply not so in crypto-Jewish society. Because every household employed servants, there were built-in witnesses and potential informers present throughout the day, each and every day. Not employing a servant would be tantamount to an admission of guilt. As a result, observance was extremely dangerous, both inside and outside one's home. For the devoted judaizer, both extreme care and a great deal of ingenuity were needed when facing the challenge of maintaining a crypto-Jewish life.

The Inquisition documents (trial proceedings) reveal that, despite these dangers, there were women who observed Judaism secretly and even managed to transmit their heritage and to teach members of the younger generation.[28] Information can be found in the accusations of the prosecutors, the confessions of the defendants, and the testimonies of the witnesses, for these proceedings were scrupulously recorded.[29] A few examples of each type of observance are presented here in order to provide a glimpse into the intricacies of the crypto-Jewish world.

Because the Sabbath recurs weekly, remembering to observe this day of rest was relatively easy for the judaizer, although it was just as easy for the outsider to notice its observance. This day entails a great deal of preparation; activities include bathing, cleaning the house, baking *hallah*, replacing or cleaning the wicks in the oil lamps, wearing clean or good clothes, and avoiding work by preparing meals in advance.

For example, one learns from a confession by María González about lighting lamps on the Sabbath:

> On the said Friday nights, soon after sunset, this confessant lit two clean lamps with new cotton wicks and at other times, the said slave Catalina lit them as commanded by this confessant . . . most often this confessant cleaned them and lit them putting in new wicks so that the said maidservants and slave would not notice.[30]

The trial of Leonor Alvarez includes a detailed description of her Sabbath customs; in the accusation prepared by the prosecutor, he began his list of counts as follows:

> First of all, that the said Leonor Alvarez, through the blind affection that she had for the deadly law of the Jews, observed and has observed the days of the Sabbath, not performing the household duties on these days that she was accustomed to do on the other days of the week, adorning herself on these days with good holiday clothes and dressing herself in a clean blouse and other holiday finery, and relinquishing household activities on Friday night in good time [sufficiently early] in honor of the Sabbath, going to visit other houses and other persons on these Sabbath days, [houses] where everyone was observing the Sabbath.[31]

In her confession, Gracia de Teva, who lived in Ciudad Real in 1511, explained that judaizers congregated in her home and ate "some stews prepared on the previous Friday made of eggs and cheese and parsley and hot dishes and spices and that sometimes they made them of eggplant and other times of carrots depending upon the season and that they ate the said stews cold and [that] they celebrated and enjoyed themselves all those said Sabbath days, until night when they went to their homes."[32]

Similarly, in the trial of Beatriz López of Hita, an emphasis is placed upon the fact that food was prepared especially for the Sabbath. The prosecutor contended that she "cooked with and had cooked stew and Jewish cuisine with meat, onions, chickpeas, spices all crushed and cooked. After long cooking, the broth was extracted and the meat was awaited. Thus she ate it with the great devotion that she had for the Law of Moses."[33]

Dietary laws also played an important role in crypto-Jewish life, and, since the women were usually responsible for food preparation, it is not surprising to find abundant information concerning these observances in the dossiers. Women slaughtered birds themselves, purchased kosher meat from Jews prior to the Expulsion, kashered their meat when they had to, refrained from eating nonkosher meats and shellfish, and even had separate dishes for those that had been in contact with pork and those that had not.

An example of a conversa who slaughtered her fowl according to Jewish law was Isabel García of Hita, who, "when she was about to slaughter some bird, prior to slaughtering it, would examine and pass the knife by her nail in the Jewish way and then slaughter the bird, watching over the blood as per Jewish rite and ceremony."[34]

Beatriz López, mentioned earlier, kashered her meat precisely and correctly, for it was reported "that the said Beatriz opened the leg of mutton lengthwise in the Jewish way, and extracted certain things and washed the meat with large quantities of water until the meat was white and devoid of blood and thus she ate in the way that the Jews did."[35]

The daughter of one conversa saw her mother, María González, perform the same ritual. The tribunal was told that "she saw her said mother remove the nerve from the meat and remove the fat, and open the leg of mutton and extract the nerve, and salt and desalt the meat and wash it at the time when she was about to cook it."[36] At the same time, a former servant of this conversa recalled:

> In the said time in which she lived with the said employers, that every time that they brought meat, the said her mistress of this witness would remove the fat with her nails very meticulously. And she remembers that sometimes this witness saw the meat that was removed from the pot which was lean, devoid of all fat and suet, and how astonished she was that [this meat] that had been brought to the house fatty and soft was without a sign of fat.[37]

On the other hand, a witness in the trial of Beatriz González testified as follows:

> This witness knew and saw that the wife of the said Juan de la Sierra did not want bacon to be brought to her house, and that if at some time it was brought, that it would be cooked in a separate stewpot; never was it observed being eaten in all the said time by the said master or mistress or by their daughter Leonor or by their son Hernando de la Sierra.[38]

The 1494 trial of Marina González of Ciudad Real reveals the anxiety that judaizing could produce within the household. Marina ate no pork nor drank from her husband's cup because he did eat pork. Pedro de Teva, a witness in the trial stated:

> He ate and lunched many times with him [Francisco de Toledo] in his house [eating] things of pork and drowned partridges and other things, and his wife Marina did not eat any of these; and one day [while] eating a piece of wild boar with her husband, this witness said to her, "Madam, why don't you come and eat?" And she said, "I cannot eat now." And her husband said to her, "I swear to God, woman, that you are looking for trouble." And she told him, "Leave it [alone], grief will come by itself."³⁹

Juana de los Olivos was accused of eating neither bacon "nor those things which were cooked with it nor those foods which were placed in plates and bowls in which pork happened to be [placed], and she had separate plates and bowls for herself which had not come into contact with bacon."⁴⁰ While Juana was careful not to eat pork, Beatriz López of Hita included other nonkosher foods in her list of forbidden dishes. It was reported to the Holy Tribunal that "the said Beatriz did not eat any food of spotted dog-fish or conger-eel or octopus or hare or rabbit although they were brought into the house, which she did in honor and respect of the Law of Moses and of the rites, precepts, and ceremonies of them."⁴¹

One can learn of some fasting and holiday observances in the Inquisition records, such as the attempt to induce a young girl to fast on Yom Kippur. Juana Rodríguez of Toledo confessed in 1498:

> In the house of my father, being of the age of thirteen, more or less, my said father, who is called Diego Rodríguez, New Christian, told me on the day of Yom Kippur of the Jews: "Daughter, fast this day and the Lord will give you, daughter, many riches." . . . Thus did I fast the said fast . . . of the Jews after marrying until I married my second husband, Juan of Zamora, shoemaker, who was an Old Christian.⁴²

Another holiday that survived the need for secrecy and the difficulty of observing without written works such as prayer books, the Pentateuch, or *megillot* (scrolls) was Passover, mainly because the baking and eating of *matzah* (and using different utensils) played such a central role in Jewish life. For example, María Díaz of Ciudad Real was seen observing:

The Festival of Unleavened Bread, eating it, like another ceremony that they do in the said festival the first two nights, in which they eat lettuce and parsley and herbs and vinegar, and another ceremony that they do with bitter herbs that implies bitterness, and with certain wafers of small unleavened bread, all as was seen done and observed and celebrated no more or less than the Jews do and observe, [as] in wearing clean clothes as in eating in new vessels that had not had contact with leavened bread and if some of those in which [she] ate were of copper or of wood or of other metals, they would be well scalded in boiling water and then with cold [water].[43]

In addition to holidays, there were many laws and rituals that were retained in the memory of the judaizers, especially those that dealt with aspects of the life cycle. One memorable rite was the *hadas*, a medieval ceremony that entailed a celebration of the birth of a male or female child. This rite was retained only by the Spanish Jewish community and, thus, also by the judaizers. A witness in the trial of Catalina López stated:

It could have been five years, more or less, when the wife of Alonso López, cloth-shearer, resident of the said locale, gave birth and within six or seven days after she gave birth, the said Alonso López invited this witness and her husband and some other Jews and gave them a collation and fruit in the fashion in which the Jews practice for their sons and daughters that is called *hadas*, which was seen twice when the said wife of Alonso López gave birth.[44]

At the same time, María González of Casarrubios del Monte confessed to observing the laws of purity. She said, "I observed sometimes when I had menstrual blood or was post-partem and then at its conclusion I washed myself, sometimes I bathed, this as per ceremony, and sometimes after childbirth, at the termination of the seven days, I dressed in clean clothes, and had clean sheets put on my bed because I was told that this was a ceremony."[45]

Many death rituals were also observed.[46] The aforementioned María's trial contained a report that she "kept silent and hid how she had been indoors for seven days upon the death of her kinsmen and had pillows with earth in them placed [by the head] for the said deceased in order to fulfill the Jewish rites and ceremonies and how Jews came to the house of the said deceased to pray and prayed for them and she also prayed [in] the said ceremonies."[47]

Isabel García's trial contains many detailed descriptions of mourning rituals and their observance. She clearly sat *shiva* for the week after her husband's death and even followed the ancient custom of wearing a *barbillera* or bandage around her chin. It was reported by a maidservant that:

> She saw the wife of Rodrigo García, whom she believes is named Isabel, a New Christian of Jew[ish] origin, resident of Hita, and certain other persons who went to the home of a certain deceased person, climbed on top of the bed of the said deceased and sang and cried and wailed, praying, raising and lowering their heads, clapping their hands, and a certain person called out the songs and then the said Isabel and the others continued the singing and cried and prayed and walked around the deceased.[48]

A number of witnesses had paid attention to her elaborate and extensive observances. Thus, it was reported by another witness as follows:

> And I know that she was "behind the door" due to the death of the said deceased person, [with] one door closed and the other open and she was seated behind the closed door with a head-dress roomy enough at the head and the end of the head-dress was placed as a "bandage" beneath the chin [in a place] where certain other persons came and all of them were there together in grief crying and lamenting and consoling themselves.[49]

By analyzing Inquisition trials, one can learn that in the earlier periods women were tried as frequently as or sometimes more often than were men. The prosecutors were well aware of the important role that these women played, a fact that is reflected in the wording of their accusations: the women were accused of actively observing Judaism, while the men were usually accused of passively observing. For instance, the women were lighting the lamps, cleaning their homes, and cooking the traditional meals, whereas the men were allowing the women to light the lamps or clean their homes and eating the foods that their wives prepared. Because the home was the sole institution that survived, it gained added importance in crypto-Jewish life, and, not surprisingly, the women were usually the teachers of other conversas. Crypto-Jewish women dealt with the challenge of observing despite the threat of the Inquisition and its severe punishments.

The Inquisition was concerned with deeds and intentions; a baptized Catholic taking part in any crypto-Jewish activity was guilty of heresy and apostasy. At the same time, the intent behind the deed was also important to the Holy Tribunal. If a woman celebrated *hadas* for her newborn child or washed off the baptismal waters from her baby's forehead upon her return home, these were acts of defiance for a Catholic even though neither could be traced to any written source of Jewish law or ritual. Those who engaged in such acts were as severely judged as if they were following normative observance of the Law of Moses.

The lives of the crypto-Jewish women were very different from those of women who lived in the Mediterranean Genizah society. The latter were influenced directly by the Islamic world and affected by its emphasis on the physical seclusion of women, including the wearing of the veil. The prevalence of polygamy and concubines directly influenced the lives of Jewish as well as Moslem women. Repercussions of the Crusades can also be detected in these communities, although, on the whole, at least in medieval Egypt, Muslim rule was quite tolerant of the Jewish communities.

On the other hand, the lives of crypto-Jewish women were directly tied to the Christian world. These women and their families had been baptized by force in 1391 or were descendants of conversos or had converted rather than leave Spain in 1492. After the establishment of the Inquisition, those women who were on trial had to face the most serious charges made by the Church, for the soul of the apostate or heretic was lost in its eyes, and thus he or she was condemned to be burned at the stake.

These differences reflect the reality of the medieval world. The two ruling religions, Islam and Christianity, encountered Jewish communities wherever they established themselves. Their Jewish subjects, both male and female, had to adapt to the reality of the dominant religious rule, as well as the changes and fluctuations that developed in each locale. As we have seen, Jewish women were exposed to and living in both of these worlds, subjected to the rule of Crescent and Cross, accepting or rejecting the influences and dictates of medieval society while remaining faithful to their own religion.

The availability of primary sources from the Cairo Genizah and the records of the Spanish Inquisition grant us an entrée into some of these women's lives. All of them had to deal with serious limitations: the first group faced the constraints of Islamic society and its repressive attitude toward women, while the second group lived with the threat of being tried and sentenced by the Inquisition. In neither of these worlds did the women opt for passivity. The letters, wills, and petitions found in the Genizah belong to a wide range of women, yet, whether impoverished, wealthy, married, divorced, or widowed, they seem to have displayed an amazing degree of initiative and inner strength. At the same time, the tenacity of the crypto-Jewish women in the face of almost-certain death is simply awe-inspiring. All of these women were concerned with survival, family, with providing for their progeny, and with living honorable lives, often despite considerable adversity. As we delve into the Genizah and Inquisition documents and strive to interpret them, we can simultaneously marvel at the impressive legacy left us by these medieval Jewish women.

NOTES

1. For general assessments of this discovery, see Alexander Marx, "The Importance of the Geniza for Jewish History," *Proceedings of the American Academy of Jewish Research* 16 (1946-47): 183–204, and Menahem Ben-Sasson, "Cairo Genizah Treasures and Their Contribution to Historiography," *Bulletin of the Israeli Academic Center in Cairo* 21 (July 1997): 3–12.

2. For the most comprehensive work to deal with these documents, see S. D. Goitein, *A Mediterranean Society*, 6 vols. (Berkeley: University of California Press, 1967–1988).

3. See Joel Kraemer, "Women Speak for Themselves," in *The Cambridge Genizah Collections: Their Contents and Significance*, ed. Stefan C. Reif (Cambridge: Cambridge University Press, 2002), pp. 178–216.

4. Joel Kraemer has translated many of the women's letters found in the Genizah. These as-yet unpublished translations will be noted as Kraemer translation, followed by the manuscript number, in this case TS 8J 16.21. (TS signifies that the manuscript is found in the Taylor-Schechter Collection, University Library, Cambridge, England.)

5. Kraemer translation, TS 8J 17.3rv; discussed also in S. D. Goitein, *Mediterranean Society*, vol. 2, pp. 144–45.

6. Ibid., TS 6J 3.22; see also S. D. Goitein, *Mediterranean Society*, vol. 3, p. 178.

7. Ibid., TS 8 J 23.17r.

8. Ibid., TS 10 J 12.18rv.

9. Ibid., TS 10 J 7.5rv; see also S. D. Goitein, *Mediterranean Society*, vol. 3, pp. 115 and 236.

10. S. D. Goitein, *Mediterranean Society*, vol. 3, p. 22.

11. J. Kraemer, TS 10 J 9.1rv; see also S. D. Goitein, *Mediterranean Society*, vol. 5, pp. 180–81, and "New Revelations From the Cairo Geniza: Jewish Women in the Middle Ages," *Hadassah Magazine* (1973), pp. 14–15, 38–39.

12. S. D. Goitein, *Mediterranean Society*, vol. 5, pp. 153–55.

13. Ibid., vol. 5, pp. 148–49.

14. See S. D. Goitein, "A Jewish Business Woman of the Eleventh Century," *The Seventy-Fifth Anniversary Volume of the Jewish Quarterly Review* (1967): 229–32.

15. Decisors were the decision makers on the basis of Jewish law. Courts would often present eminent rabbis with questions that were unusual or difficult.

16. Kraemer, TS 10 J 9.13rv; see also S. D. Goitein, *Mediterranean Society*, vol. 3, pp. 175–76.

17. S. D. Goitein, *Mediterranean Society*, vol. 3, p. 169.

18. Mordechai Akiva Friedman, *Jewish Polygyny in the Middle Ages* [Hebrew], (Jerusalem: Mosad Bialik; Tel-Aviv: Bet Hasefer Le-mada'ei Ha-yahadut, 1986), p. 226.

19. J. Kraemer, TS 8 J 22.22rv.

20. J. Kraemer, TS 10 J 11.25.

21. S. D. Goitein, *Mediterranean Society*, vol. 5, p. 201.

22. An entire section in ibid., vol. 3, pp. 312–59 and 496–507, is entitled "The World of Women," which was a revolutionary idea for a Jewish historian at that time.

23. For a Hebrew translation, see Joshua Blau, *Teshuvot Ha-Rambam*, 4 vols. (Jerusalem: Mekitzei Nirdamim, 1957–61 and 1986), vol. 2, pp. 524–25 and vol. 4, p. 9; see also Mordechai Akiva Friedman, "New Fragments of Maimonides' Responsa," in *Studies in Geniza and Sephardi Heritage Presented to Shelomo Dov Goitein* [Hebrew], ed. S. Morag, I. Ben-Ami, and N. A. Stillman (Jerusalem: Magnes Press, 1981), pp. 119–120.

24. Responsa were the replies to the questions presented to the rabbinic courts by the decisors. Many were recorded later for posterity, and later decisions could thus be based on earlier ones.

25. My translation, published in the article "He Said, She Said: A Woman Teacher in Twelfth-Century Cairo," *AJS Review* 22 (1997): 23–27.

26. Basically, Maimonides suggested that she declare herself a *moredet* or rebellious woman, meaning that she was refusing to have relations with her husband. The court would then appropriate the sum termed the "delayed marriage payment"; this was promised by the husband in case of divorce or death in order to protect the wife. The court would reduce this sum on a set basis and, once nothing remained, the court would force the husband to grant his wife a writ of divorce. She forfeited what was intended as a safety net, but, in this case, there probably was no money set aside by the husband, so she had nothing to lose. Besides, she was self-sufficient, and her independence was worth far more than any payment recorded on paper.

27. For a short history of the conversos, see Renée Levine Melammed, *Heretics or Daughters of Israel: The Crypto-Jewish Women of Castile* (New York: Oxford University Press, 1999), pp. 3-30.

28. For details concerning teaching as well as techniques, see Renée Levine Melammed, "The Ultimate Challenge: Safeguarding the Crypto-Judaic Heritage," *Proceedings of the American Academy for Jewish Research* 53 (1986): 91–109.

29. For a discussion of the use of Inquisition documents as a reliable source, see Yosef Hayim Yerushalmi, *From Spanish Court to Italian Ghetto* (New York: Columbia University Press, 1971), pp. 21–31.

30. This file is Legajo (Leg.) 154, no. 37 (1511–13); it also appears in Haim Beinart, *Records of the Trials of the Spanish Inquisition in Ciudad Real* (Jerusalem: Israel National Academy of Sciences and Humanities, 1974-85), vol. 2 (1977), p. 250.

31. Leg. 122, no. 21 (1512–14); see *Records*, vol. 2, p. 234.

32. Leg. 154, no. 37 (1511–13); see *Records*, vol. 2, p. 251.

33. Leg. 159, no. 15 (1520–21).

34. Leg. 158, no. 9 (1520–23).

35. Leg. 159, no. 15 (1520–21).

36. Leg. 155, no. 1 (1512–13); see *Records*, vol. 2, p. 427.

37. Leg. 154, no. 37 (1511–13); see *Records*, vol. 2, pp. 267–68.

38. Leg. 153, no. 15 (1511–13); see *Records*, vol. 2, p. 166.

39. Leg. 155, no. 4 (1494); see *Records*, vol. 2, p. 21.

40. Leg. 173, no. 6 (1503–04); see *Records* vol. 2, p. 152.

41. Leg. 159, no. 15 (1520–21).

42. Leg. 180, no. 10 (1498–99).

43. Leg. 143, no. 11 (1483–84); see *Records*, vol. 1, p. 58.

44. Leg. 144, no. 3 (1491–92).

45. Leg. 154, no. 33 (1500). For a detailed article dealing with this conversa, see Haim Beinart, "Judíos y Conversos en Casarrubios del Monte," in *Homenaje a Juan Prado*, ed. L. Alvarez Verdes and E. J. Alonso Hernandez (Madrid: Consejo Superior de Investigaciones Cientificas, 1975), pp. 645–57.

46. For a detailed discussion, see Renée Levine Melammed, "Some Death and Mourning Customs of Castilian Conversas," in *Exile and Diaspora, Studies in the History of the Jewish People Presented to Professor Haim Beinart*, ed. A. Mirsky, A. Grossman and Y. Kaplan (Jerusalem: Ben Zvi Institute, 1991), pp. 157–57.

47. Ibid.

48. Leg. 158, no. 9 (1520–23).

49. Leg. 158, no. 9 (1520–23).

5

|||||||||||||||||||||||||||||||||||||||||||||||||

The Mystical Spirituality of Eastern European Jewish Women

Chava Weissler

Much attention has been paid recently to the turn toward spirituality in American religious life. Not only have Americans turned to various Eastern traditions—yoga and Buddhist meditation, for example—but they have been looking at the spiritual sides of the Western traditions in which they grew up.[1] In Judaism, there has been an upsurge of interest in Kabbalah and Hasidism, both of them aspects of the Jewish mystical tradition. From Madonna to the Kabbalah Centre, from books with titles like *Simple Kabbalah* to the renewed popularity of Shlomo Carlebach's hasidic melodies, there is definitely something in the air.[2] Interestingly, much of this spiritual revival, both in the general society and in Judaism, has been fueled by the energy and creativity of women.

Can we find any parallels to the current situation in the Jewish past? The 16th, 17th, and 18th centuries saw a number of spiritual revival movements among all religious traditions in the Mediterranean countries, elsewhere in Europe, and in North America. While the question of historical interrelatedness of these various movements is complex, we can certainly note that the same is true of Judaism during this period. First, the Zohar, the great classic work of medieval Kabbalah, achieved canonical status during this period and was first printed in 1558–60.[3] Second, the 16th century saw the rise of a center of intense Jewish mystical and pietistic activity in the small Galilean town of Safed. Third, in 1665, Shabbatai Zevi, a Jew from Izmir, in the Ottoman Empire, became convinced that he was the messiah. Even after his forced conversion to Islam in 1666 and his death ten years later, his followers continued to believe in him; they were eventually forced underground. Finally, in

18th-century Poland, Hasidism emerged, producing an amazing religious revival movement—for men.

The early modern period was a time of tremendous spiritual ferment and creativity. Important kabbalistic thinkers emerged, and their works had wide influence. But how did women—and nonscholarly men—participate in this mystical spirituality? What did Kabbalah mean for the masses? And what did popular participation mean for Kabbalah? I will argue that this period saw the emergence of what can be called a "vernacular Kabbalah" that enabled ordinary Jews, including women, to create deeper Jewish lives.[4]

A primary source for this inquiry is the *tkhines*, prayers in Yiddish written for and sometimes by Central and Eastern European Jewish women during the 17th and 18th centuries.[5] *Tkhines* form a centuries-long tradition of women's prayer, oral and written; analysis of this material shows us the ways in which women's piety was a creative part of the larger Jewish spiritual context. These prayers, informed by the mystical piety of the day, are evidence of a deeply lived spiritual life and a richly imagined spiritual world. This chapter surveys what is known of women's spiritual lives during this period and introduces two intriguing *tkhine* authors: Leah Horowitz and Shifrah bas Yosef. Both women lived in 18th-century Poland. An examination of their works reveals the ways in which women did—and did not—participate in and transform the kabbalistic spirituality of their day.

What Are the Tkhines?

Written for a wide variety of occasions, *tkhines* structured women's spiritual lives by defining a range of topics considered suitable for women and by creating a way of speaking about these topics. Women chanted these prayers—which could be as brief as a paragraph or as long as several pages—from small books or little pamphlets, often at home, sometimes with other women in the synagogue or the cemetery.[6] Some *tkhines* were composed by women, others by men, and the majority of them were published without mention of an author and often without reference to date or place of publication. Each individual *tkhine* begins with a heading directing when and sometimes how it should be recited: "A pretty *tkhine* to say on the Sabbath with great devotion"; "A *tkhine* that the woman should pray for herself and her husband and children"; "What one says when one comes into the synagogue"; "A confession to say with devotion, not too quickly: it is good for the soul"; "When she comes out of the ritual bath"; "The Seven Praises *tkhine* to say with great devotion, corresponding the Seven Heavens"; "What one says on the Eve of Yom Kippur in the cemetery"; or "A *tkhine* for Sabbaths and Festivals after candle-lighting."

From the many occasions on which women recited *tkhines* we can discern the important religious events in their lives. Women, along with men, participated in the ongoing rhythms of Jewish life, in the festivals and fasts of the Jewish calendar and in the passages of the life cycle. Yet, to the extent that women recited *tkhines*, they also resonated to the rhythms of an alternative world structured not only by the communal events of the Jewish calendar but also by the private events of a woman's domestic life.

The *tkhines* show how women understood their religious acts. Consider a *tkhine* for lighting the Sabbath candles, a ritual performed primarily by women: it may contain prayers for protecting the woman's husband and children from evil spirits, or it may contain, as we shall see, images of the candelabrum—the *menorah*—in the ancient Temple in Jerusalem. Or, consider the *tkhines* for the women's ritual of making memorial candles for the dead. Interestingly, although this custom is nowhere mandated in Jewish law, the *tkhine* text refers to it as a *mitzvah*, a divine commandment.[7]

The distinctiveness of *tkhines* as prayers specifically for women can be seen more clearly by comparing them with the prayers of the standard Hebrew liturgy of the *siddur*, the prayer book. The differences are striking. The prayers of the *siddur* are composed in Hebrew, the sacred, scholarly language. They are fixed and obligatory (for men), regulated by the time of day and the liturgical calendar: men prayed three times a day, reciting a set liturgy that was expanded on Sabbaths and holidays. These prayers mark the daily transitions at dusk and dawn, sanctify the separation of the day of rest from the workaday week, and celebrate the turning of the seasons and the formative events of Jewish history. The Hebrew prayers often refer to the merits of the patriarchs, Abraham, Isaac, and Jacob. The preferred setting for worship is with a congregation, defined primarily as a community of men. Indeed, the prayers of the *siddur* are typically phrased in the plural.

Tkhines, by contrast, are in the spoken language, Yiddish, and are voluntary and flexible, recited when the woman desired, typically at home. They are usually phrased in the singular and often have space for the petitioner to insert her own name, thus making them a very personal address to God. Unlike Hebrew prayers, *tkhines* contain many references to the matriarchs—Sarah, Rebecca, Rachel, and Leah—and to other women of the Bible. It should be noted that, according to some authorities, women are exempt from the duty of recitation of all or part of the liturgy—and by all accounts from communal prayer. Nevertheless, some women recited the Hebrew prayers daily at home and attended synagogue on Sabbaths and holidays; some women even attended synagogue every day. There was a special prayer leader, a learned woman known as the *firzogerin* or the *zogerke*, who led the women's section of the synagogue in reciting both the Hebrew prayers and the Yiddish *tkhines*. Some of the *tkhines* were probably composed by these learned ladies as part of their Yiddish interpretations or paraphrases of the liturgy.

The Tkhines *and Early Modern Ashkenazic Spirituality*

The *tkhines* began to appear in print in the 16th century and flourished in the 17th and 18th centuries, continuing on into the 19th and 20th centuries, as well. Why did this genre arise and flourish in that particular historical era? The evidence of the *tkhines* suggests that women were well integrated into and, indeed, creative participants in two of the important spiritual currents of the 17th and 18th centuries: the pietism that emerged from the mystical circles in Safed and the Sabbatian messianic movement.[8] Thus, certain changes in piety directly influenced the rise of the *tkhines* by creating an atmosphere in which many forms of expression of religious devotion first became available to ordinary Jews, rather than only to scholars and mystics. This epoch saw the creation of new prayers for midnight and dawn devotions (*tikkun ḥatzot* and *hashkamat boker*), for visiting the cemetery, for preparing corpses for burial, for observing the eve of the new moon as a penitential fast, and for other events. It saw as well the publication of guides to pious practices for groups and individuals and collections of mystical prayers in Hebrew for men, known as *teḥinnot* (the same Hebrew term from which the word *tkhines* is derived). Even the Zohar, the great classic of medieval Kabbalah, appeared in a partial translation into Yiddish. During this era, itinerant preachers called for repentance and popularized mystical conceptions of piety.

What were the factors that motivated these changes, and how can we understand the place of Jewish women within them? First, consider the internal Jewish factors that led to religious change. The 16th-century mystical community in Safed, which included scores of eminent mystics and scholars, gave rise to a mystical pietism that spread rapidly throughout the Jewish world. Most influential among these mystics was Isaac Luria, who died young and left only a few writings of his own but also a legacy of myth and symbol transmitted and transformed by his disciples. During this period, pietism transformed the Lurianic "mythos" to a lived and ritualized "ethos." The Lurianic myth of an exile within God that parallels the exile of Israel on earth and of the imperative for human beings to mend both the world and the Godhead through their repentance, prayer, and performance of the commandments gave rise to the pervasive ritualization of Jewish life discussed earlier. Luria's followers held that human beings act in partnership with God to bring the redemption through their devotion in prayer and in religious action. Human acts can affect the inner state of the Godhead and thus play an essential role in redeeming both divinity and the cosmos from their current state of exile and suffering. In Safed, men, women, and children participated in new forms of religious life.[9]

In addition, this was a time of technological change and religious and intellectual ferment in Christian Europe. The invention of printing made possible the inexpensive dissemination of ideas through books and broadsides and thus helped to bring about both the Renaissance and the Reformation. The rise of the printed book also had a decisive influence on Judaism. For the first time, book production was cheap enough that broad masses of people could have access to published materials. This led to two results. First, halakhic (legal), philosophical, and especially mystical teachings that had been known only to small groups of scholars achieved much wider dissemination, despite the controversy this aroused. Second, a new kind of literature emerged, one whose audience was the nonscholarly literate public. These readers ranged from men with a solid education in Hebrew and classical rabbinic literature to less well educated men and literate women with only a rudimentary knowledge of Hebrew. (Only a tiny number of women had a real command of Hebrew.) These nonscholarly Jews were the primary consumers of guides to the ethical life, books of pious practices, and new liturgies and rituals, often in abridged and simplified form, whether in Hebrew, for the better educated among them, or in Yiddish, for those who were less learned. Thus, the mystically inflected religious practices that originated in Safed were, through the technology of printing, spread widely among nonlearned Jews, including women.

The push for spiritual perfection as a way to bring about the end of exile and the messianic era was one of the factors leading to the 17th-century messianic movement led by Shabbatai Zevi. After the Turkish sultan forced Zevi to convert to Islam, in 1666, many were disillusioned. Nonethless, some of his followers maintained their faith, although they were eventually forced underground. Interestingly, Shabbetai Zevi himself saw the improvement of women's status within Judaism as an important aspect of the redemption. If the sin of Eve was to be canceled, so too were her punishments: painful childbirth and subordination to her husband. Further, the Sabbatians, even as an underground movement, worked to spread knowledge of the Kabbalah, and of the Zohar in particular, to nonlearned Jews and to women, whom they actively recruited.[10]

Women, whether Sabbatian or not, were influenced by the pietistic currents of the times. They, too, wished to participate in extra ritual activities. In addition to composing *tkhines*, learned women were among those who helped to make other literature that originated in Safed spirituality available in Yiddish. At the beginning of the 18th century, Ellus bas Mordecai of Slutsk published her translations of an abridged version of *Maavar Yabbok* (The Ford of the Jabbok), a guide to dealing with the dying and the dead, and *Shomrim la-Boker* (Watchers for the Morning), a liturgy for dawn devotions. As she says in her introduction to *Shomrim la-Boker*, "many men and women chirp like birds," reciting the Hebrew prayers without understanding them; she therefore provided a Yiddish translation. And a Yiddish version of Nathan Nata Hannover's *Sha'arei Tsiyyon* (Gates of Zion), an important collection of mystical devotions, *tehinnot*, written in Hebrew, was published in Prague at about the same time. The title page describes the translator as follows: "Because of her modesty, she would not let her name be published, but her learning and expert knowledge are renowned far and wide." This "important woman" provided the translation "for the pious women who understand only Yiddish" so that they too would be able to say these prayers. It was also during this period that women began treating the Sabbath before the new moon as a time of special piety, perhaps taking their inspiration from men's observances of the eve of the new moon as a day of penitence.

The *tkhines* as a genre were also born of women's desire to shape their own form of participation in the pietistic practices of the day. For example, the introduction to an early collection of *tkhines*, published in Amsterdam in 1648, says explicitly that women wanted to recite the Hebrew *tehinnot* but could not understand them and that therefore the (unnamed) editor acceded to the requests of these pious women and provided *tkhines* in Yiddish. Thus, the *tkhines* take their origins, in part, from the Hebrew *tehinnot*, mystical prayers in Hebrew, based on Lurianic Kabbalah, that were recited by men on a variety of occasions, from midnight devotions to Sabbath meals to preparations for sexual intercourse. While some of the Hebrew *tehinnot* are indeed found in Yiddish adaptation or paraphrase in early collections of *tkhines*, from the beginning there were *tkhines* for many different sorts of private events that only partially overlapped those for which there were Hebrew mystical devotions.

Nonetheless, by the 18th century, we find individual women authors who move beyond paraphrase of Hebrew sources to develop distinctive voices of their own. All of these women came from noted rabbinical families. This is hardly surprising; few *men* outside such families wrote for publication. In their work, we can see how they adapted the Yiddish (and Hebrew) literature of Safed (and sometimes Sabbatian) spirituality to shape a vision of women's spiritual significance.

Leah Horowitz and the Tkhine *of the Matriarchs*

Sarah Rebecca Rachel Leah Horowitz (ca. 1715–ca.1790), known by family and friends as Leah, was the daughter of Yukl Horowitz, a noted mystic, and lived in Bolechow, Dobromil, and Krasnik, in Poland. Three of Leah's brothers were well-known rabbis. Conversant with both rabbinic and kabbalistic literature, she was among the most learned of *tkhine* authors, and, as we shall see, her understanding of prayer derives from kabbalistic sources. Her only extant work, an eight-page *tkhine*, *Tkhine Imohos* (The *Tkhine* of the Matriarchs), is to be recited on the Sabbath before the New Moon, during the prayer that announces the coming month, and expresses hopes that the messianic redemption may soon arrive. Leah's composition contains a Hebrew introduction in which she discusses the nature of prayer and women's ability to pray, an Aramaic liturgical poem on the blessing of the New Moon, and a Yiddish prose paraphrase of the poem, the actual *tkhine* she offers to her readers.[11]

Leah's text assumes a kabbalistic understanding of God: a conception of the Godhead as consisting of a dynamic interrelationship among the ten emanations (*sefirot*) of the utterly transcendent and unknowable God. In Leah's view, proper prayer is for the sake of the Shechinah, the Divine Presence, the feminine aspect of the Godhead, who, as the tenth and final *sefirah*, mediates between the human and the divine worlds. According to Jewish mystical teaching, the Shechinah, like Israel, is in exile, and it is the goal of all true prayer and religious performance to end this exile and to reunite her with her divine consort, the Holy Blessed One, the sixth *sefirah*, a masculine aspect of the Godhead. The full and final reunification will come only in the era of messianic redemption, the time when harmony will be restored to the divine realm and Israel's exile will end with their restoration to the Holy Land. Prayer that strives to bring this about is "prayer for the sake of heaven."

Leah argues vigorously that women (and not only men) are capable of "prayer for the sake of heaven," calling those who would object "fools." In Leah's view, women have the power, through their tearful prayer, to bring about the messianic redemption--if only they prayed properly. They should attend synagogue daily, morning and evening, and they should pray with devotion, rather than spending their time in synagogue comparing their clothes and jewelry. Most important, they must know how to weep for the Shechinah. This is especially crucial, Leah says, because "The day of the Lord is near," that is, she believed redemption was at hand and that women's prayers could hasten its coming. Further, although there may be obstacles to prayer, "the Gate of Tears is never locked." While space forbids a full discussion of the kabbalistic basis of her argument, briefly, Leah, who has a mystical understanding of prayer, is trying to teach women with little knowledge of Kabbalah how to affect the divine realm and bring about the unification of Shechinah and the Holy Blessed One through their prayers.[12] This will bring the end of exile and the messianic redemption.

Leah simplifies this somewhat in the Yiddish portion of her *tkhine*, directed at an audience of nonlearned women. It begins:

> Today, when we consecrate the new moon, when we say the blessing on the Sabbath before the new moon, then it is a time to petition God. Therefore, we spread out our hands before God, and say our prayers that you bring us back to Jerusalem, and renew our days as of old. For we have no strength; we can no longer endure the hard, bitter exile, for we are also like the feeble lambs. Our Sabbaths and festivals and our new moons have been ruined.

Leah then continues with an appeal that the merit of each of the matriarchs cause God to redeem the people of Israel and bring them out of exile. When she gets to Rachel, she gives women a model of prayer with weeping that, in her understanding, has the mystical power to affect relations among the *sefirot*, the emanations of divinity. This is the model of the children of Israel weeping at Rachel's grave:

> O God, . . . answer us this month, by the merit of our faithful mother Ra-
> chel, to whom you promised that by her merit, we, the children of Israel,
> would come out of exile. For when the children of Israel were led into exile,
> they were led not far from the grave in which our mother Rachel lay. They
> pleaded with the foe to permit them to go to Rachel's tomb. And when the
> Israelites came to our mother Rachel and began to weep and cry, "Mother,
> mother, how can you look on while right in front of you we are being led
> into exile?" Rachel went up before God with a bitter cry, and spoke: Lord
> of the world, your mercy is certainly greater than the mercy of any hu-
> man being. Moreover, I had compassion on my sister Leah when my father
> switched us and gave her to my husband. He told her to expect that my
> husband would think that I was the one. No matter that it caused me great
> pain; I told her the signs [that Jacob and I had agreed upon to prevent the
> switch]. Thus, even more so, it is undoubtedly fitting for you, God, who are
> entirely compassionate and gracious, to have mercy and bring us out of this
> exile now. So may it come to pass, for the sake of her merit.

This dramatic depiction of the children of Israel on their way into exile, pleading at Rachel's tomb for her aid, and of Rachel's impassioned plea
to God expresses the anguish of later Jews in exile and their hope for redemption. Rachel, the matriarch most often identified with the Shechinah, is moved by her maternal concern for the children of Israel to recall
her own struggles with passion and jealousy. She calls God to account to
have compassion on Israel as she had compassion for her sister.

Even beyond this heart-rending and powerful picture, the passage
presents the paradigm for "prayer for the sake of heaven." When the children of Israel come to Rachel's tomb, they weep; their tears stir Rachel to
respond with a bitter cry of her own. And Rachel's tearful plea to the Holy
One causes Him to respond with redemption: "and your children shall
come back to their own country" (Jer. 31:17). Thus, there is a graphic depiction of the effectiveness of tearful prayer and its ability to bring about
the end of the exile.

But is this *kabbalistic* prayer? Despite her knowledge of the Zohar and
other kabbalistic texts, Leah omits, in the Yiddish portion of her prayer,
the references to kabbalistic texts and concepts that shape her arguments
in the Hebrew introduction. Her Yiddish *tkhine* does not aim to make

women deeply knowledgeable about mystical teachings. It gives them a way to see that prayer practices already common among women, that is, weeping during prayer, have great mystical significance and power. It also teaches women to pray regularly in this way and thus to help bring about the redemption.

Shifrah bas Yosef and Her Tkhine *for Kindling Sabbath Lights*

While Leah Horowitz was able to read kabbalistic sources such as the Zohar and rabbinic sources such as midrash and Talmud in their original languages and interpret them for other women, most female authors of *tkhines* were less learned. They relied instead on the Yiddish adaptations of ethical and mystical works. One such author is Shifrah, daughter of Joseph, wife of Ephraim Segal, judge in the rabbinical court of Brody. In composing her *tkhine*, entitled *Imrei Shifrah* (Words of Shifrah), the author drew upon *Naḥalat Tsevi*, a Yiddish paraphrase of portions of the Zohar, published in 1711, as her direct source.[13] Internal evidence—the statement that "we have suffered in this dark exile for more than 1,700 years"—dates this text to some time after 1770.[14] Because Shifrah addressed the work specifically to women, it brought material from the Zohar, especially interpretations of the mystical significance of various Sabbath observances, to a wider female audience. Further, the author wove this material into an extended consideration of the mystical importance of women's Sabbath observance.

In the passage to be discussed, Shifrah employs a number of standard kabbalistic images and ideas: a conception of the Godhead as consisting of a dynamic interrelationship among the ten emanations, the *sefirot*, of the utterly transcendent and unknowable God; the image of the Tabernacle of Peace for the tenth *sefirah*, the Shechinah, God's immanent presence thought of as female and in exile from the other *sefirot*; the image of the menorah, the seven-branched candelabrum, as a symbol of the seven lower *sefirot*; the idea that Jews receive the *neshamah yeterah*, a special additional soul, on the Sabbath; and the conviction that the human and divine worlds are interrelated as microcosm and macrocosm and that human devotion in prayer and in performing the commandments brings about love and unity among the *sefirot* and restores, if only momentarily, the Shechinah from her exile. In this way, the people of Israel help to bring about the redemption.

Shifrah begins her "new *tkhine* for the Sabbath" with a general statement about God's grandeur and power and about the significance of the
Sabbath as sanctifying the memory of the creation. Next, she emphasizes
the importance of women's observance of the Sabbath: "And women must
be as scrupulous about the Sabbath as men." She mentions that women
are obligated to recite *kiddush*, the prayer of sanctification over wine that
begins the Sabbath meal, usually recited by men. She then moves on to
the significance of candle lighting:

> The *mitzvah* of Sabbath candles was given to the women of the holy peo-
> ple that they might kindle lights. The sages have said that because Eve ex-
> tinguished the light of the world and made the cosmos dark by her sin,
> [women] must kindle lights for the Sabbath.[15] But this is the [real] reason
> for it. Because the Tabernacle of Peace [the Shechinah] rests on us dur-
> ing the Sabbath, on the [Sabbath-]souls, it is therefore proper for us to do
> below, in this form, as it is done above [within the Godhead], to kindle
> the lights.[16] Therefore, because the two souls shine on the Sabbath, they
> [women] must light two candles.

The complicated argument goes as follows: Making use of Numbers
8:2,[17] a description of the candelabrum (*menorah*) in the Tabernacle, the
portable sanctuary of the Israelites in the wilderness, Shifrah postulates
a correspondence between an upper and a lower candelabrum, relying
on the fact that the verse speaks of seven lamps facing or corresponding to the candelabrum. The lower candelabrum was that in the Tabernacle, and the upper candelabrum is a symbol of the seven lower *sefirot*,
or emanations, of the Godhead. Lighting the lower candelabrum—an act
performed by the High Priest—brings about great arousal to love in the
upper spheres, and as a consequence the male and female aspects of God
unite. Now, returning to Shifrah's text:

> When the priest below lit the seven lamps, he therewith caused the seven
> lamps above to shine. Therefore, by kindling the lamps for the holy Sab-
> bath, we awaken great arousal in the upper world. And when the woman
> kindles the lights, it is fitting for her to kindle [them] with joy and with
> wholeheartedness, because it is in honor of the Shechinah and in honor of
> the Sabbath and in honor of the extra [Sabbath] soul.[18]

The *tkhine* then moves on to other matters.

The woman lighting candles is explicitly compared to the High Priest lighting the candelabrum in the Tabernacle, and in this text the acts of the High Priest are understood to have cosmic and redemptive significance. Thus, the woman, too, must light the candles with "joy and wholeheartedness." Indeed, Shifrah uses the technical kabbalistic term *hit'orerut,* in Hebrew, for the awakening or arousal of the *sefirot* above. Note that Shifrah rejects the view of the sages that women were commanded to light candles to make up for Eve's sin and substitutes an interpretation that portrays women as significant religious actors.

Even more important, women's ritual acts, too, can have kabbalistic significance.[19] In the mystical spirituality spread by the new religious literature in Yiddish, all Israel had to pray and fulfill the commandments with the proper mystical intentions in order to bring the redemption. Of course, it is always a question in such cases as to whether a term like "all Israel" includes women. This *tkhine,* at least, asserts that it does—that women also have the ability and the responsibility to carry out *their* religious duties with full mystical intention and significance. In *Tkhine Imrei Shifrah,* women performing a quintessentially womanly religious duty act in full consciousness of the religious significance of what they do and with full mystical import.

Conclusion

During the early modern period, as the historian Jacob Katz has written, there was "a general shift in religious values" among Eastern European Jews:[20] Kabbalah rather than *halakhah,* mysticism rather than Jewish law, became the foundation of Jewish life. There was a penetration of poetry and myth into the more rational talmudic ethos of Eastern European Judaism. This new paradigm gave human beings a role in healing the brokenness of the cosmos and of the divine, providing concrete ways to enact their longing for redemption and thus deepening the meaning of religious observance as a way of cleaving to God. Within this new understanding, women also could find their place. Whether they were learned, like Leah Horowitz, and thus able to read original kabbalistic texts, or less learned, like Shifrah, who could read kabbalistic materials only in Yiddish adaptations, women created texts in the Yiddish vernacular that portrayed the redemptive power of women's prayer and *mitzvot.* These women and their readers participated in a "vernacular Kabbalah," a Kabbalah of the common people, which enriched their lives, prayers, and religious acts with the depth of meaning drawn from mystical spirituality.

NOTES

1. See, for example, Robert Wuthnow, *After Heaven: Spirituality in America Since the 1950s* (Berkeley: University of California, 1998), and Wade Clark Roof, *Spiritual Marketplace: Baby Boomers and the Remaking of American Religion* (Princeton: Princeton University Press, 1999).

2. Kim Zetter, *Simple Kabbalah* (Berkeley: Conari Press, 1999); for a study of the Kabbalah Centre, see Jody Myers, *Kabbalah and the Spiritual Quest* (Westport, CT: Praeger, 2007).

3. Arthur Green, "Introduction," in *The Zohar, Pritzker Edition*, translation and commentary by Daniel C. Matt (Stanford: Stanford University Press, 2004), vol. 1, p. lxxvii.

4. I owe the term "vernacular Kabbalah" to Jean Baumgarten, "The Translation of the Zohar in Yiddish: *Naḥalat Tsvi* by Yerahmiel Chotsch (Frankfurt, 1711)," unpublished manuscript, paper delivered at the Association for Jewish Studies, December 2005, p. 1.

5. The word *tkhines* comes from the Hebrew *teḥinnot*, supplication, supplicatory prayers, from the root *le-hithanen*, "to supplicate, ask for grace or mercy". See Chava Weissler, *Voices of the Matriarchs* (Boston: Beacon Press, 1999), for a fuller discussion of the *tkhines* and the bibliographical references there. I have used some language from that book in the present chapter. For additional studies of *tkhines* and translations of additional *tkhine* texts, see Devra Kay, *Seyder Tkhines: The Forgotten Book of Common Prayer for Jewish Women* (Philadelphia: Jewish Publication Society, 2004); Tracy Guren Klirs, ed. and trans., *The Merit of our Mothers* (Detroit: Wayne State University Press, 1996).

6. The Yiddish word *tkhine* can refer either to an individual prayer or to a booklet of such prayers.

7. For more on this ritual, see C. Weissler, *Voices of the Matriarchs*, chapter 8.

8. At least from the evidence of the *tkhines*, women were not, by and large, creative participants in Hasidism. However, see Malkah Shapiro, *The Rebbe's Daughter*, trans. and ed. Nehemiah Polen (Philadelphia: Jewish Publication Society, 2002), for a memoir showing the intense involvement in Hasidic spirituality of the women in a *tzaddik's* family at the turn of the 20th century.

9. An excellent introduction to this era in Jewish religious life is *Safed Spirituality*, trans. and introd. by Lawrence Fine (New York: Paulist Press, 1984); see also Zeev Gries, *The Book in Early Hasidism* (Tel Aviv: Hakibbutz Hameuchad Publishing House, 1992) (Hebrew).

10. See Gershom Scholem, *Sabbatai Sevi: The Mystical Messiah* (Princeton:

Princeton University Press, 1973), pp. 403–5; Ada Rapoport-Albert, "On the Position of Women in Sabbatianism," in *The Sabbatian Movement and Its Aftermath*, ed. Rachel Elior (Jerusalem: Institute of Jewish Studies, Hebrew University of Jerusalem, 2001), pp. 143–347 (Hebrew), and Boaz Huss, "Sabbatianism and the Reception of the *Zohar*" in R. Elior, *The Sabbatian Movement*, pp. 53–71 and especially pp. 66–68 (Hebrew).

11. I have used three editions of this text. The first two contain the full text, with sections in all three languages. One is found in the Jewish National and University Library (JNUL), Jerusalem (shelf mark R41 A460, v. 6, no. 2) and was published in pamphlet format, without mention of place or date of publication. Typographical considerations suggest that it was printed in Lvov at the press of Judith Rosanes (active 1788–1805). Another edition, also published without mention of place or date of publication, is found in the *tkhine* pamphlet collection in the library of the Jewish Theological Seminary of America. A third edition (found in the JNUL, R75 A284) was published in Horodno (Grodno) in 1796 and contains a Yiddish paraphrase of the introduction, in addition to the Aramaic poem and the Yiddish *tkhine*.

12. See C. Weissler, *Voices of the Matriarchs*, chapter 7, for a fuller discussion of this text.

13. *Naḥalat Tsevi* was the work of Tsevi Hirsch b. Yerahmiel Chotsh, who was an underground believer in the messiah Shabbetai Tsevi. This text was apparently used by Sabbatian women and men in Zohar study circles. There are some slight hints in Shifrah's text that she might have been an underground Sabbatian, but that is not really clear.

14. The edition I used, found in the Jewish National and University Library, Jerusalem, contains no date or place of publication. The same is the case for a different edition in the collection of the Jewish Theological Seminary, New York. Ch. B. Friedberg, *Bet Eked Sefarim* (Jerusalem: 1969 or 1970; photo-offset of Tel Aviv, 1951), 1: 90, no. alef 2258, lists a [Sudylkow: 1837] edition. The title of this *tkhine* appears to be a play on the common book title *Imrei Shefer*, which, in Genesis 49:21, means "lovely fawns" but eventually came to mean "beautiful words," that is, words of Torah.

15. *Genesis Rabba*, end of 17; *Tanḥuma*, beginning of *Noah*, and near the end of *Metsora'*.

16. This is the macrocosm-microcosm correspondence mentioned earlier.

17. The Hebrew text is difficult and ambiguous and thus lends itself to multiple interpretations.

18. Some portions of this passage are a paraphrase of Zohar I:48b; however, the interpretation of Numbers 8:2 does not appear in this form in the Zohar. However, it *does* appear in *Naḥalat Tsevi*. The author of the *tkhine* has combined two passages from *Naḥalat Tsevi*. The discussion of women, Sabbath candles, and the Shechinah is found in *parashat Bereshit*, col. 5b, also numbered col.

130 (in the first edition, Frankfurt-am-Main, 1711), while the discussion of the High Priest is found near the beginning of *parashat Beha'alotekha*, col. 8a, also numbered col. 281. The bringing together of these two motifs is the work of the author of the *tkhine*.

19. On the mystical significance of the Sabbath, including some mention of the lighting of the candles, see Elliot K. Ginsburg, *The Sabbath in the Classical Kabbalah* (Albany: State University of New York Press, 1989).

20. Jacob Katz, *Tradition and Crisis*, trans. Bernard Dov Cooperman (New York: Schocken, 1993), p. 190.

6

||||||||||||||||||||||||||||||||||||||||||||||||||||||

How Central European Jewish
Women Confronted Modernity

Harriet Pass Freidenreich

During the course of the 19th century, a tolerated Jewish minority made up of elite Court Jews and lower-class traders and peddlers residing in small towns grew into a bourgeois, cultured, and heavily urban commercial and professional class, and traditional, Yiddish-speaking Central European Jewish women evolved into fashionable, modern German-Jewish women. Arranged marriages and large families gradually developed into more equal, companionate marriages with fewer children; more Jews chose their own partners, while some never married. In the transition from traditional Jewish society to modernity, Orthodox observances were gradually abandoned, Reform Judaism evolved, and some conversions to Christianity occurred, as integration into the surrounding German culture increased. Even though Central European Jews were legally emancipated during the 19th century, social acceptance took longer to achieve. Jewish women responded differently than men to modernity and the process of acculturation; while most became modern German-Jewish women, others had transformed into "new women" by the early 20th century.

Social and cultural historians have adopted a variety of approaches to the study of Central European Jewish women in the modern era, while examining their lives as women, as Jews, as Germans, and as German-Jewish women. Some, like Deborah Hertz,[1] focus on exceptional individuals on the periphery of the Jewish community, like the salon women and women writers who often converted or intermarried, while others, especially Marion Kaplan,[2] the leading scholar in the field, emphasize the role of Jewish women as wives and mothers, maintaining Jewish traditions in the home while at the same time instilling German culture in their children. Scholars have investigated changes in marriage patterns and family life, the impact of secular education on Jewish girls, the growth of Jewish women's organizations, the role of Jewish women in the German women's movement and in 20th-century politics, the exclusion of women from the leadership of the Jewish community, and women's changing economic role over the years. Tracing these different trends sheds light on the range of experiences of German-Jewish women as exceptional individuals and as a group and the varied interpretations and understandings of how they confronted modernity.

Glikl of Hameln: A Jewish Woman's Life in the Early Modern Era

Before the end of the 18th century, the lives of Jewish women in the various German states and the Habsburg Empire did not differ greatly from the lives of other Yiddish-speaking Ashkenazi women in Eastern Europe countries such as Poland or, later, in the Tsarist Empire. Growing up in towns or villages with small, traditional Jewish communities, Jewish women generally married in their late teens or early twenties and raised fairly large families, while helping their husbands run their businesses and support their families, whether at home or in the marketplace. Young Jewish girls generally learned household and economic skills from their mothers. Most could read Yiddish, and some learned Hebrew or secular subjects with tutors in the home, but usually they received little formal instruction.[3]

The first Central European Jewish woman we know about from her own writings is Glikl bas Judah Leib (1747–1824), often referred to as Glückel of Hameln, who wrote a memoir for her children toward the end of her life. Glikl can serve as an archetypical, if not typical, premodern Jewish woman. Her family belonged to the elite group of wealthy Jews involved in international trading of jewels and other goods. Betrothed at twelve, married at fourteen, and the mother of twelve children who survived to adulthood, she was actively involved in helping run her husband's business, especially when he was traveling and after his death. She was also greatly preoccupied with arranging suitable marriages for her children and providing her daughters with dowries. Despite limited formal education, Glikl was very knowledgeable about Jewish lore and values; she covered her hair and maintained a traditional Jewish home, strictly observing kosher dietary laws and the laws of family purity. As a widow, she often attended synagogue, sitting in a separate women's gallery curtained off from the men.[4]

Glikl was exceptional in that not only could she apparently read Hebrew, but she also recorded her experiences in a memoir written in Judeo-German or Western Yiddish. She married at a very young age and had an unusually large family, but otherwise her life was not unlike that of other Jewish women of her day, especially members of the wealthy elite. Her marriage, like the matches she made for her children, was arranged through personal or business contacts with other Jews in distant communities. Along with running a large household and being a devoted wife and mother, she served as her husband's business partner and confidante. Although travel was difficult and dangerous, she went on business trips and paid visits to her far-flung family. After a happy first marriage, based on mutual respect and trust, she spent a number of years as a widow before remarrying. Her second marriage proved to be both an economic and a personal disaster; she spent the last years of her life widowed again, living in the home of one of her daughters, even though she would rather have remained independent. Glikl strongly identified herself as a Jew and lived in a predominantly Jewish milieu, having relatively little contact with Christian society. Above all else, she wanted to pass on Jewish values and traditions to her children and grandchildren.[5]

Conversion and Intermarriage: Salon Women and Working Girls

By the late 18th century, some elite Jewish men in Central Europe under the influence of the German Enlightenment introduced the *Haskalah* movement, or the Jewish Enlightenment. At roughly the same time, some wealthy Jewish women, especially in Berlin, also began to distance themselves from traditional Jewish practices and tried to gain acceptance into German intellectual and social circles. Young women began to dress more like their Christian neighbors, and married women gradually abandoned head coverings; girls and women began speaking German, rather than Judeo-German, and reading German and French Romantic literature. By the early 19th century, an exceptional group of "salon women" were entertaining leading German intellectuals and noblemen in their homes in Berlin and in Vienna. Since interfaith marriages were generally not permitted in 19th-century Central Europe, some of these women converted in order to marry Christians, sometimes after divorcing their Jewish husbands. Most salon women, however, remained at least nominally within the Jewish fold.

Historians have had a longstanding fascination with the lives of these salon women, especially Henriette Lemos Herz, Dorothea Schlegel (née Brendel Mendelssohn), and Rahel Levin Varnhagen von Ense, who are often viewed as the first truly modern German-Jewish women. During the 1920s and 1930s, three leading German-Jewish women intellectuals, Hannah Arendt, Selma Stern, and Bertha Badt-Strauss, all wrote studies on salon women.[6] Some scholars have emphasized salon women's lack of Jewish education and their attraction to Romanticism, literature, music, and foreign languages as opposed to their fathers' or their Jewish husbands' involvement in the Enlightenment, rationalism, and philosophy.[7] Others have emphasized the desire of young women with secular education to break away from their patriarchal Jewish families, their ambivalence concerning Judaism and their Jewish origins, and their yearning to integrate more fully into German society.[8] Both women and men in elite Berlin Jewish circles converted to Christianity in significant numbers in the early 19th century, but they seem to have chosen baptism for different reasons: the men for legal and economic advancement and the women for marriage and social acceptance. Sometimes entire families were baptized together, but in other cases parents converted their children before they themselves were baptized.[9]

Women converted to both Protestantism and Catholicism, sometimes seemingly out of religious conviction but more often for the purpose of marriage. Although illegitimacy was quite rare within the Jewish community, lower-class Jewish women, especially domestic servants who had become pregnant, were known to have converted to Christianity in order to marry their Christian lovers. The salon women, however, were among the first upper-class Jewish women to leave the Jewish community because of a desire to intermarry. Deborah Hertz points out that women were in the vanguard of the wave of conversions and intermarriage in late-18th-century Berlin, but during the 19th century, as Steven Lowenstein argues, many more men than women accepted baptism and married outside the faith.[10] By the late 19th century, intermarriage had become more common among working-class and lower-middle-class Jews, particularly women.[11] When Jewish women married Christian men, they almost always converted to Christianity in order to do so; when Jewish men married

Christian women, they were not necessarily forced to leave the Jewish community. In either case, the children of mixed marriages were raised as Christians. Until the early 20th century, however, endogamy (in-marriage) was the general rule in Central Europe, and conversions and intermarriage remained exceptional for the most part, especially for women.[12]

The Modern Jewish Woman and Domestic Judaism

Marriage was the norm for women in Central Europe, and marital status defined a woman's place in society. If the vast majority of Jewish women continued to marry Jewish men and raise their children as Jews, what made modern Jewish women different from their more traditional mothers and grandmothers? The modern German-Jewish woman had to create a balance between being German by culture and Jewish by religion; unlike Glikl, she was expected to raise her children as both Germans and Jews. She married later, had fewer children, spoke German, had a good secular but weaker Jewish education, and lived in a city rather than a small town. In addition, she was very well versed in German literature, music and art and often engaged in philanthropic activities but maintained strong Jewish social and family ties.

During the course of the 19th century, as Central European Jews became increasingly urbanized and adopted a bourgeois lifestyle, Jewish women, except for widows and divorcées, gradually abandoned their significant economic role in the family business and focused their attention mainly on their household and on child rearing. Once the home and the workplace became separate, it was not considered appropriate for middle-class Jewish women to work outside the home for pay, especially when married. Jewish women were expected to wed by their early to mid-twenties, but often the groom was considerably older than the bride, since the husband was supposed to be able to support his wife and every couple was expected to establish its own household. Arranged marriages were still very common, and dowries remained important factors in negotiating suitable matches, but increasing numbers of marriages maintained at least the appearance of being love matches. With the development of the "cult of domesticity" among the middle class in Germany and elsewhere in the 19th century, a woman's place was clearly in the home and not in the public sphere; German-Jewish women embraced this ideal and embodied it in their personal lives.[13]

During the course of the 19th century, Jewish men gained emancipation in the form of freedom of movement and residence, educational and economic opportunities, and voting rights, whereas women, including Jewish women, did not achieve such civil rights until the 20th century. The Reform movement developed in Germany as a response to modernity linked to the struggle for emancipation on the one hand and the need to stem the tide of conversions on the other. Men provided the momentum and the leadership for this movement, which aimed to transform Jews into "German citizens of the Jewish faith," but how did this movement affect women's lives, given that women were largely excluded from public roles within the Jewish community (or *Gemeinde*)? The historian Benjamin Maria Baader argues that the Reform movement led to the feminization of German Jewry and the development of "domestic Judaism," centered in the home rather than the synagogue. According to Baader, Jewish boys and men were becoming more like Jewish girls and women.[14] Jewish boys were acquiring advanced secular education but much less Jewish education than in the past. They no longer spent their youth studying Torah and Talmud in a *heder* or *yeshiva* but instead attended secondary schools and universities, studying medicine, philosophy, and law. Jewish girls, although excluded from higher education, attained the best secular education available to them, particularly in areas such as foreign languages and literature, art, and music, but received rather limited formal religious education. Instead of the bar mitzvah ceremony for boys, the Reform movement introduced the confirmation ceremony for both boys and girls at the age of thirteen as the culmination of their Jewish education, which focused on moral teachings, principles of Judaism, and biblical history, rather than text study.[15] German sermons became central to the religious service in Reform synagogues, and German largely replaced Hebrew as the language of prayer. Women felt more comfortable in a service they could understand, but they still sat separately from men as part of the audience, rather than as rabbinic or lay leaders of the congregation. Women began to attend synagogue on a more regular basis on both Sabbath and holidays, while men's attendance declined.[16] Although minor changes occurred, the Reform movement in Germany never lived up to its promise of significantly improving the status of women within marriage, the synagogue, or the Jewish community and lagged behind its American counterpart, which continued to adopt more radical policies after 1870.[17]

However, under the influence of the middle-class ideology of domesticity, German Reform placed greater emphasis on family observances in the home than on prayer in the synagogue; women thereby became the bastions of the Jewish traditions, responsible for maintaining Jewish customs and practices, at a time when men were becoming less observant. Friday night dinners and Passover seders assumed increasing significance as family meals and celebrations and brought family members of different generations together on a regular basis. Women were in charge of strengthening family bonds by inviting extended family for Sabbath and festival meals and by preparing traditional Jewish dishes, creating a type of "gastronomic Judaism" that helped pass on memories from grandmothers to grandchildren. According to domestic Judaism, women, not men, were to transmit Jewish knowledge and values to the next generation by creating a close-knit family environment. Twentieth-century memoirists, both women and men, often recalled their grandmothers, rather than their mothers, as pious women, praying at home, observing Jewish dietary laws, and preparing special dishes for Jewish holidays. As the men drifted away from Jewish practices, eating on the Day of Atonement and rarely attending synagogue, mothers and grandmothers were left to ensure that the next generations would identify as Jews.[18]

At the same time, it was up to the women to instill German culture (often referred to as *Bildung*) and bourgeois values into their homes and families. Although the men frequently had sizable libraries, it was the mother's role to read Goethe and Schiller to her children, to take them to the theater and museums, to introduce them to music and the arts, and to arrange for dancing lessons so that they could meet appropriate partners. Even though many families had non-Jewish domestic servants, as well as nurses and governesses, to help look after the home and the children, it was the mother's job to educate the children properly in both German and Jewish values.[19]

As Jews climbed from the middle class to the upper middle class by the early 20th century, their families gradually became smaller, with two or three children, sometimes only one, instead of five or six, as had been common earlier. Modern Jewish women were in the forefront in using recently available contraceptive methods to control the size of their families. In many instances, Jewish families were also in the vanguard in adopting new fashions and modern inventions in their homes. Especially in small towns, they tended to be among the first to get telephones, electricity, and other newfangled devices in the late 19th century. If Jewish men owned the department stores, then their wives became the ultimate consumers. Because married German-Jewish women by and large no longer engaged in economic activities outside the home and generally had domestic servants who did much of the housework, they had more time to become involved in volunteer philanthropic activities both within the Jewish community and outside it. Jewish women's clubs and philanthropic associations formed even before their Christian counterparts developed.

In 1904, the *Jüdischer Frauenbund* (League of Jewish Women), the flagship organization representing the modern middle-class Jewish woman, came into existence. Its main goals were to fight against "white slavery," or prostitution; to provide vocational training for young Jewish women; to support Jewish women and children in need, including unwed mothers; and to campaign on behalf of women's rights, including suffrage, both in Germany and within the Jewish community. With roughly one out of five German-Jewish women belonging to the JFB, this moderate Jewish feminist organization, affiliated with the *Bund deutscher Frauen* (Federation of German Women), grew to be one of the largest women's groups in interwar Germany. Even though most of its fifty thousand members were married, some of its leaders and activists, including its founder and president, Bertha Pappenheim, were single women, who formed something of an anomaly within the organized Jewish community.[20]

Jewish Women and German Feminism

During the 19th century, individual Jewish women became active participants in both the German and the Austrian woman's movements. First-wave feminists in Central Europe focused their activities on educational reform, admission of women to universities, improved working conditions for women, and protection of motherhood. Jewish women were particularly active in the Fröbel kindergarten movement for reform of early childhood education and the modernization of social work. According to the historian Maya Fassmann, one-third of the most prominent leaders of the early feminist movement in Germany, twenty out of sixty activists, were of Jewish origin.[21]

Fassmann divides these Jewish feminists into three groups: writers, Fröbel movement leaders, and philanthropists and social work advocates. The writers, including Fanny Lewald-Stahr, Jenny Hirsch and Hedwig Dohm, came from highly assimilated wealthy families, most of which had moved away from traditional Judaism. These women were often deeply ambivalent about their Jewishness, and some sought to keep their Jewish origins secret.[22] By contrast, the women associated with the kindergarten movement had a more positive attitude toward Judaism and their Jewish identity; Johanna Goldschmidt and Lina Morgenstern were both confirmed in Reform synagogues, and both Morgenstern and Henriette Goldschmidt were married to Reform rabbis. The third group comprised daughters of these early feminists who criticized the domesticity and philanthropic activities of their mothers' generation and sought other alternatives, thereby laying the foundations for modern social work. Among these social work pioneers were Jeanette Schwerin, Henriette Fürth, and especially Alice Salomon, who served as secretary and then vice president of the Federation of German Women's Associations. Despite the fact that some, like Alice Salomon, chose to convert to Christianity, Fassman argues that behind the actions of most German-Jewish feminists was a desire that German society accept them and recognize them as Jews who were socially engaged and working on behalf of a more humane society based on equality. However, she recognizes that there was no real German-Jewish symbiosis within the German feminist movement.[23]

Some Jewish women also became very involved in Central European politics, especially within the German Democratic, Social Democratic, and Communist parties. Several, including Henriette Fürth, Ottilie Schoenewald, Toni Sender, Käte Frankenthal, and Frieda Wunderlich in Germany and Therese Schlesinger-Eckstein in Austria, served on municipal councils during the interwar years and a few, like Gertrud Klausner, Frieda Wunderlich, and Toni Sender, were elected to state or national office. Rosa Luxemburg, Ruth Fischer, and Käthe Leichter belonged to Socialist or Communist party leadership cadres, but many more Jewish women were party activists, party members, or fellow travelers. Some of these individuals openly identified as Jews, while others did not. Anitta Müller-Cohen and Erna Patak were prominent within the Jewish Nationalist Party in Vienna, but women's involvement in Zionist politics in Central Europe was rare.[24]

The Jewish "New Woman"

Although socialized at an early age to marry by their early twenties and become housewives, some members of the younger generation of Jewish women, including Alice Salomon, the founder of modern German social work, rejected housework and feminine handicrafts and objected to forced idleness after completing their higher girls' school education at the age of sixteen.[25] As modern German-Jewish women evolved into "New Women," they sought advanced education and the option to pursue a career before, or as an alternative to, marriage. Before the turn of the century, however, German and Austrian universities were closed to women, and few vocational opportunities for middle-class Jewish women were available. Since Jewish women were largely excluded from teaching and nursing positions due to anti-Semitism, single Jewish women who sought to escape from bourgeois conventions often turned to literary careers, social welfare activities, and, by the early 20th century, professions that required university education.

The expression "New Woman" usually describes a type of individual who defies many of the prescribed gender rules of feminine behavior with respect to physical appearance and lifestyle. It generally refers to unmarried women, whether working-class, middle-class, or university educated, who worked outside the household, were able to control their own incomes, and made their own decisions about their lives. According to Barbara Caine, "new women" were those "who sought to lead lives very different from those of their mothers by engaging in activities which proclaim their independence, their sense of personal worth, and their entitlement to a public role."[26]

Single career women could more easily defy the gender norms of society by living or working on their own than could married women, especially married women with children. To remain a "New Woman" after marriage meant finding a "New Man" to marry and creating a "New Family" in a new type of marriage that would allow a woman to be at least semi-independent and to pursue her own interests or career. Many women might have aspired to the independent way of life of the "New Woman," if not the label attached to it, which was often pejorative, but "New Men" were hard to find, and women working outside the home voluntarily, especially married middle-class women, were often perceived as threats to the social order in the early 20th century.

Key differences between the modern German-Jewish woman, whom I have already discussed, and the Jewish "New Woman" can be found in changing attitudes toward marriage and career, as well as sexuality and motherhood. For the Jewish "new women" I studied while researching my book *Female, Jewish, and Educated: The Lives of Jewish University Women*, higher education and/or a career often took precedence over marriage, and adult life was not entirely focused on *"Kinder, Küche, und Kehille,"* that is, motherhood, homemaking, and involvement in Jewish life and the Jewish community.[27] As I have indicated, women who married were less likely to fit the category of the "New Woman" than were those who remained single, were employed outside the home, and were self-supporting. Although it was indeed possible for some professional women, such as the physicians that Atina Grossmann has analyzed so well in her work,[28] to maintain the lifestyle of the "New Woman" after marriage and childbearing, that scenario generally required a reasonably egalitarian partnership that would allow a woman to pursue her own interests. Such family arrangements were much less common in early-20th-century Germany and Austria than they are today.

A study of Jewish women who attended universities in Central Europe before the Nazi era provides a logical place to begin a search for the Jewish "New Woman" of the early 20th century. Whereas modern Jewish women were likely to be wives and mothers and/or involved in Jewish activities at some level, Jewish women with higher education were often single, childless, and alienated from the Jewish community. Another place to explore the phenomenon of the Jewish "New Woman" is within intermarriages, which by the turn of the century were quite different from the marriages of the Jewish salon women and writers a century earlier. Till van Rahden has analyzed the "New Woman" in relationship to interfaith marriages between Jews and Christians in his recent book and articles.[29] He asserts that Jewish women who entered into interfaith marriages in late-19th- and early-20th-century Breslau, with or without converting to Christianity, could serve as examples of the "New Woman," especially among the Jewish working class. According to van Rahden,

> both Jews and Gentiles who intermarried—particularly Jewish women— were more independent of their families, more adventurous and rebellious than partners in intra-Jewish marriages. They were far more likely than women in intra-Jewish marriages to have worked professionally and far less likely to still be living with their parents. In an age when premarital sex for women was taboo, about a quarter of intermarried couples had actually shared an apartment with their partner before marrying. Jewish women who entered mixed marriages did so because they wanted to; intra-Jewish marriages, in contrast, continued to conform to the pattern of strategic marriage alliances.[30]

Jewish women who intermarried exercised greater independence in their choice of a partner and went against many of the norms of intra-Jewish marriage. It is possible to categorize them in some respects as Jewish "new women"; they were certainly beyond *Kehille*, although I doubt that they were also beyond both *Kinder* and *Küche*. Nevertheless, those Jewish women who were most likely to be beyond *Kinder* and *Küche*, as well as *Kehille*, tended to be middle-class, often university-educated, professionals and intellectuals like the women I studied in my book. Interestingly enough, Jewish university women in Central Europe were no more likely than other German-Jewish women to intermarry, but they were much less likely to marry at all.[31]

Even among intra-Jewish marriages, marriage and family patterns were in the process of change among modern Jewish women in Central Europe. Arranged marriages and dowries were certainly less common in the 20th century than they had been in the 19th century; age differences between husband and wife were diminishing, and family size was declining rapidly within middle-class Jewish families, undoubtedly because of the widespread use of birth control. This was particularly true among educated women. Before 1933, the overwhelming majority of Central European Jewish women, including many with university educations, were very modern Jewish women, leading cultured, urban, middle-class lives. They might have aspired to be "new women" in some sense, but by and large they continued to conform to the gender-roles assigned to middle-class Jewish women. They married by their mid-twenties, had children, and spent most of their adult lives carrying out the roles of wife and mother. Many married Jewish women were involved in volunteer work and belonged to such organizations as the *Jüdischer Frauenbund*, but after marriage relatively few worked for pay outside the home by choice, rather than out of economic necessity. The husband was expected to be the primary, and indeed the sole, breadwinner in the family. In short, Jewish wives did not tend to be beyond *Kinder, Küche*, or *Kehille*. Most often the decision whether to work outside the home and to maintain a certain degree of economic self-sufficiency, like the decision whether to belong to and be involved in the *Gemeinde* (the organized Jewish community), was not left up to them. Paid employment outside the home, other than in a family business or by widows and divorcées, was not considered respectable, except perhaps for educators, physicians, and some other professionals. Among married women, the Jewish "New Woman" was the exception rather than the rule, although single women achieved greater independence and were able to defy gender norms more easily.

In the past fifteen years, a great deal has been published about women students and women professionals in both Germany and Austria; much of this burgeoning literature deals with Jewish women, either directly or indirectly, including the important work of the late Claudia Huerkamp on women students and professionals in Germany,[32] Waltraud Heindl on women students in Vienna,[33] and Atina Grossmann on women physicians in Weimar Germany,[34] among many others. While researching my book on Central European Jewish university women, I was constantly struck by how many German and Austrian historians were focusing on exactly the same individuals I was studying, not because they were necessarily interested in Jews per se but because women of Jewish descent were so prominent among the pioneering generations of university students, physicians, academics, and other professionals, as well as among writers and political activists. Numerous German articles and edited volumes by Barbara Hahn, Hiltrud Häntzschel, Marina Sassenberg, and other German and Austrian scholars focus on the lives and careers of individual Jewish women intellectuals, social reformers, and academics. Some excellent biographies and many biographical dictionaries that include Jewish women scientists, psychologists, and so on, have also appeared within the past decade or so. There is thus a plethora of information available in both primary and secondary sources, mainly in German, to document the history of educated Central European Jewish women before the Nazi era, especially since Jewish women seem to have written most of the memoirs.[35]

Jewish university women in Central Europe are thus obvious candidates to be designated as the archetypical "new women" of the early 20th century. As I state at the outset in *Female, Jewish, and Educated*:

Women who attended university . . . were "New Women" who chose a different path. They were not satisfied to follow their mothers' examples as homemakers and volunteers, but preferred becoming physicians, educators, scientists, lawyers or social reformers. For them, marriage was an option, not a necessity.

. . . Many middle-class European Jewish girls desired to escape from the almost exclusively female realm of home and school in which they had been raised and to gain access to the traditionally male domain of university and professional life. These young women did not necessarily wish to become like men, nor did they always aspire to economic independence. By attending university they wanted to realize their intellectual potential as human beings and emancipate themselves from at least some of society's constraints against women.[36]

Thus, for women with a university education and other "new women," marriage had become an option, rather than a necessity, and was no longer the focal point of their entire existence. That, to me, is the essence of "new womanhood."

A majority of Central European Jewish university women eventually married and three out of five married women had children, but it is striking to note that more than a quarter of the women whom I studied remained single, and almost 40 percent of the married women were childless and hence more easily able to pursue careers after marriage if they so desired. Single university women, such as Käte Frankenthal, Toni Sender, Margarete Berent, Lise Meitner, Tilly Edinger, Alice Salomon, and Charlotte Wolff, are very easy to categorize as "new women" throughout their lives. Although they might retain close ties with their families of birth, by and large they lived independently, pursued careers (not always paid), and sometimes flouted the sexual mores of their day. Married women, even those without children, often faced a greater struggle in making their own choices and decisions and frequently had to make compromises because of the demands of marriage and motherhood. Often, their careers were overshadowed by those of their husbands, but many, especially those in more egalitarian marriages to men close to their own age, managed to persevere in living the life of a "New Woman" even after marriage and childbirth.[37] As Atina Grossmann has demonstrated, physicians like Hertha Nathorff were among the most successful in combining career, marriage, and family,[38] yet many "new women" who had aspired to pursue professional careers before their marriage found themselves relegated to becoming housewives and homemakers thereafter.

The Making of the "New Jewish Woman"

Were these Jewish "New Women" really "New Jewish Women"? I don't think so. Let me illustrate the difference between these categories by using two examples: Käte Frankenthal and Rahel Goitein Straus. Frankenthal, a physician and socialist politician born in 1889, defied most gender stereotypes of her day and is the epitome of the "New Woman" in virtually all respects: she smoked, she drank whisky, she was very athletic, she had short hair, and she often wore men's clothing. As a feminist, a public health official, and an elected deputy of the Berlin municipal council, she actively fought on behalf of birth control and abortion rights. Käte Frankenthal remained single but had an active sex life. Although close to her family, she was fiercely independent; she needed a housekeeper because she had absolutely no interest in cooking, sewing, or performing other household chores. She left the Jewish community and officially became *konfessionslos* (without religion) at the age of thirty-four, after the death of her parents, and claimed to be "turned off by anything Jewish in appearance or manner." She was a Jew by descent, not by choice. Käte Frankenthal might be a fairly extreme case of a "New Woman," but I can provide numerous examples of other Jewish university women who resemble her in many ways.

Rahel Goitein Straus was a different type of Jewish "New Woman"; she was a "Jewish Jew" and most definitely a precursor to the "New Jewish Woman." Born in Karlsruhe in 1880, she graduated from the first girls' gymnasium in Germany and was among the first women to earn a medical degree from Heidelberg. A practicing physician for twenty-five years and the mother of five children, she supported woman's suffrage, gave lectures to women on nutrition and birth control, and wrote a pamphlet for mothers explaining how to discuss sex with their daughters. An ardent Zionist as well as a feminist, she organized and led various women's Zionist groups in Munich and served as vice president of the *Jüdischer Frauenbund* before her emigration to Palestine in 1932. Straus also ran a fairly traditional Jewish household, welcomed visiting Zionist dignitaries and numerous Jewish students to her home, and served as matchmaker. Rahel Goitein Straus is my favorite example of a "New Jewish Superwoman" of the early 20th century, but I haven't found many others like her.

In a paper I delivered titled "Jewish Identity and the 'New Woman': Central European Jewish University Women in the Early Twentieth Century" at a conference on gender and Judaism at Ohio State University in 1993, I concluded the following:

> committed Jews like Rahel Goitein Straus were far more exceptional among Central European Jewish university women in the early 20th century than socialists like Käte Frankenthal or the many others who either rejected their Jewishness or only allowed it to play a minimal role in their lives until Hitler appeared on the scene. By acquiring a higher education equal to that of men, these "new women," the products of the first generation of feminism, strove to define new and more equal roles for women in society but not necessarily within the Jewish community. University women

were dissatisfied with the traditional middle-class Jewish woman's role as homemaker. But although most of these women retained nominal Jewish affiliation, they rarely attempted to reform their community or the position of women within it. Prior to the Nazi era, Germany and Austria certainly produced a very large number of "new women" of Jewish origin, but the "new Jewish woman"—a modern woman with a strong, positive Jewish identity—had scarcely begun to emerge.[39]

Today, more than a decade and a half later, I would still say much the same thing, at least with respect to Central European university-educated Jewish women. By and large, I would categorize them as Jewish "new women" but not "new Jewish women."

In her introduction to an essay entitled "The 'New Jewish Woman' in Weimar Germany," published in 1998, Claudia Prestel challenges my conclusion, deeming it to be "rather harsh" and arguing that "the phenomenon of the 'new Jewish woman' was evident much earlier and was fairly common in the Weimar Republic." She goes on to say that "The Jewish press, for example, published numerous articles on modern women and modern marriages as well as on the 'new family' in the 1920s." Prestel introduces the idea of a "new-old Jewish woman" who incorporates modernity into tradition, and she concludes that "To deny them the title of 'new woman,' even though in some aspects of their lives they carried some of the burdens of tradition and a pre-emancipatory past, would not do justice to the variety of the lives of Jewish women in Weimar."[40] I believe, however, that it is necessary to distinguish between modern Jewish women and "new Jewish women." Just as many Jewish "new women" cannot be classified as "new Jewish women" because they lack a strong positive sense of Jewish identity and because they are not actively involved in Jewish life or within the Jewish community, so too perhaps should many modern Jewish married women be excluded from the category of "new Jewish women," even if they live a modern Jewish family life, practice birth control, and are actively involved in the *Jüdischer Frauenbund* or other Jewish women's organizations. Claudia Prestel and I agree that Rahel Straus does indeed provide the prototype for the "New Jewish Woman," and we both would use many of the same examples to illustrate who else might belong to that category, but for me at least the classification "New Jewish Woman" of the interwar years remains elusive and difficult to define. As far as I can tell, even "new women" did not exercise much agency within the Jewish community.

Claudia Prestel's work on Jewish women, like much of Marion Kaplan's early work, has focused largely on women within the *Gemeinde* and women involved in Jewish organizations. Such women were not usually beyond *Kinder, Küche,* or *Kehille,* although they were trying to redefine and modernize women's lives within both the home and the Jewish community and to some extent made progress in these areas. Most members of the *Jüdischer Frauenbund* were married, but some of the most important activists, including not only Bertha Pappenheim and Hannah Karminski but also several Jewish university women, including Margarete Berent, Käthe Mende, and Cora Berliner, were single. Working within the Jewish community and on its behalf was one of the few ways single Jewish "new women" could function as "new Jewish women" as well.[41]

My own research has dealt mainly with university-educated women who were marginal members of the organized Jewish community. In the early 20th century, highly educated Jewish "new women" who remained single, who married late and had no children, or who combined both family and career did not fit easily within the established Jewish community and its organizations. Only a very small minority of the Jewish university women I studied were actively involved in Jewish women's organizations or Jewish activities of any kind. Most of the volunteers who belonged to such organizations as the JFB and B'nai Brith Women tended to be women from fairly traditional backgrounds who married soon after leaving university and did not pursue full-time careers in Germany, although several Jewish university women, including Margarete Edelheim and Eva Reichmann, worked for the *Centralverein* (the Central Association of Jewish Citizens of the Jewish Faith), while others were social workers or teachers working within Jewish institutions.[42]

It is important to acknowledge that, as Claudia Prestel points out, there were indeed different varieties of modern Jewish women in Central Europe before the Nazi era and that studying university women helps one learn more about individual Jewish "new women" than about "new Jewish women" collectively. Many career women, including teachers, social workers, nurses, librarians, or physicians and whether single or married, might indeed qualify as "new Jewish women," as long as they both challenged the prevalent gender roles of their day and were involved in Jewish activities. More research needs to be done on the role of Jewish women social workers, educators, and communal employees as "new women." Many, but not all, of the "Jewish Jews" in my book could be described as "new Jewish women" in some sense because they were indeed "new women" with university educations and, in some cases, careers and also demonstrated a positive Jewish commitment in some way, but "Jewish Jews" make up less than 15 percent of my study population of 460 Jewish university women.[43]

Jewish women intellectuals who chose to do research on Jewish topics during the interwar years form another, special category of "new Jewish women." In their personal lives, they, like most Jewish "new women," were largely beyond *Kinder, Küche,* and *Kehille*; they were not usually bound by traditional gender roles and were only peripherally involved in Jewish communal or organizational activities. These rather exceptional individuals have recently attracted the attention of women scholars, including Barbara Hahn[44] and others. Several members of this unusual group—Selma Stern, Hannah Arendt, Trude Weiss-Rosmarin, and Bertha Badt-Strauss—wrote about Jewish women, including salon women, and can be seen as searching for a usable Jewish past for Jewish "new women" and other modern Jewish women to adopt.[45] These women can perhaps serve as a bridge connecting the Jewish "New Woman" of the past with the "New Jewish Woman" of the present. Living as "new women" but often writing with a strong Jewish awareness, such women help us to reconceptualize the "New Jewish Woman" as nonconformists within the larger Jewish community.

The categories of Jewish "New Woman" and "New Jewish Woman" are undoubtedly artificial and somewhat contrived. Like the terms "feminist" and "Jewish feminist," these are labels that researchers today might give to women of the past but not necessarily ones that the women themselves would have chosen. Just as the Jewish "new women" that emerged in the early 20th century were the beneficiaries of the 19th-century woman's movement, or first-wave feminism, the "new Jewish women" of the late 20th century were for the most part the by-products of second-wave feminism, which developed after 1968. The pioneering generations of modern Jewish educated women in Central Europe certainly saw themselves as pathbreakers, paving the way for others to follow, but I'm not sure that they would have referred to themselves as "new women," let alone "new Jewish women." The lives and careers of these Jewish "new women" foreshadow the experiences of all women professionals, whether single or married, in the late 20th century. Today we can look back on the modern German-Jewish women and Jewish "new women" of the 19th and early 20th centuries to help us understand how the "new Jewish women" of the 21st century started to become what we are now.

NOTES

1. See Deborah Hertz, *Jewish High Society in Old Regime Berlin* (New Haven: Yale University Press, 1988); Hertz, "Work, Love, and Jewishness in the Life of Fanny Lewald," in *Profiles in Diversity*, ed. Frances Malino and David Sorkin (Detroit: Wayne State University Press, 1998), pp. 202–20.

2. Marion Kaplan, *The Making of the Jewish Middle Class: Women, Family, and Identity in Imperial Germany* (New York: Oxford University Press, 1991).

3. For an overview of ordinary Jewish women's lives and families from the early modern era to World War II, see Marion A. Kaplan, ed., *Jewish Daily Life in Germany, 1618–1945* (New York: Oxford University Press, 2005).

4. See Marvin Lowenthal, trans., *The Memoirs of Glückel of Hameln* (New York: Schocken Books, 1977).

5. For an excellent recent analysis of Glikl's life and significance in the context of 17th-century Western European women's history, see Natalie Zemon Davis, *Women on the Margins: Three Seventeenth Century Lives* (Cambridge, MA: Harvard University Press, 1995), pp. 5–62.

6. Hannah Arendt, *Rahel Varnhagen: The Life of a Jewish Woman*, rev. ed. (New York: Harcourt Brace Jovanovich, 1974); Barbara Hahn, ed., *Frauen in den Kulturwissenschaften* (Munich: Verlag C. H. Beck, 1994), pp. 152–65, 204–18, 334–338; Marina Sassenberg, ed., *Apropos Selma Stern* (Frankfurt am Main: Verlag Neue Kritik, 1998), pp. 74–84. More recent studies include D. Hertz, *Jewish High Society in Old Regime Berlin*, and Emily D. Bilski and Emily Braun, *Jewish Women and Their Salons: The Power of Conversation* (New Haven: Yale University Press, 2005).

7. Michael A. Meyer, *The Origins of the Modern Jew* (Detroit: Wayne State, 1967), pp. 85–114.

8. See D. Hertz, *Jewish High Society in Old Regime Berlin*, pp. 204–50.

9. Ibid.; Steven M. Lowenstein, *The Berlin Jewish Community: Enlightenment, Family, and Crisis, 1770–1830* (New York: Oxford University Press, 1994), pp. 162–76.

10. Ibid.

11. Till van Rahden, "Intermarriages, the 'New Woman,' and the Situational Ethnicity of Breslau Jews From the 1870s to the 1920s," *Leo Baeck Institute Year Book* 46 (2001): 125–50.

12. Monika Richarz, "Demographic Development," in *German-Jewish History in Modern Times*, ed. Michael A. Meyer, vol. 3 (New York: Columbia University Press, 1997), pp. 13–17.

13. See Paula Hyman, *Gender and Assimilation in Modern Jewish History* (Seattle: University of Washington Press, 1995); M. Kaplan, *The Making of the Jewish Middle Class* and other works by Kaplan, including "Priestess and Hausfrau: Women and Tradition in the German-Jewish Family," in *The Jewish Family:*

Myths and Reality, ed. Steven M. Cohen and Paula E. Hyman (New York: Holmes and Meier, 1986), pp. 62–81, and "Tradition and Transition: The Acculturation, Assimilation and Integration of Jews in Imperial Germany—A Gender Analysis," *Leo Baeck Institute Yearbook* 27 (1982): 3–36.

14. See Benjamin Maria Baader, *Gender Judaism, and Bourgeois Culture in Germany, 1800–1870* (Bloomington: Indiana University Press, 2006).

15. Ibid., pp. 146–51.

16. Ibid., pp. 117–60.

17. For a comparative view of place of women in 19th-century American Reform Judaism, see Karla Goldman, *Beyond the Synagogue Gallery: Finding a Place for Women in American Judaism* (Cambridge, MA: Harvard University Press, 2000).

18. See M. Kaplan, *The Making of the Jewish Middle Class.*

19. Ibid.

20. For a history of the *Jüdischer Frauenbund*, see Marion Kaplan, *The Jewish Feminist Movement in Germany: The Campaigns of the Jüdischer Frauenbund, 1904–1938* (Westport, CT: Greenwood Press, 1979).

21. Irmgard Maya Fassmann, *Jüdinnen in der deutschen Frauenbewegung, 1865–1919* (Hildesheim: Georg Olms Verlag, 1996), especially pp. 12–13. Maya Fassmann, "Jüdinnen in der deutschen Frauenbewegung 1865–1919," in *Zur Geschichte der jüdischen Frau in Deutschland*, ed. Julius Carlebach (Berlin: Metropol Verlag, 1993), pp. 147–65. See also Harriet Anderson, *Utopian Feminism: Women's Movements in Fin-de-Siècle Vienna* (New Haven: Yale University Press, 1992).

22. M. Fassman, "Jüdinnen in der deutschen Frauenbewegung 1865–1919," pp. 147–60. See also Deborah Hertz, "Work, Love and Jewishness in the Life of Fanny Lewald," in *Profiles in Diversity*, ed. F. Malino and D. Sorkin (Detroit: Wayne State University Press, 1998). Fassmann emphasizes the Jewish ties of these feminists, whereas Hertz focuses on their ambivalence concerning their Jewish descent.

23. M. Fassmann, "Jüdinnen in der deutschen Frauenbewegung 1865–1919," pp. 147–160. For biographical information on individual women mentioned in this essay, see *Jewish Women: A Comprehensive Historical Encyclopedia* (2006) (on CD-ROM and online at http://jwa.org).

24. Fassmann, *Jüdinnen in der deutschen Frauenbewegung 1865–1919*, pp. 147–160. See also Harriet Pass Freidenreich, *Female, Jewish, and Educated: The Lives of Central European University Women* (Bloomington: Indiana University Press, 2002), pp. 152–60, 253–54.

25. Alice Salomon, *Character Is Destiny: The Autobiography of Alice Salomon* (Ann Arbor: University of Michigan Press, 2004).

26. Barbara Caine and Glenda Sluga, *Gendering European History* (London: Leicester University Press, 2000), p. 130.

27. See H. P. Freidenreich, *Female, Jewish, and Educated.*

28. Atina Grossmann, "German Women Doctors From Berlin to New York: Maternity and Modernity in Weimar and in Exile," *Feminist Studies* 19:1 (Spring 1992): 65–87; Atina Grossmann, "New Women in Exile: German Women Doctors and the Emigration" in *Between Sorrow and Strength*, ed. Sibylle Quack (Washington, DC: German Historical Institute, 1995), pp. 215–38.

29. T. van Rahden, "Intermarriages, the 'New Woman,' and the Situational Ethnicity of Breslau Jews From the 1870s to the 1920s" *Leo Baeck Institute Yearbook* 46 (2001): 125–58;; Till van Rahden, "Mingling, Marrying, and Distancing: Jewish Integration in Wilhelminian Breslau and Its Erosion in Early Weimar Germany," in *Jüdisches Leben in der Weimarer Republik*, ed. Wolfgang Benz et al. (Tübingen: J. C. B. Mohr, 1998), pp. 197–222; Till van Rahden, *Juden und andere Breslauer* (Göttingen: Vandenhoeck & Ruprecht, 2000), pp. 141–74.

30. T. van Rahden, "Mingling, Marrying, and Distancing," p. 140.

31. H. P. Freidenreich, *Female, Jewish, and Educated*, pp. 109–14 and tables 10 and 11.

32. Claudia Huerkamp, *Bildungsbürgerinnen: Frauen im Studium und in akademischen Berufen, 1900-1945* (Göttingen: Vandenhoeck & Ruprecht, 1996); Huerkamp, "Frauen, Universitäten und Bildungsbürgertum. Zur Lage studierender Frauen 1900–1933" in *Bürgerliche Berufe: Zur Sozialgeschichte der freien und akademischen Berufe im internationalen Vergleich*, ed. Hannes Siegrist (Göttingen: Vandenhoeck und Ruprecht, 1988), pp. 200–22. Claudia Huerkamp, "Jüdische Akademikerinnen in Deutschland, 1900–1938," *Geschichte und Gesellschaft* 19 (1993): 311–31.

33. Waltraud Heindl and Marina Tichy, eds. *"Durch Erkenntnis zu Freiheit und Glück . . .": Frauen an der Universität Wien (ab 1897)*, Schriftenreihe des Universitätsarchivs Universität Wien, vol. 5 (Vienna: WUV-Universitätsverlag, 1990); Waltraud Heindl and Rudolf Wytek. "Die jüdischen Studentinnen an der Universität Wien 1897–1938," in *Der Wiener Stadttempel, Die Wiener Juden* (Vienna: J&V Edition, 1988), pp. 137–50.

34. A. Grossmann, "German Women Doctors From Berlin to New York: Maternity and Modernity in Weimar and in Exile,"; Atina Grossmann, "New Women in Exile: German Women Doctors and the Emigration," in *Between Sorrow and Strength*, ed. Sibylle Quack (Washington, DC: German Historical Insitute, 1995), pp. 215–38; Atina Grossmann, *Reforming Sex: The German Movement for Birth Control and Abortion Reform, 1920-1950* (New York: Oxford University Press, 1995).

35. See H. P. Freidenreich, *Female, Jewish, and Educated*, endnotes and bibliography, for a long list of such sources.

36. Ibid., pp. 1–2.

37. Ibid., pp. 112–32 and tables 10 and 11.

38. A. Grossmann, "German Women Doctors From Berlin to New York."

39. Harriet Pass Freidenreich, "Jewish Identity and the 'New Woman:' Central European Jewish University Women in the Early Twentieth Century" in *Gender and Judaism*, ed. T. M. Rudavsky (New York: New York University Press, 1995), p. 120.

40. Claudia T. Prestel, "The 'New Jewish Woman' in Weimar Germany," in *Jüdisches Leben in der Weimarer Republik*, ed. Wolfgang Benz et al. (Tübingen: J. C. B. Mohr, 1998), p. 135.

41. H. P. Freidenreich, *Female, Jewish, and Educated*, pp. 146–47.

42. Ibid.

43. Ibid., pp. 144–46.

44. Barbara Hahn, *The Jewess Pallas Athena: This Too a Theory of Modernity*, trans. James McFarland (Princeton: Princeton University Press, 2005).

45. H. P. Freidenreich, *Female, Jewish, and Educated*, p. 199.

Part III

‖‖

Contemporary Life

||||||||||||||||||||||||||||||||||||||||||||||||||

7

Women and American Judaism

Pamela S. Nadell

If there is an overarching theme for the history of the 20th century, it is that of cataclysmic change. Enormous social, political, and economic transformations followed in the wake of the century's catastrophic wars, mass social movements, and technological revolutions. When the century dawned, Americans still lived in homes heated by coal stoves; at century's end, a computer chip had transformed our world. The incineration of Hiroshima and Nagasaki not only ended World War II; it also ushered in the age of nuclear peril. In 1900, Jim Crow ruled the land; in 2005, when the civil rights heroine Rosa Parks died, her body lay in state in the rotunda of the U.S. Capitol.

Amid these astonishing changes, one of the great stories of the 20th century is the burgeoning possibilities for how women live their lives. Because every arena of women's "lived life" was affected, historians of women and gender use myriad lenses—domesticity, education, economics, politics, social life, and sexuality—to read this history of change over time. In this chapter, we eschew these multiple lenses to select but a single one, that of religion, to examine how expanding opportunities for American women ultimately led to the transformation of American Judaism.

In 1889, on the front page of the Philadelphia *Jewish Exponent*, the writer Mary M. Cohen asked a provocative question: could women become rabbis? The raising of the question and the debate over women's ordination that followed in its wake reflect the long history of the question of women's proper sphere within American Judaism.[1] Incremental change in women's roles within Judaism characterized the 19th and the 20th centuries until the second wave of American feminism burst forth. Then, as a floodtide of gendered shifts occurred, feminism crashed up against

American Judaism. The result was a revelation: women used their power to transform American Judaism.[2]

In the 19th century, American Jewish immigrants, responding to modernity and finding its essence in creative adaptation of Judaism to the United States, experimented with a variety of synagogue reforms. Especially after the Civil War, as congregants prospered and built grand new synagogues, questions of ritual change surfaced. Must the cantor still face the ark? Which prayers could be eliminated? Could services be shortened? At the heart of the questions lay the goal of "becoming an American while remaining a Jew."[3] In time, congregations introduced organs, replaced cantors with gentile choirs, abolished the second day of festivals, abbreviated the Torah reading, discarded Hebrew liturgy for the vernacular, and dispensed with male head covering. The historian Leon Jick concludes: "By 1870 . . . there were few congregations in America in which substantial reforms had *not* been introduced and in which an accelerating program of radical revision was *not* in process . . . the modest tendency toward reform became an irreversible tide."[4]

But, if "an irreversible tide" of dramatic reform was then under way in many American synagogues, changes in women's status in American Judaism appeared far less startling. Women's places within their Jewish worlds had literally shifted in the 19th century. Unlike the practice in the communities from which they or their parents had set sail, in America Jewish women first became regular synagogue goers. Then their places changed yet again as, before too long, they found themselves breaking from the traditional practice of separating men and women during prayer by coming down from the balcony to sit next to their husbands in family pews.[5] At the same time, thanks to Philadelphia's Rebecca Gratz, some women discovered another new religious role. When, in 1838, Gratz founded the Hebrew Sunday School, she not only gave girls an opportunity to receive religious education but also opened up the possibility that the very best female students would grow up to become teachers of the next generation of Hebrew Sunday School students.[6]

Nevertheless, when these shifts in Jewish women's religious status are pitted against the other ritual and liturgical reforms associated with 19th-century American synagogues, they suggest relatively modest change in women's status within the synagogue. As Karla Goldman has observed, women appeared to gain a measure of equality within the synagogue, but what they had really gained was the opportunity for equality as spectators of the synagogue service. Moreover, one result of "bringing women down from the balcony was to undermine the identity of women as a distinct group within the congregation."[7]

Toward the end of the century, another new forum for women's Jewish commitments appeared as an array of national Jewish women's organizations were founded. In 1893, the National Council of Jewish Women (NCJW) became the first nationwide American Jewish women's club.[8] In the decades that followed, other new organizations launched armies of Jewish women massed to support their synagogues through sisterhood, to promote Zionism through Hadassah, and to protect immigrant girls from the perils of "white slavery" through the NCJW.[9]

These organizations gave women public venues for their Jewish activism and commitments. They invested great resources in educating their members, aiming to give their women the tools essential not only to making the *Jewish Home Beautiful* but also to raising up the next generation of deeply committed American Jews. The *Jewish Home Beautiful*, published by the National Women's League, the union of sisterhoods committed to the Conservative synagogue,[10] and similar works emphasized the home as woman's domain, the central sphere of her Jewish activity for her husband and family, and urged her to make of this, "the grandest of all institutions," "a miniature Temple."[11]

Nevertheless, these organizations also provided women with important new venues for social activism and public activity. Through Hadassah, the Women's Zionist Organization of America, women worked to build the infrastructure of the Yishuv, the Jewish community in British-controlled Palestine, raising money for the American Zionist Medical Unit and rescuing children imperiled by the rise of Nazism.[12] In the 1930s, members of the Women's Division of the American Jewish Congress provided temporary homes for refugees of Nazism and stood outside Catholic churches on Sunday mornings handing out leaflets exposing the anti-Semitism of the popular radio preacher Father Charles Coughlin.[13] In cities and towns, large and small, synagogue sisterhoods of every denomination took responsibility for much of the cultural and social programming— the mother-daughter luncheons, the teas and pageants, the dances and picnics—that made the American synagogue a social center for American Jewry.[14] Although the scope of this activism and activity extended well beyond that of the female Hebrew benevolent societies and sewing circles of the 19th century, it scarcely impacted women's roles and places within the religious spaces of the synagogue. When on Sabbaths and holidays the ladies of the sisterhood crossed the portal to the sanctuary, their roles there had not changed since they had first acquired their places in the pews next to their husbands.

But a single change prior to the emergence of the second wave of American feminism stands out as an innovation in the ritual life of a Jewish woman—the invention of the bat mitzvah. The story of the first bat mitzvah is well known. On March 18, 1922, Rabbi Mordecai M. Kaplan, a professor at the Jewish Theological Seminary, called his eldest daughter, Judith, then aged twelve and half, to read a portion of the Torah—from a printed book, not from the sacred handwritten scroll—on Sabbath morning. Years later, the musicologist Judith Kaplan Eisenstein recalled the "excitement" and the "disturbance" of that day. She was excited, but her grandmothers were so disturbed that they tried to convince the rabbi not to do this "terrible thing."[15]

In fact, this first bat mitzvah failed to cause "the kind of sensation"[16] that other of Mordecai M. Kaplan's ritual changes evoked. As the founder of Reconstructionist Judaism, he recast Jewish worship to reflect his new theology. In the case of his 1941 Passover Haggadah, that meant eliminating the ten plagues and inserting Moses into a liturgy in which he had never been named.[17] A few years later, Orthodox rabbis outraged by Kaplan's *Sabbath Prayer Book* gathered in New York at the McAlpin Hotel. Declaring that "Dr. Kaplan has published a new monster that was prepared in the name of a prayer book," whose contents gladdened "the eye of every heretic and heresy before the God of Israel," they publicly burned the prayer book and excommunicated Kaplan.[18]

By comparison, the reaction to the first bat mitzvah pales. In the summer of 1922, a Reform rabbi, contemplating the radical question of women's ordination, remarked that "the rabbi of an Orthodox congregation had a bar mitzvah of girls" and that this proved that "the other wing of Judaism is also making progress."[19] Not only did bat mitzvah seem to become routine rather quickly at Kaplan's Society for the Advancement of Judaism,[20] but, in the decades that followed, it won acceptance in the American synagogue. By 1960, almost all Conservative and Reform congregations had introduced bat mitzvah. Rabbis became the staunchest champions, for the ceremony meant that girls spent more time in Hebrew school. The rabbis believed that bat mitzvah could "inspire our girls to a better understanding and a more significant appreciation of Jewish life," preparing them for "their main job—that of maintaining the home so that our youth may grow up with the proper guidance and example!"[21] In the end, it seems that those most upset by the invention of bat mitzvah were Judith Kaplan's grandmothers.

But even if by the middle decades of the 20th century bat mitzvah had won acceptance among American Reform and Conservative Jews, it had scarcely transformed women's roles in the synagogue. Not only did rabbis justify bat mitzvah in traditional gendered terms, but, "for the bat mitzvah girl," bat mitzvah "was literally a once-in-a-lifetime event that signaled the end rather than the beginning of her inclusion in the synagogue service." After their bar mitzvah, boys were welcome to continue to take on important roles in the service. They were again called up to the Torah; even as thirteen-year-olds, they counted toward the quorum of ten required for public prayer; one day, the few so inclined could go on to become rabbis and cantors. But, for girls, bat mitzvah, "a ceremony whose time had come," signaled the first—and the last—time that anyone thought these young women would stand before the congregation. Well into the 1960s, it promised no remarkable shift in women's status in American Judaism.[22]

That held true for another attempt "to equalize the status of women in Jewish law as a true expression of a Torah of justice."[23] Equalization, in 1955, meant, at least for Conservative rabbis, yet another symbolic concession to enlarging women's roles in the sanctuary, the granting to women of the right to be called up to bless the reading of the Torah, to have an *aliyah*.[24] Even then, cogent observers wondered just how much this far-reaching step—after all, in Jewish tradition women never had *aliyot*—would achieve. No women clamored for this privilege, according to Rabbi Gershon Winer.[25] As the eminent sociologist Marshall Sklare concluded, "Conservative women have generally been satisfied with their limited status—a great advance over the age-old segregation."[26] As late as 1972, only 7 percent of 142 rabbis regularly gave women *aliyot*; another 17 percent granted them on special occasions.[27] Together, the symbolic concessions of bat mitzvah and women's *aliyot* uphold the argument for the slow pace of incremental change in Jewish women's religious roles through the 1960s.

But the social movements that erupted during these years of great turmoil ushered in massive societal changes, and, in time, one of them, the second wave of American feminism, crashed right up against American Judaism. A second wave of American feminism implies the existence of a first. That first wave succeeded the 19th-century woman's rights movement, which had largely focused on the single issue of woman suffrage. As that movement culminated in 1920 in the ratification of the Nineteenth Amendment, which granted women the right to vote, a "new language of Feminism" had already come into view, one that proposed revolutionizing "all the relations of the sexes."[28] Ultimately, those who aimed at that far broader societal transformation failed to effect the revolution in women's roles that they sought. That the Nineteenth Amendment, in fact, did so little to affect women's lives reveals, as the historian William Chafe has observed, that "discrimination against women remained deeply rooted in the structure of society—in the roles women and men played and how those roles were valued."[29] Writing about the threads of feminist activism that persisted even after the first wave foundered, the scholars Leila Rupp and Verta Taylor observed that they survived in the doldrums.[30]

But feminism re-emerged with the dawning of the 1960s.[31] The establishment, in 1961, of President John F. Kennedy's Commission on the Status of Women "implicitly recognized the existence of gender-based discrimination in American society."[32] In the Kennedy years, "people began to question all the previously held assumptions about what women had been," and women began to sense that "they could be more than anybody thought they could be."[33]

In 1963, the Jewish housewife and journalist Betty Friedan published *The Feminine Mystique*. There, writing about "the problem that has no name,"[34] she chronicled the discontent of her generation of female college graduates confined to suburban homes, which she likened to "comfortable concentration camps."[35] Half a year later, some of those college graduates joined the one thousand women assembled for the biennial meeting of Reform Judaism's National Federation of Temple Sisterhoods and called for women to become rabbis.[36] As they did, they mirrored the reality that "the times they are a-changin'."[37]

Meanwhile, Congress paved the way for those "changin'" times to deal with women's discontent via the Equal Pay Act of 1963. Then, in 1964, the Civil Rights Act passed. To the surprise of many, including perhaps even the congressman who introduced the three-letter word, Title VII banned discrimination in employment on the basis of race—and sex. After the Equal Employment Opportunity Commission showed little interest in enforcing the antidiscrimination sections of Title VII when it came to female complaints, Friedan and others founded the National Organization for Women to pressure the government to secure equal rights for all. Its birth, in 1966, heralded the arrival of the second wave of American feminism. With the founding of this first feminist civil rights organization, the "world split open."[38]

By the late 1960s the women's movement was spinning off in a dizzying array of new directions. Feminists turned their attention to a host of legal, political, and social inequities. They demanded an end to job ads labeled "Help Wanted—Male." They marched to legalize abortion. They coined the slogan "Sisterhood Is Powerful," and they meant it. Women's Liberation, which celebrated female difference, burst forth, and with it came the first consciousness-raising groups: small, intimate circles of female friends decrying sexism sprang up on college campuses, in suburban backyards, and in middle-class urban apartments.[39] The gains of the second wave of feminism—the opening of elite colleges and universities to women,[40] the infusion of funding into girls' sports,[41] and the insistence that affirmative action programs include women—thrust women into the center in American life and made headlines.

A "great media blitz," well under way by 1970, broadcast news of the surging tide of feminism.[42] Some reports revealed how American religion was wrestling with the feminist critique. Headlines blazoned "Women's 'Lib' on the March in the Churches," as the National Organization for Women created an ecumenical task force on women and religion and churches, including the United Methodist and United Presbyterian, established their own task forces. Protestant denominations, which had never had women ministers, now began to do so. Moreover, the pace of change on this single issue was startling. In the century since 1853, when the Congregationalists first began ordaining women, little more than two dozen Protestant denominations had followed their lead. But, in the 1960s and 1970s, more than a dozen joined them, and they included major mainline denominations, such as the Episcopal Church and the 26 million men and women of the American Lutheran Church.[43] Collectively, these changes presented a picture of feminism storming the bastion of American religion.[44] Not surprisingly, that storm also engulfed American Judaism.

The encounter between second-wave feminism and American Judaism began with "a series of isolated questionings" raised by feminist Jewish undergraduate and graduate students who found themselves "torn in two."[45] Their feminist involvements on their campuses promised them intellectual and social equality with their male peers. But, when, on Shabbat, they turned to the synagogue, Judaism relegated them to second-class status.[46] They were joined by women who sprang up from among the ranks of Jewish communal leaders, who, deeply influenced by the "remarkable re-burgeoning of the Women's Movement," wanted to bring its message to bear upon American Jewish life.[47]

Signs of second-wave feminism's inroads into American Judaism were apparent by the early 1970s. Already the press was reporting that the first women were studying to become rabbis and cantors.[48] In November 1971, as the women of Reform Judaism gathered for their biennial convention, they demanded equal partnership in decision making with the leaders of the Reform movement, announcing: "We refuse to be restricted to serving tea and cookies."[49] Half a year later, after ten religious feminists, under the banner of Ezrat Nashim, failed to gain a place on the program of the Conservative rabbis' annual convention, they told the *New York Post*: "We're directing our demands at the Conservative movement . . . but ultimately all of Judaism will have to come around."[50] Two months later, Sandy Eisenberg Sasso, then a third-year student at the Reconstructionist Rabbinical College, called for ritual changes to the traditional wedding ceremony, demanding "a mutuality of obligation, rather than the one-sided sense of man's ownership of women and the double standard that it implies."[51] A month later, on June 3, 1972, a young woman who, only a decade before, had written, "Although I am a girl, I would like very much to study for a rabbinical degree," was ordained rabbi, teacher, and preacher in American Judaism. Her name was Sally Priesand.[52] Collectively, these events delivered a message to American Jewry: "Women are stating, in clear and resounding cadences, that they will no longer be second-class citizens."[53]

These examples, covering less than two years—and many, many others could have been included—say much about Judaism's encounter with second-wave feminism and suggest the breadth of what would evolve, over time, into Jewish feminism. When comparing the changes of the 1970s with the earlier shifts in women's status in Judaism—coming down from the balcony, bat mitzvah, and the very occasional *aliyah*—what first stands out is the gender of the actors. The earlier shifts in women's status were largely conceived and implemented by men, especially by rabbis. In 1851, Reform rabbi Isaac Mayer Wise introduced mixed seating in Albany, New York, after his new congregation purchased an old church for its first synagogue and decided, perhaps for economic reasons, to use its pews for worship rather than add the balcony required to separate the sexes as expected by Jewish tradition.[54] Bat mitzvah, of course, was initiated by Rabbi Mordecai M. Kaplan; not surprisingly, it was also rabbis who decided that women could have *aliyot*.

But now the actors in the debate over Jewish women's religious roles were vociferous women. They included several distinct groups of players determined to bring the messages of feminism home to Judaism. In the first group was the handful of women already studying in the rabbinical and cantorial schools, including Sally Priesand and Sandy Eisenberg Sasso. Even before they were ordained, they presented the possibility that, through them, feminism would cross over to American Judaism.[55] As Rabbi Priesand wrote, "My appearance in a forum series becomes a lesson in consciousness-raising and gives women the courage they need to demand complete and full participation in synagogue life." Only two years after her ordination, she could see the transformations under way: already ten women had followed her path to rabbinical school; Jewish organizations, including her own Central Conference of American Rabbis, had established task forces on women; more women were moving into positions on Jewish communal and synagogue boards; even liturgy committees had begun the process of grappling with the androcentric language of prayer.[56]

Another group included other young women deeply committed to Judaism, like the members of Ezrat Nashim—among them two graduate students, Martha Ackelsberg and Paula Hyman—who, in January 1972, prepared a position paper titled "Jewish Women Call for Change." It demanded that women become full members of their synagogues; that they count in the prayer quorum (*minyan*) of ten, traditionally ten men, needed for worship; that they become synagogue and Jewish communal leaders; that women have the right to serve as witnesses and to initiate divorce, roles forbidden to them by Jewish law; and that women be allowed to attend rabbinical and cantorial schools.[57]

Ezrat Nashim's first target, to present its demands at the annual meeting of Conservative Judaism's rabbis in March 1972, was directed at the Conservative movement. Nevertheless, its "Call for Change" and the accompanying publicity brought Jewish feminism out into the open, where it resonated deeply among American Jewish women and men whose consciousnesses had already been raised by second-wave feminism. Ezrat Nashim's members were deluged with requests to share their message widely. They spoke to synagogues, Jewish communal organizations, student groups, and the national and Jewish presses. They also helped plan the first National Jewish Women's Conference, held in New York City in February 1973.[58]

Simultaneously, a third group sympathetic to second-wave feminism that also wanted to bring its message home to American Jewish life sprang from female Jewish communal activists. Their ranks included longtime professional Jewish communal leaders, such as Jane Evans, executive director of the Reform movement's National Federation of Temple

Sisterhoods, who claimed to have been raising the issue of women's ordination for decades and who, at last, propelled the women of Reform Judaism to join her on this issue in 1963.[59]

This segment of Jewish feminists also included outstanding volunteer leaders, such as Jacqueline Levine. By the time Jacqueline Levine raised a clarion call for female leadership in the Jewish community, she had chalked up more than a quarter-century of deeply committed liberal social activism. She had marched from Selma to Montgomery for civil rights and would later get arrested outside the Soviet embassy in Washington, D.C., protesting, "Let my people go." Embracing second-wave feminism, with its call for justice for all, came naturally to this liberal activist who believed that the Jewish community rightfully stood "in the vanguard of social change." In 1972, when she was both national president of the American Jewish Congress Women's Division and a vice president of the Council of Jewish Federations and Welfare Funds, she brought home its message to her preponderantly male colleagues. In her best-known speech, "The Changing Role of Women in the Jewish Community," she called for a program of affirmative action to open Jewish communal leadership to women, whose hundreds of thousands of hours of voluntarism had earned them the right both to be called "volunteer professionals," rather than "professional volunteers," and to hold seats on decision-making boards.[60]

Collectively, these women raised a formidable challenge, one that revealed their power to transform Judaism. The issues that would come to define the feminist critique of Judaism were evident from the very first events of the early 1970s. First and foremost, as the women of Ezrat Nashim told the press, "ultimately all of Judaism will have to come around." No longer would American Jewish women be satisfied with symbolic concessions that, in fact, underscored the inequity between men and women. These activists—female rabbis, young women across the denominational spectrum deeply committed to Judaism, and female Jewish communal leaders—demanded a broad transformation of Jewish religious and communal life to make women, at last, equal.

Moreover, they had learned from the women's movement just how to effect that change. They started out by deepening their knowledge of women in Jewish history and law. The women of Ezrat Nashim had begun meeting as a small "fellowship" group "determined to subject the Jewish tradition to serious scrutiny . . . reacting to God-concepts, liturgy and sex roles."[61] As Sally Priesand headed into her final year of rabbinical school, she faced the hurdle of the required rabbinical thesis. She thought she would write about the Yom Kippur liturgy; she ended up writing a thesis titled "Historic and Changing Role of the Jewish Woman."[62]

Then these activists shared what they had learned with as many audiences as they could reach. Even as a rabbinical student, Priesand gave numerous public lectures, talks that she deemed lessons in "consciousness-raising."[63] Although denied a spot on the official program of the Conservative rabbis' meeting, the women of Ezrat Nashim found a room at the conference hotel and invited "All Women" to their open forum; 130 people turned up.[64]

To reach those whom they could not meet in person, they turned to print. Rabbi Preisand's rabbinic thesis became the book *Judaism and the New Woman.*[65] In 1973, the journal *Response: A Contemporary Jewish Review* published a special issue called "The Jewish Woman." Many of its contributors—the historian Paula E. Hyman, the theologians Rachel Adler and Judith Plaskow, the activist Jacqueline Levine, the poet Marcia Falk, and Rabbi Sandy Eisenberg Sasso—would use their particular areas of expertise to propel the Jewish community to reckon with the feminist *cri de coeur.*[66] Moreover, they did not always have to write for publication, for, no matter what they learned, what they said, or where they wrote, the media followed the Jewish feminists, bringing their messages to ever larger circles of American Jews.[67]

These feminists were determined to transform all of Jewish life. Educating themselves and others were the tools; what were the objectives?

As the press had reported, in the early 1970s, women bent on becoming rabbis were on their way to ordination. Although these contenders scarcely knew this then, they followed in the footsteps of a handful of challengers who, over the course of the preceding century, had tried and failed to become the first woman rabbi.[68] In the following decades, as some sectors of American Judaism continued to grapple with the question of admitting women to the rabbinate, those who had opened their gates discovered the unanticipated consequences of having women religious and spiritual leaders in American Jewish life.

Those consequences concerned workaday issues: Must congregations interview female rabbis? What would they do about maternity leave? What does one call the husband of the rabbi? "Lucky," so said some, but others understood that these men would not play roles analogous to that of the *rebbetzin*, the rabbi's wife, whose open houses, baked goods, and keen ear had long been a crucial element of her husband's congregational success.[69] That meant that the dynamics of rabbi-congregational life would no longer be the same.

But the implications of women's entrance into the rabbinate extended far more deeply into the fabric of American Jewish life than anyone could possibly have envisioned when Sally Priesand's classmates spontaneously rose to honor her on ordination day. The early pioneers of Jewish feminism had to learn on their own what they needed to know. Those who followed them came to expect that their seminaries would teach them what they needed to know by incorporating Jewish women's studies into the curriculum.[70] Moreover, the women who became rabbis would compel their congregations to embrace religious and spiritual innovations designed to make Judaism fully accepting of women and the female experience. In the end, the female rabbis—and, by 2006, there were 829 of them in the Reform (the first woman was ordained in 1972), Reconstructionist (1974), and Conservative (1985) movements[71]—became bridges to a Judaism re-imagined and re-visioned by women's wisdom.[72]

This re-visioning of Judaism began with the transformation of women's roles within the synagogue. For those affiliated with the liberal denominations of American Judaism, this meant reconfiguring the synagogue as an egalitarian institution. In time, this came to mean, for some, that women could wear the prayer shawls and head coverings traditionally worn only by men; that women could count toward the quorum of ten necessary for a complete prayer service;[73] that women could learn Hebrew and the liturgical skills they had never acquired as girls and could celebrate, as adults, a bat mitzvah; that women could take on new roles in their synagogues, like reading regularly from the Torah; and that women could be elected president of their synagogue.[74]

Moreover, such re-visioning of Jewish women's religious roles also impacted Orthodoxy, where the charge on the feminist challenge was led by Blu Greenberg, author of *On Women and Judaism: A View From Tradition* and the founder of the Jewish Orthodox Feminist Alliance.[75] Signs of feminism's redefining women's roles in the Orthodox world proliferate. Orthodox parents celebrate a daughter's bat mitzvah, although the Orthodox bat mitzvah service is not identical with that of the bar mitzvah.[76] A "learning revolution" has transformed what Jewish girls learn in Orthodox educational settings and has come to include for many a year of post-high school study of religious texts in women's educational settings in Israel.[77] Orthodox women gather in women's prayer groups where they take on ritual roles not open to them when men are present. In New York, a few Orthodox synagogues pioneered a new position of congregational intern to permit learned women to teach and to counsel, roles customarily counted among the rabbis' duties. Not surprisingly, a handful of Orthodox women have even studied for rabbinical ordination, and a few claim to have achieved it.[78] Thus, all the movements of American Judaism have been swept up by the feminist challenge.

The desire to equalize women's role in Jewish religious life also led, as Sandy Eisenberg Sasso portended back in 1972, to tampering with its rituals and ceremonies. Then she had critiqued the gender inequities in the Jewish wedding ceremony, where traditionally the woman remained silent. Not surprisingly, then, some of the very first feminist ceremonial innovations focused on Judaism's traditional rites and rituals, and, not surprisingly, they began at the beginning, with the newborn. For millennia, Jews have joyously welcomed a baby boy into the community with the commanding ceremony of circumcision. Taking note of a baby girl— traditionally by announcing her name in the synagogue during the regular Sabbath service following her birth—at the same time proclaimed her gendered inequality. Hence, early feminist ritual creativity brought forward new ceremonies that would give, as Sandy Eisenberg Sasso wrote, "as much ceremonial importance to a girl's birth as to a boy's."[79]

But Jewish feminist ritual experimentation had only begun. Not only had Judaism always treated boys and girls differently, but the tradition had also shockingly failed to affirm the great moments in women's lives. If full equality was the goal for transforming ceremonies that already existed, what could be done about inventing rituals that did not exist but whose lack clearly asserted an imbalance in the tradition when it came to Jewish women? An astonishing array of prayers, readings, and ceremonies emerged for women's "invisible life passages." [80] They include prayers for going to the *mikveh* (the ritual bath), "to be said on the evening the couple wishes to conceive,"[81] for the first months of pregnancy and for entering the ninth month, for the onset of labor, for a Caesarean birth, and for nursing for the first time. New rituals sustain those grieving infertility, suffering stillbirth, seeking medical intervention, and turning to adoption. Ceremonies mark the onset of menses and the completion of menopause, offer solace after rape, affirm remaining single, and acknowledge marital separation.[82] In the end, feminist ritual invention sought to unite Judaism to the occasions, great and small, that rest at the core of women's lives and that are so often intimately linked to the feminine, to the female body.

From sanctification of the private, feminists turned their attention to public rituals and celebrations, seeking new venues for communal feminist spirituality. They reclaimed Rosh Chodesh, Judaism's marking of each new month in its lunar calendar, as the women's holiday, inventing "ceremonies which draw upon the similarity between women's cycles and the moon's cycles, the capacity of both women and the moon to physically wax and wane, ebb and flow, give birth, die, and be reborn."[83] They reappropriated *mikveh*, the pool in which observant married women immerse for the ritual purification required before they may resume sexual relations following their proscription during and immediately after menstruation. This reappropriation transforms *mikveh* into a space for women to celebrate Rosh Chodesh, to mark a milestone, or to bring closure to a crisis.[84] Feminists have imagined public ceremonies for "croning," honoring women who have reached the age of sixty, the age of wisdom. Some have formed feminist spirituality groups. Their retreats and gatherings over the years have offered spaces for ritual invention and liturgical creativity.[85]

Of the public communal feminist spiritual innovations, the one that has reached most widely is the women's seder. The foremother of these seders took place in New York in 1976.[86] By the end of the 20th century, women's seders had sprung up in Jewish communities all across the United States.[87] Asking, "Why is this seder different from all other seders?," the women's seders in synagogues and community centers from New York to Los Angeles, from Miami to Seattle, bring "women of all ages and from every corner of the Jewish community together to celebrate the Exodus in story, song, and symbolism from a woman's perspective."[88] Using an array of women's *haggadot*, usually compiled, edited, and written by local seder organizers, the women's seders re-vision the traditional ritual. They ask those gathered to "think of Miriam / The woman who began / Our journey to the promised land."[89] Whereas the sages taught that the traditional four cups of wine represent God's promises of redemption, at the women's seder each cup symbolizes the redemption out of the shadows of the Jewish past of women of "wisdom, courage, and inspiration."[90] Moreover, elements of the women's seder have spilled over to traditional seders where its symbols, including an orange on the seder plate and a cup of water for Miriam alongside Elijah's cup of wine, now appear.[91]

Undergirding women's new visibility within the synagogue and their enhanced ritual choices are explorations in Jewish feminist theology. Even as feminist theologians critique Judaism's androcentricity, its obliteration of the voices and perspectives of women, they work from within the body

of Jewish tradition, seeking avenues to the theological, legal, and liturgical transformations essential to redress the wrongs of women's exclusion.
They have articulated the questions that must be addressed and begun to
construct answers. Judith Plaskow, author of the very influential *Standing Again at Sinai: Judaism From a Feminist Perspective*, queried "whether
egalitarianism is enough?" As barriers against Jewish women's full participation in the tradition fell, they "pointed to the need for changes far
deeper and more frightening than the process of simply making available
to women what all in the community acknowledge to be of value. . . . Beyond egalitarianism, the way is uncharted," but she knows that it leads
to a transformation of Judaism "so that it is truly the Judaism of women
and men." Moreover, it requires "creating the structures that allow women
to speak." Feminist theologians, who also include Rachel Adler, author of
Engendering Judaism, and feminist liturgists, such as Marcia Falk, are trying to figure out just how to do that.[92]

The feminist theologians' critique forms part of the growing canon of
Jewish women's and gender studies. That canon began to emerge with the
publication, in 1976, of *The Jewish Woman in America*, by Charlotte Baum,
Paula Hyman, and Sonya Michel.[93] In the United States, women's studies,
especially the writing of women's history, burgeoned dramatically in the
1970s. Believing that understanding women's place in the past could advance women's place in the present, historians raised a host of questions
as they began their search for "a usable past."[94] As this new scholarship
was emerging, the first attempt to synthesize the existing body of knowledge in American Jewish women's history using new-found feminist sensibilities appeared.[95] It presented models of Jewish women's activism in
the past to a nascent generation of Jewish feminists.[96]

Since then, as women's and gender studies have found a home in the
academy, a generation of feminist Judaic Studies scholars have become the
first women in Jewish history to have acquired "the basic technical skills"
needed to explore Jewish civilization from a feminist perspective. Some
fields within Judaic studies, notably modern Jewish history, Jewish literatures, and the social sciences, have been more amenable than others to the
integration of this new feminist scholarship.[97] Nevertheless, today no sub-
field of Jewish Studies—Bible, rabbinics, history, sociology, anthropology,
literature—remains untouched by this work.[98] Jewish feminists have embraced this scholarship, and its scholars, following in the footsteps of the
women of Ezrat Nashim, lecture widely throughout the American Jewish
community, sharing their insights with America's Jewish women and men.

Scholars are not the only writers energized by Jewish feminism. It has sparked an explosion of feminist literary discovery and creativity. Earlier works of American Jewish literature, like Anzia Yezierska's 1925 novel *The Bread Givers*, about a young woman's rebellion against her father's tyrannical old world patriarchy, were rediscovered by a new generation seeking sympathetic voices from the past.[99] Three-quarters of a century later, through *The Women's Torah Commentary*, female rabbis from across the denominations interject women into almost every one of the fifty-four weekly Torah portions.[100] This creativity includes midrashim, imaginative re-creations of the biblical text, like Anita Diamant's wildly successful *The Red Tent*.[101] Feminist writers of serious fiction also riff upon Jewish tradition, as Cynthia Ozick does in *The Puttermesser Papers*, where her protagonist, Ruth Puttermesser, creates a female golem (a character out of Jewish folklore, a human figure made of clay), who gets her elected mayor of New York.[102]

Yet another area of Jewish life affected by feminism has been marriage and the Jewish family. By the beginning of the 21st century, American Jewish families had achieved diversity unimaginable before the revolutions of second-wave feminism and postindustrial America. A quarter of all Jewish adults surveyed in 2000–2001 were single and had never married. Twenty-six percent of Jewish women ages 40–44 were childless.[103] These statistics point to the wide diversity of contemporary Jewish family configurations, including Jewish lesbians.

In *Nice Jewish Girls: A Lesbian Anthology*, Evelyn Torten Beck exposed the painful dichotomy of lesbian Jewish identity: that these women feel marginalized as lesbians in the Jewish world and as Jews in their lesbian communities.[104] Other important works deepening this theme followed, showing the breadth of its challenge.[105] Even the Orthodox have had to respond: The 2001 film *Trembling Before G-d* depicted the despair felt by lesbians and gays when they are rejected by their Orthodox communities.[106] Asserting their right to remain fully within Jewish tradition, Jewish lesbians proudly display in their homes a modern *ketubah* (Jewish wedding contract), whose text has been amended "specifically for gay [or] lesbian couples."[107]

But Jewish feminism has impacted not only the synagogue and religion, scholars and writers, and the Jewish family; it was meant to affect all of American Jewish life, and that includes the network of agencies, welfare funds, advocacy groups, and community centers that sustain American Jewry, the so-called secular Jewish world. That was the world that

Jacqueline Levine had addressed back in 1972, when she told the General Assembly of the Council of Jewish Federations and Welfare Funds that "Women are stating, in clear and resounding cadences, that they will no longer be second-class citizens." Pointing to the gross gender imbalance in Jewish communal leadership, she challenged her peers to restructure Jewish communal life to include women as leaders.[108] The question is how successful that transformation was.

A 2005 study found some, but insufficient, change.[109] In the intervening years, some Jewish communal organizations, such as the American Jewish Congress, which had long maintained separate women's divisions, disbanded them in favor of integrating the sexes. Yet others, like B'nai B'rith, saw its women's division secede rather than face integration.[110] At the turn of the 21st century, the Jewish women's associations founded more than a century ago, including synagogue sisterhoods and Hadassah, continued to offer women rich and varied opportunities for voluntarism and professional work, but their agendas—training women to lead religious services,[111] opening a Washington Action Office that lobbies to end violence against women—show how much they have been affected by Jewish feminism.

Yet, beyond the women's organizations, women's progress in advancing as volunteer and professional Jewish leaders is checkered. The 2005 study by Ma'yan: The Jewish Women's Project concluded: "Jewish organizations continue to limit women's access to power in all areas of Jewish communal life."[112] It observed that, despite incremental change, women seeking to advance in Jewish life hit a glass ceiling that covers all Jewish institutions—synagogues, communal agencies, and schools.[113]

Perhaps the good news is that, thanks to Jewish feminism, in the 21st century, when the secular Jewish community slights Jewish women, it makes headlines. In June 2006, when a prestigious Israeli think tank convened a "high-powered parley" to chart "the future of the Jewish people," it managed to find only two women to invite. Once upon a time in Jewish life and in American life, that would never have caused comment. This time, the leaders of the Jewish People Policy Planning Institute were deluged with criticism, and the national Jewish press reported it on the front page. Accusing the institute of "being mired in the 1950s," Deborah Lipstadt, a professor of history at Emory University and a long-time Jewish feminist activist, bluntly asked: "How can you do policy planning for the Jewish community when half the community is excluded?"[114] Meanwhile, even as the institute's director, Avinoam Bar-Yosef, defended the invite list, he betrayed, perhaps because he is Israeli, how little he understood of the Jewish feminist critique. Responding to Lipstadt, he wrote: "The epic and incredible survival of Jewish civilization throughout history owes a great deal to the legendary Jewish mother."[115] That Bar-Yosef was put on the defensive and that even some of the male invitees, like David Ellenson, president of Hebrew Union College-Jewish Institute of Religion, called the "omission of women . . . a glaring gap"[116] reveal just how deeply feminism, after only a few decades, has penetrated the sensibilities of the American Jewish community.

In the nearly four decades since it emerged, Jewish feminism has deeply affected American Jewish life. In fact, it is difficult to imagine American Jewish life stripped of feminist influence. Wherever one looks in the Jewish community, the consequences of a social revolution that resulted in empowering women to transform Judaism are evident. They can be seen on the pulpit where female rabbis preach, in classrooms where girls learn Talmud, and at homes as couples gather family and friends to bring their infant daughters into the covenant of the Jewish people. Feminism resonates in Jewish communal boardrooms each time leaders deliberately seek out women for inclusion—or fail to do so; in college classrooms where Jewish feminist scholars teach; in Jewish community centers' day care programs; and in synagogue sanctuaries when Jews pray that God blessed Abraham, Isaac, and Jacob — and Sarah, Rebekah, Rachel, and Leah.

Before the emergence of second-wave feminism, women's roles within American Jewish life had changed slowly and incrementally over time. Yet, once second-wave feminism burst forth and stormed American Judaism, change cascaded over the American Jewish landscape. Second-wave feminists sought to give power to one-half of the people. In so doing, they gave American Jewish women the power to transform all of American Judaism.

NOTES

1. This is fully discussed in Pamela S. Nadell, *Women Who Would Be Rabbis: A History of Women's Ordination, 1889–1985* (Boston: Beacon Press, 1998). See also the introduction to Pamela S. Nadell and Jonathan D. Sarna, *Women and American Judaism: Historical Perspectives* (Hanover, NH: Brandeis University Press, 2001).

2. On feminism and American religion broadly, see Ann Braude, *Transforming the Faiths of Our Fathers: Women Who Changed American Religion* (New York: Palgrave Macmillan, 2004).

3. Leon A. Jick, *The Americanization of the Synagogue, 1820–1870* (1976; reprint, Hanover, NH: Brandeis University Press/University Press of New England, 1992), pp. 152–53, 64.

4. L. Jick, *Americanization of the Synagogue*, pp. 174–85, quotation 74. For an evaluation of this book, see the essays in the special issue of *American Jewish History*, including Pamela S. Nadell, "The Americanization of the Synagogue, 1820–1870: An Historical Appreciation," *American Jewish History* 90 (2002), pp. 51–62.

5. On these transformations, see Karla Goldman, *Beyond the Synagogue Gallery: Finding a Place for Women in American Judaism* (Cambridge, MA: Harvard University Press, 2000); Jonathan D. Sarna, "The Debate Over Mixed Seating in the American Synagogue," in *The American Synagogue: A Sanctuary Transformed*, ed. Jack Wertheimer (Cambridge: Cambridge University Press, 1987), pp. 363–94.

6. Dianne Ashton, *Rebecca Gratz: Women and Judaism in Antebellum America* (Detroit: Wayne State University Press, 1997).

7. K. Goldman, *Beyond the Synagogue Gallery*, pp. 133–34.

8. Faith Rogow, *Gone to Another Meeting: The National Council of Jewish Women, 1893–1993* (Tuscaloosa: University of Alabama Press, 1993).

9. On women's organizations in these years, see Anne Firor Scott, *Natural Allies: Women's Associations in American History* (Urbana: University of Illinois Press, 1991). On the national denominational sisterhood bodies, see Pamela S. Nadell and Rita J. Simon, "Ladies of the Sisterhood: Women in the American Reform Synagogue, 1900–1930," in *Active Voices: Women in Jewish Culture*, ed. Maurie Sacks (Urbana: University of Illinois Press, 1995), pp. 63–75; Jenna Weissman Joselit, "The Jewish Priestess and Ritual: The Sacred Life of American Orthodox Women," in *American Jewish Women's History: A Reader*, ed. Pamela S. Nadell (New York: New York University Press, 2003), pp. 153–74. On Hadassah, see Joyce Antler, "Zion in Our Hearts: Henrietta Szold and the American Jewish Women's Movement," in *American Jewish Women's History: A Reader*, ed. Pamela S. Nadell (New York: New York University Press, 2003), pp. 129–49.

10. Betty D. Greenberg and Althea O. Silverman, *Jewish Home Beautiful* (New York: Women's League of the United Synagogue of America, 1941).

11. Cited in Jenna Weissman Joselit, *New York's Jewish Jews: The Orthodox Community in the Interwar Years* (Bloomington: Indiana University Press, 1990), p. 97.

12. Mary McCune, *"The Whole Wide World, Without Limits": International Relief, Gender Politics, and American Jewish Women, 1893–1930* (Detroit: Wayne State University Press, 2005).

13. Rona Sheramy, "'There Are Times When Silence Is a Sin': The Women's Division of the American Jewish Congress and the Anti-Nazi Boycott Movement," *American Jewish History* 89:1 (2001): 105–21.

14. P. Nadell and R. Simon, "Ladies of the Sisterhood."

15. Ellen Dickstein (Kominers) interview with Judith Kaplan Eisenstein, November 1, 1974; copy of tape in my possession. On the bat mitzvah, see Mel Scult, *Judaism Faces the Twentieth Century: A Biography of Mordecai M. Kaplan* (Detroit: Wayne State University, 1993), pp. 301–2.

16. Ellen Dickstein (Kominers) interview with Judith Kaplan Eisenstein, November 1, 1974.

17. Pamela S. Nadell, *Conservative Judaism in America: A Biographical Dictionary and Sourcebook* (New York: Greenwood Press, 1988), pp. 149–50.

18. Zachary Silver, "A Look Back at a Different Book Burning," *Forward*, June 3, 2005, http://www.forward.com/articles/3251.

19. *Central Conference of American Rabbis Yearbook* 1922, p. 171, quoting Rabbi Stern.

20. Felicia Lamport, *Mink on Weekdays* (Boston: Houghton Mifflin, 1950), pp. 125–29. Lamport shared her bat mitzvah date with Selma Kaplan.

21. Quotations appear in Regina Stein, "The Road to Bat Mitzvah in America," in *Women and American Judaism: Historical Perspectives*, ed. Pamela S. Nadell and Jonathan D. Sarna (Hanover, NH: Brandeis University Press, 2001), pp. 223–34.

22. Ibid., pp. 226 and 232.

23. "Equalization of Status of Women," *Proceedings of the Rabbinical Assembly* (1954), p. 143.

24. Sanders Tofield, "Woman's Place in the Rites of the Synagogue With Special Reference to Aliyah," *Proceedings of the Rabbinical Assembly* (1955): 182–90; Aaron H. Blumenthal, "An Aliyah for Women," 1955, reprinted in *And Bring Them Closer to Torah: The Life and Work of Rabbi Aaron H. Blumenthal*, ed. David R. Blumenthal (Hoboken, NJ: Ktav, 1986).

25.Gershon Winer, "Discussion," *Proceedings of the Rabbinical Assembly* (1955): 34–35.

26. Marshall Sklare, *Conservative Judaism: An American Religious Movement*, 1972 rev. ed. (1955; reprint, Lanham, MD: University Press of America, 1985), pp. 86–90.

27. Daniel J. Elazar and Rela Geffen Monson, "Women in the Synagogue Today," *Midstream* 27:4 (1981): 25–26.

28. Nancy F. Cott, *The Grounding of Modern Feminism* (New Haven: Yale University Press, 1987), pp. 3–10.

29. William H. Chafe, *The Paradox of Change: American Women in the 20th Century* (New York: Oxford University Press, 1991), p. 44.

30. Leila J. Rupp and Verta Taylor, *Survival in the Doldrums: The American Women's Rights Movement, 1945 to the 1960s* (New York: Oxford University Press, 1987).

31. For harbingers of the second wave, see Susan M. Hartmann, *The Other Feminists: Activists in the Liberal Establishment* (New Haven: Yale University Press, 1998).

32. L. Rupp and V. Taylor, *Survival in the Doldrums*, p. 166.

33. Pamela Nadell interview with Ann Blitzstein Folb (November 21, 1989).

34. Betty Friedan, *The Feminine Mystique* (New York: Norton, 1963).

35. Kirsten Lise Fermaglich, "'The Comfortable Concentration Camp': The Significance of Nazi Imagery in Betty Friedan's *The Feminine Mystique* (1963)," *American Jewish History* 91:2 (2003): 205–32.

36. P. Nadell, *Women Who Would Be Rabbis*, p. 147.

37. Bob Dylan's song *The Times They Are A-Changin'* was written in 1963; http://www.bobdylan.com/songs/times.html

38. Many have discussed the emergence of the second wave of American feminism; see, among others, W. Chafe, *The Paradox of Change*; Ruth Rosen, *The World Split Open: How the Modern Women's Movement Changed America* (New York: Viking, 2000).

39. For a chronology of these developments, see R. Rosen, *The World Split Open*.

40. On this, see Jerome Karabel, *The Chosen: The Hidden History of Admission and Exclusion at Harvard, Yale, and Princeton* (Boston: Houghton Mifflin, 2005).

41. That transformation was the result of Title IX of the Education Amendments of 1972 to the Civil Rights Act of 1964. It reads: "No person in the United States shall, on the basis of sex, be excluded from participation in, or denied the benefits of, or be subjected to discrimination under any educational program or activity receiving federal assistance."; "What Is Title IX?," http://www.american.edu/sadker/titleix.htm, accessed March 7, 2006.

42. R. Rosen, *The World Split Open*, quotation, p. xxi.

43. This is based on Mark Chaves, *Ordaining Women: Culture and Conflict in Religious Organizations* (Cambridge, MA: Harvard University Press, 1997), table 2.1. See also George Dugan, "Lutherans Vote to Ordain Women," *New York Times*, October 25, 1970, p. 36.

44. P. Nadell, *Women Who Would Be Rabbis*, pp. 152 and 161–62.

45. Anne Lapidus Lerner, "'Who Hast Not Made Me a Man': The Movement for Equal Rights for Women in American Jewry," *American Jewish Year Book* 77 (1976): 3–38.

46. For other accounts of Jewish feminism's emergence, see Reena Sigman Friedman, "The Jewish Feminist Movement," in *Jewish American Voluntary Organizations*, ed. Michael N. Dobkowski (New York: Greenwood Press, 1986), pp. 574–601; Sylvia Barack Fishman, *A Breath of Life: Feminism in the American Jewish Community* (New York: Free Press, 1993), pp. 1–15. Note that these narratives fail to consider that an old guard, like the National Federation of Temple Sisterhoods' executive director, Jane Evans, and the journalist Trude Weiss-Rosmarin had been raising feminist issues for decades before the late 1960s. On both Evans's and Weiss-Rosmarin's feminism, see P. Nadell, *Women Who Would Be Rabbis*, pp. 123, 125, 127–29, and 131–35.

47. Jacqueline Levine, "The Changing Role of Women in the Jewish Community, 1972," in *The American Jewish Woman: A Documentary History*, ed. Jacob Rader Marcus (New York: Ktav, 1981), pp. 902–7.

48. Edward B. Fiske, "Women's 'Lib' on the March in the Churches," *New York Times*, October 25, 1970, IV:15; Joan Cook, "A Female Cantor? Two Women Who Are Bucking the Tradition," *New York Times*, February 22, 1971, p. 20.

49. Irving Spiegel, "Women Demand Equal Voice in Reform Judaism," *New York Times*, November 9, 1971, p. 34.

50. Barbara Trecker, "10 Religious Feminists to Confront the Rabbis," *New York Post*, March 14, 1972, p. 71.

51. George Dugan, "Female Rabbinical Student Asks Increased 'Femininity' in Judaism," *New York Times*, May 7, 1972, p. 37.

52. P. Nadell, *Women Who Would Be Rabbis*, p. 168.

53. J. Levine, "The Changing Role of Women in the Jewish Community, 1972."

54. J. Sarna, "The Debate Over Mixed Seating in the American Synagogue."

55. For a fuller discussion of how female rabbis served as a bridge for feminism, see Pamela S. Nadell, "Bridges to 'a Judaism Transformed by Women's Wisdom,'" in *Women Remaking American Judaism*, ed. Riv-Ellen Prell (Detroit: Wayne State University Press, 2007).

56. Sally J. Priesand, "Not for Men Only: Rabbi Sally Priesand Comments on Her Experience as the First Practicing Woman Rabbi," *National Council of Jewish Women*, February 1974.

57. "Jewish Women Call for Change, 1972," in *The American Jewish Woman: A Documentary History*, ed. Jacob Rader Marcus (New York: Ktav, 1981), pp. 894–96.

58. This is discussed in Pamela S. Nadell, "A Bright New Constellation: Feminism and American Judaism," in *The Columbia History of Jews and Judaism in America*, ed. Marc Lee Raphael (New York: Columbia University Press, 2007).

59. P. Nadell, *Women Who Would Be Rabbis*, pp. 132–35.

60. Julie K. Gordon, "Jacqueline Levine," in *Jewish Women in America: An Historical Encyclopedia*, ed. Paula Hyman and Deborah Dash Moore (New York: Routledge, 1997), 835–36; J. Levine, "The Changing Role of Women in the Jewish Community, 1972."

61. Alan Silverstein, "The Evolution of Ezrat Nashim," *Conservative Judaism* 30 (1975): 41–51.

62. P. Nadell, *Women Who Would Be Rabbis*, p. 166.

63. Ibid., 153–54.

64. A. Silverstein, "The Evolution of Ezrat Nashim," p. 46.

65. Sally Priesand, *Judaism and the New Woman* (New York: Behrman House, 1975).

66. Liz Koltun, *Response: A Contemporary Jewish Review (The Jewish Woman: An Anthology)* 18 (1973). A sample of their subsequent influential works include

Paula Hyman and Deborah Dash Moore, eds., *Jewish Women in America: An Historical Encyclopedia*, 2 vols. (New York: Routledge, 1997); Rachel Adler, *Engendering Judaism: An Inclusive Theology and Ethics* (Boston: Beacon Press, 1998); Judith Plaskow, *Standing Again at Sinai: Judaism From a Feminist Perspective* (San Francisco: Harper and Row, 1990); Marcia Falk, "Sabbath, Dialogues, New Blessings," in *Four Centuries of Jewish Women's Spirituality: A Sourcebook*, ed. Ellen M. Umansky and Dianne Ashton (Boston: Beacon Press, 1992), 240–43; Sandy Eisenberg Sasso, *A Prayer for the Earth: The Story of Naamah, Noah's Wife* (Woodstock, VT: Jewish Lights, 1996); Marcia Falk, *The Book of Blessings* (Boston: Beacon Press, 1999).

67. See notes 47–50.

68. P. Nadell, *Women Who Would Be Rabbis.*

69. Shuly Rubin Schwartz, *The Rabbi's Wife: The Rebbetzin in American Jewish Life* (New York: New York University Press, 2006).

70. Pamela S. Nadell, "An Angle of Vision: Jewish Women's Studies in the Seminaries," *Conservative Judaism* 55:1 (2002): 3–10.

71. Paul Zakrzewski, "Pioneering Rabbi Who Softly Made Her Way," *New York Times*, May 20, 2006, p. A11.

72. P. Nadell, "Bridges to 'a Judaism Transformed by Women's Wisdom.'"

73. Irving Spiegel, "Conservative Jews Vote for Women in Minyan," *New York Times*, September 1, 1973, p. 1.

74. A few women became synagogue presidents before the second wave of feminism burst forth; P. Nadell, *Women Who Would Be Rabbis*, p. 129. As a result of Jewish feminism, by 2005, it was becoming commonplace for women to become presidents of synagogues everywhere except among the Orthodox. On the first woman to head an Orthodox congregation in Washington, D.C., see Paula Amman, "Beth Sholom Breaks Ground: First Local Orthodox Shul to Elect Woman President," *Washington Jewish Week*, April 7 2005, p. 9.

75. On Greenberg, see Shuly Rubin Schwartz, "Ambassadors Without Portfolio?: The Religious Leadership of Rebbetzins in Late-Twentieth-Century American Jewish Life," in *Women and American Judaism: Historical Perspectives*, ed. Pamela S. Nadell and Jonathan D. Sarna (Hanover, NH: Brandeis University Press, 2001), pp. 253–60; *JOFA: Jewish Orthodox Feminist Alliance*, www.jofa.org.

76. Norma Baumel Joseph, "Ritual Law and Praxis: Bat Mitsva Celebrations," *Modern Judaism* 22:3 (2002): 234–60.

77. Laurie Goodstein, "Women Take Active Role to Study Orthodox Judaism," *New York Times*, December 21, 2000, pp. 1ff. On the "learning revolution," see Rochelle Furstenberg, "The Flourishing of Higher Jewish Learning for Women," in *Jerusalem Letter* (Jerusalem: Jerusalem Center for Public Affairs, 2000).

78. On Orthodox women and ordination, see Laurie Goodstein, "Ordained as Rabbis, Women Tell Secret," *New York Times*, December 21, 2000, p. A29; Haviva Ner-David, *Life on the Fringes: A Feminist Journey Toward Traditional Rabbinic*

Ordination (Needham, MA: JFL Books, 2000). Most recently, the well-regarded modern Orthodox rabbi Aryeh Strikovsky has granted Haviva Ner-David ordination but he qualifies its meaning; Peggy Cidor, "For the Sake of Righteous Women," *Jerusalem Post*, June 2, 2006, http://pqasb.pqarchiver.com/jpost/access/1037364611.html?dids=1037364611:1037364611&FMT=ABS&FMTS=ABS:FT&date=May+5%2C+2006&author=PEGGY+CIDOR&pub=Jerusalem+Post&edition=&startpage=09&desc=For+the+sake+of+righteous+women.

79. Sandy Eisenberg Sasso, "B'rit B'not Israel: Observations on Women and Reconstructionism," *Response: A Contemporary Jewish Review* 8:2 (Summer 1973): 101–5, quotation, 103.

80. Debra Orenstein, *Lifecycles: Jewish Women on Life Passages and Personal Milestones*, vol. 1 (Woodstock, VT: Jewish Lights, 1998), p. 117. Orenstein lists an array of moments Jewish men and women should honor in their lives. They include first love, first sexual experience, weaning, finding out the biopsy is negative, becoming a grandparent, cooking a grandmother's recipe, and "discovering Jewish feminism"; pp. 119-20.

81. Nina Beth Cardin, *Tears of Sorrow, Seeds of Hope: A Jewish Spiritual Companion for Infertility and Pregnancy Loss* (Woodstock, VT: Jewish Lights, 1999), p. 28.

82. D. Orenstein, *Lifecycles*, vol. 1; Laura Levitt and Sue Ann Wasserman, "*Mikveh* Ceremony for Laura," in *Four Centuries of Jewish Women's Spirituality*, ed. Ellen M. Umansky and Dianne Ashton (Boston: Beacon Press, 1992), pp. 321–26.

83. Lenore Bohm, "The Feminist Theological Enterprise," *CCAR Journal* (Summer 1997): 70–79, 76. A major collection of Rosh Chodesh readings is Penina V. Adelman, *Miriam's Well: Rituals for Jewish Women around the Year*, 2nd ed. (New York: Biblio Press, 1990).

84. Elyse Goldstein, "Rabbi Elyse Goldstein," in *Half the Kingdom: Seven Jewish Feminists*, ed. Francine Zuckerman (Montreal: Vehicule Press, 1992), pp. 71–88 and 82–83.

85. Judith Plaskow, "Spirituality," in *Jewish Women in America: An Historical Encyclopedia*, ed. Paula Hyman and Deborah Dash Moore (New York: Routledge, 1997), pp. 1302–6.

86. E. M. Broner, *The Telling* (New York: Harper San Francisco, 1993), vol. 1, pp. 193–94. The film *Miriam's Daughters Now* shows a feminist seder, women celebrating *tashlich* (casting away of sins on the Jewish new year), and a baby-naming ceremony; *Miriam's Daughters Now*, Lilly Rivlin, 1986.

87. Nadine Brozan, "Waiting List Grows as Seders for Women Increase in Popularity," *New York Times*, March 16, 1999, p. B5. There is no standard text for these seders. Reflecting the grassroots nature of this transformation, women in the synagogue and Jewish communal groups that sponsor the seders tend to write their own, borrowing and adapting from various texts that circulate privately.

88. Jewish Federation of Greater Washington, Eighth Annual Miriam's Seder, http://www.shalomdc.org/content_display.html?ArticleID=173415, accessed June 19, 2006.

89. "San Diego Women's Haggadah," in *The Women's Seder Sourcebook: Rituals and Readings for Use at the Passover Seder*, ed. Sharon Cohen Anisfeld, Tara Mohr, and Catherine Spector (Woodstock, VT: Jewish Lights, 2003), pp. 10–11.

90. Sharon Cohen Anisfeld, Tara Mohr, and Catherine Spector, eds., *The Women's Seder Sourcebook: Rituals and Readings for Use at the Passover Seder* (Woodstock, VT: Jewish Lights, 2003), p. 35.

91. On the orange, see Susannah Heschel, *The Origin of the Orange on the Seder Plate* (Miriam's Cup, 2001, May 12, 2005; http://www.miriamscup.com/Heschel_orange.htm, accessed May 12, 1995. On Miriam's cup, see S. Anisfeld, T. Mohr, and C. Spector, eds., *The Women's Seder Sourcebook: Rituals and Readings for Use at the Passover Seder*, 60–70.

92. Judith Plaskow, "Beyond Egalitarianism," in *In Our Own Voices: Four Centuries of American Women's Religious Writing*, ed. Rosemary Skinner Keller and Rosemary Radford Ruether (San Francisco: HarperSanFrancisco, 1995), pp. 139–43; J. Plaskow, *Standing Again at Sinai*; R. Adler, *Engendering Judaism*.

93. Charlotte Baum, Paula Hyman, and Sonya Michel, *The Jewish Woman in America* (New York: New American Library, 1975, 1976).

94. The oft-repeated phrase "a usable past" comes from the literary critic Van Wyck Brooks's celebrated essay "On Creating a Usable Past" (1918); reprinted in *Van Wyck Brooks: The Early Years; A Selection From His Works, 1908–1925*, ed. Claire Sprague (Boston: Northeastern University Press, 1993), pp. 219–-26.

95. For a discussion of earlier works on American Jewish women's history, see Pamela S. Nadell, "Women on the Margins of Jewish Historiography," in *The Margins of Jewish History*, ed. Marc Lee Raphael (Williamsburg, VA: College of William and Mary, 2000), pp. 102–12.

96. At a recent conference, Paula Hyman called this book a "feminist document"; panel on *The Jewish Woman in America* at the 2006 Biennial Scholars' Conference on American Jewish History, Charleston, South Carolina, June 5–7, 2006. On the influence of this work, see Pamela S. Nadell, "Bookends," in *Jewish Women 2000: Conference Papers from the HRIJW International Scholarly Exchanges 1997–1998*, ed. Helen Epstein (Waltham, MA: November 1999), pp. 187–90.

97. Paula E. Hyman, "Judaic Studies," in *Jewish Women in America: An Historical Encyclopedia*, ed. Paula Hyman and Deborah Dash Moore (New York: Routledge, 1997), pp. 705–9; Lynn Davidman and Shelly Tenenbaum, eds., *Feminist Perspectives on Jewish Studies* (New Haven: Yale University Press, 1994).

98. Influential titles include, in Bible, Tikva Frymer-Kensky, *Reading the Women of the Bible: A New Interpretation of Their Stories* (New York: Schocken Books, 2002); in rabbinics, Judith Hauptman, *Rereading the Rabbis: A Woman's*

Voice (Boulder, CO: Westview Press, 1997); in philosophy, Hava Tirosh-Samuelson, *Women and Gender in Jewish Philosophy, Jewish Literature and Culture* (Bloomington: Indiana University Press, 2004); in history, P. Hyman and D. D. Moore, eds., *Jewish Women in America*; in sociology, S. B. Fishman, *A Breath of Life*; in anthropology, Susan Starr Sered, *Women as Ritual Experts: The Religious Lives of Elderly Jewish Women in Jerusalem* (New York: Oxford University Press, 1992); in Jewish literatures, Naomi B. Sokoloff, Anne Lapidus Lerner, and Anita Norich, *Gender and Text in Modern Hebrew and Yiddish Literature* (New York: Jewish Theological Seminary of America, 1992).

99. Anzia Yezierska, *Bread Givers* (New York: Persea Books, 1975). See also Joyce Antler, ed., *America and I: Short Stories by American Jewish Women Writers* (Boston: Beacon Press, 1991).

100. Elyse Goldstein, ed., *The Women's Torah Commentary: New Insights From Women Rabbis on the 54 Weekly Torah Portions* (Woodstock, VT: Jewish Lights, 2000).

101. Anita Diamant, *The Red Tent* (New York: St. Martin's Press, 1997), p. 2. First published in 1997, *The Red Tent* has gone through multiple reprintings and is available in more than twenty countries; http://www.jwa.org/this_week/week40.html

102. Cynthia Ozick, *The Puttermesser Papers*, 1st ed. (New York: Knopf, 1997).

103. "The National Jewish Population Survey, 2000–01: Strength, Challenge, and Diversity in the American Jewish Population" (New York: United Jewish Communities, 2003), pp. 3–4.

104. Evelyn Torton Beck, *Nice Jewish Girls: A Lesbian Anthology*, rev. and updated ed. (Boston: Beacon Press, 1989).

105. Christie Balka and Andy Rose, *Twice Blessed: On Being Lesbian, Gay, and Jewish* (Boston: Beacon Press, 1989); Melanie Kaye/Kantrowitz and Irena Klepfisz, *The Tribe of Dina: A Jewish Women's Anthology*, rev. and expanded ed. (Boston: Beacon Press, 1989); Rebecca Alpert, Sue Levi Elwell, and Shirley Idelson, eds., *Lesbian Rabbis: The First Generation* (New Brunswick, NJ: Rutgers University Press, 2001). See also the journal *Bridges*.

106. *Trembling Before G-D*, Sandi Simcha Dubowski, 2001.

107. Modern Ketubah by the fine-art photographer Daniel Sroka, http://www.modernketubah.com/ketubah_commitment.php, accessed June 19, 2006.

108. J. Levine, "The Changing Role of Women in the Jewish Community, 1972."

109. Tamara Cohen, Jill Hammer, and Rona Shapiro, "Listen to Her Voice: The Ma'yan Report; Assessing the Experiences of Women in the Jewish Community and Their Relationship to Feminism" (New York: Ma'yan: The Jewish Women's Project, 2005).

110. B'nai B'rith Women became independent in 1990 and is now known as Jewish Women International.

111. Shuly Rubin Schwartz, "Women's League for Conservative Judaism," in *Jewish Women in America: An Historical Encyclopedia*, ed. Paula Hyman and Deborah Dash Moore (New York: Routledge, 1997), pp. 1493–97.

112. T. Cohen, J. Hammer, and R. Shapiro, "Listen to Her Voice," p. 25.

113. Ibid., pp. 32ff.

114. Rebecca Spence, "Think Tank Under Fire Over Lack of Women," *Forward*, June 16, 2006, pp. 1ff. On Lipstadt's early feminism, see Deborah E. Lipstadt, "And Deborah Made Ten," in *On Being a Jewish Feminist: A Reader*, ed. Susannah Heschel (New York: Schocken, 1983), pp. 207–9.

115. Avinoam Bar-Yosef, *Op-Ed: Institute Intent on Hiring Women Because of Their Merits, Not Gender* (Jewish Telegraphic Agency, Global News Service of the Jewish People, June 13, 2006, June 19, 2006); http://www.jta.org/page_view_story. asp?intarticleid=16719&intcategoryid=4. On the differences between feminism in Israel and in the United States, see Pamela S. Nadell, "Encountering Jewish Feminism," paper presented at the conference "Why Is America Different?," Boston University, October 25, 2004.

116. Rachel Silverman, "An Institute Tackles Pressing Issues, Critics Say It Ignores Women's Voices," *JTA News*, June 13, 2006, http://jta.org/page_view_story.a sp?intarticleid=16715&intcategoryid=4.

8

‖‖‖

Women's Transformations of Contemporary Jewish Life

Sylvia Barack Fishman

Until the 1960s, in many scholarly and popular accounts of Jewish history and societies, women's distinctive contributions and experiences were ignored, considered inappropriate for discussion and exploration, or described as subordinate. Women were portrayed as the passive recipients of the gender-role constructions that patriarchal Judaism had defined for them. As one pioneering book put it, Jewish women were effectively "written out of history."[1] Happily, however, in recent decades, Jewish women's lives from biblical through contemporary times have received careful examination in hundreds of books and articles—a veritable explosion of interest. As a result, both the academic world and the general reading public have discovered that Jewish women have always made a difference and that one cannot fully understand Jewish history, texts, or culture without paying close attention to gender.

In 20th- and 21st-century Jewish communities, especially, women have altered long-established religious and social patterns. Jewish women have disproportionately led and participated in second-wave feminism, a political and social movement that emerged in the 1960s, first through the efforts of feminist leaders (many of whom were Jewish) and later by becoming a grassroots movement, especially among highly educated American Jewish women. Second-wave feminism had as its goals political, educational, and advocacy activities aimed at guaranteeing women educational, occupational, political, and social equality.[2] Along with broad social trends, these transformations in turn affected demographic realities—education, occupation, marital status, fertility levels, social networks. Equally dramatic, Jewish women since the 1960s have successfully worked to expand their roles in the realms of Judaic scholarship, religious leadership, Jewish life-cycle events, liturgy, synagogues and Jewish organizations, voluntarism, and philanthropy. They have also incorporated women's insights, experiences, and attitudes into Jewish spirituality, liturgical expressions, and conceptual understandings of Jewishness. This chapter utilizes recent research to explore these developments in contemporary Jewish life. We show that in the United States women's activism has revitalized Jewish connections within the lives of Jewish women and men. At the same time, in Israel women are in the process of confronting the status quo, posing critical challenges in areas that profoundly affect the lives of Israeli Jewish men and women. Thus, rather than being passive recipients, women shape and transform Jewish life today. The chapter ends with a challenging question: as women have moved to the forefront of Jewish spirituality, have men been left behind? If so, what are the implications for the future of Jewish religious culture?

Educational Achievement and Labor Force Participation

One of the reasons Jewish women have been important agents for change in the modern period is that they have been disproportionately well educated. Sweeping social historical changes provided impetus and context for transformations in women's roles: in Western Jewish communities that emancipated Jews in the 18th and 19th centuries and offered them the opportunity to enter schools and *gymnasia,* the lives of both Jewish men and women were transformed. Although men in general received more education than women, within some traditional societies elite strata of Jewish men were sequestered in talmudic academies, and Jewish women sometimes preceded Jewish men into the modern world. Indeed, the great writers of the 19th-century Jewish Enlightenment or *Haskalah* often described their entry into modern literature through the reading habits of their mothers and sisters.[3] In Germany, while Jewish men immersed themselves in commerce according to the middle-class pattern and Jewish thinkers reformed and transformed synagogue life, Jewish women became the designated agents of *embourgeoisement*, transforming the Jewish population so that it conformed to middle-class norms, and the transmitters of Westernized lifestyles and forms of Judaism to the next generation.[4]

Especially in 20th-century America, Jewish girls and women took advantage of educational opportunities far more than women of other ethnoreligious groups: in New York in 1910, at a time when Jews made up about 19 percent of the population, 40 percent of the women enrolled in night school were Jewish. By 1934, more than 50 percent of New York female college students were Jewish.[5] In 1990, almost nine out of ten American Jewish women ages 30–39 had gone to college, and almost a third had attended graduate school. However, although Jewish women continued to pursue disproportionately high levels of secular education throughout the 20th century, their labor force participation did not immediately follow suit, for they had thoroughly adapted to the Western bourgeois pattern of ceasing to work for pay outside the home once they married and bore children. This tendency to stop paid employment became a sociological characteristic of Jewish women, who brought their high levels of education and cultural bias toward articulateness and assertiveness into the Jewish communal organizational world, where they created immensely effective unpaid working communities. Hadassah, the Women's Zionist Organization of America, which grew to be one of the most successful Zionist organizations in the world, for example, is the epitome of efficient organizational empires built by Jewish women during the decades when most of them defined themselves as full-time "homemakers."

These patterns began to change in the 1960s as Jewish women emerged as the best-known leaders of the American feminist movement. Betty Friedan's book *The Feminist Mystique* became the bible of the movement,[6] and feminist activists with Jewish names like Gloria Steinem,[7] Bella Abzug, Shulamith Firestone,[8] Vivian Gornick,[9] and many others wrote critiques of Western societies that shaped social change. On a grassroots level, Jewish women were among those most likely to join feminist "consciousness-raising" sessions and to change their lives in accordance with feminist ideals of independence, assertiveness, and self-actualization. Rather than devoting their excellent educations to volunteer work, which had been the previous American Jewish pattern—as we have noted, before second-wave feminism, Jews were the ethnoreligious group most likely to acquiesce to the American middle-class norm of homemaker-mothers, dropping out of labor force participation with the birth of their first child—with the advent of second-wave feminism in the 1960s, Jewish women began to reverse that pattern, and Jewish women increasingly began to take jobs for pay outside the home. By 1990, paid outside employment was reported by three-quarters of Jewish women ages 25–44 and two-thirds of those ages 45–64.[10] Today, the majority of American Jewish women are employed for pay even when they have young children at home. Indeed, except for the most ultra-Orthodox, religiously traditional women are as likely as other groups of American Jewish women to have earned advanced degrees and to work outside the home in a professional capacity.[11]

Jewish Feminism

Feminism with a distinctive Jewish focus became differentiated from the generalized movement in the late 1960s and early 1970s and was part of an overall Jewish awakening. In the United States, during the years of mass immigration (1880–1924) and in the decades immediately afterward, American social norms included a "melting pot" pressure toward ethnic conformity. During the 1960s, however, the exploration of Judaism as a religious culture was encouraged by the American civil rights and the anti-Vietnam War protest movements and by a lively and often transgressive youth culture, which advocated "doing your own thing," including the celebration of ethnic differences. This Jewish awakening was reinforced by American Jewish feelings of pride immediately after the 1967 war in the Middle East, during which Israel defended itself against the massed armies of the Arab states. In a parallel development, American Jewish intellectuals and artists became extremely influential and increasingly explored and emphasized their own Jewishness. In Israel, the growing interest in Jewish feminism was marked by successive international conferences that brought together Jewish feminist scholars and activists from around the world and by the establishment of numerous Judaic studies academies for women's or coeducational sacred text study.

American Jewish feminists began to turn their attention toward the Judaic cultural heritage and contemporary Jewish societies and institutions with the publication of Trude Weiss-Rosmarin's "The Unfreedom of Jewish Women,"[12] which examined "the inequality of Jewish marriage laws," and Rachel Adler's "The Jew Who Wasn't There,"[13] which contrasted male and female models of Jewish piety. In the early 1970s, Jewish women's prayer and study groups were formed in St. Louis, Baltimore, Cambridge, and New York. Women from the New York Havurah (one of the new egalitarian worship and study groups that developed on college campuses and spread into Jewish communal settings) evolved into Ezrat Nashim, whose membership consisted primarily of women who identified as Conservative Jews and who were interested in Jewish women's scholarly and public leadership roles.

Jewish feminists were not and are not a monolithic group, and they have had several different areas of primary interest. Some focused on leadership and some on the lives of Jewish girls and women at large, including but not limited to (1) marking women's life-cycle events with Jewish sacralizing and/or celebratory rituals; (2) including women in Jewish public worship as leaders and active participants; (3) upgrading the Jewish education and Jewish cultural literacy of girls and women; (4) innovating and supporting Judaic scholarship by Jewish women and about Jewish females in classical Jewish texts and throughout Jewish history; (5) creating gender-inclusive synagogue liturgy and other prayers and rituals; (6) reclaiming and publishing materials about the experiences of Jewish girls and women historically and today; (7) examining Jewish religious texts, laws, customs, and culture through the lenses of feminist theory and issues of equality; (8) creating religious and secular legislation to end religiously mandated unequal power relationships and abuses against women, such as women who are *agunot* or *m'sarevot get* (women who have not been successful in obtaining desired divorces from their husbands); (9) creating inclusive Jewish attitudes and environments for Jews living in nontraditional households, such as single Jews, gay and lesbian Jews, and single parents by choice; and (10) incorporating women's theological and philosophical challenges, along with their spiritual understandings and experiences, into a predominantly patriarchal religious culture.

Jewish Women's Education and Life-Cycle Events

For Jewish women in the United States, there has probably been no more sweeping change than the rise of the bat mitzvah from virtual invisibility to its ubiquity as both a celebration and a vehicle for dramatic cultural change. For much of Diaspora Jewish history, a male's achieving adult religious status at the age of thirteen (bar mitzvah) was ceremonially marked, while female adult religious status at age twelve (bat mitzvah) was seldom celebrated. Boys were also far more likely to be sent to religious schools than girls—often for the simple reason that they were preparing for their bar mitzvah celebrations. In America, during the first half of the 20th century, this resulted in a situation in which more than a third of America's Jewish girls received no formal Jewish education. In contrast, when bat mitzvah celebrations became ubiquitous in American communities across the denominational spectrum, the gender gap narrowed and disappeared. Indeed, by the turn of the 21st century, the American Jewish gender educational gap had actually reversed itself—girls are slightly more likely than boys today to be enrolled in Jewish educational activities in the elementary school ages and are dramatically more likely to continue through the teen years. Boys leave Jewish educational settings in much greater proportions than girls immediately after the bar or bat mitzvah. In Orthodox communities in the United States, there is virtually no gender gap, since it has for several decades been normative for both boys and girls to attend Jewish day schools for twelve years and then to attend a one-year program of advanced Jewish study in Israel between high school and college.

In adult Jewish educational activities, men slightly outnumber women in Orthodox settings, while, in Conservative, Reform, Reconstructionist, and transdenominational settings, women now outnumber men two to one. For adult women, preparation for and celebrating the adult bat mitzvah—a ceremony unknown in earlier Jewish communities—has emerged as a powerful and meaningful tool for motivating continuing education. Many hundreds of women acquire new levels of Jewish literacy, including synagogue liturgical skills, because they are initially motivated by the desire to participate in an adult bat mitzvah. Researchers who study Jewish education have remarked that women's passion for acquiring these skills often brings their husbands into classes, as well—a kind of conflagrating spark.

Women are reclaiming many ancient life-cycle rituals for their own use and are inventing other rituals to help them sacralize life-cycle events that are peculiar to the female experience. They seek out these rituals because many people find ritual meaningful and satisfying on a personal, communal, and sometimes spiritual level. For example, in the United States, it is now almost ubiquitous in congregations across denominational lines for women to recite the *kaddish* prayer at services after the death of a loved one and on the anniversaries of that bereavement (*yahrzheit*). Immersion in the waters of the *mikveh* has enjoyed a resurgence not only in Orthodox communities but in liberal Jewish life, as well. Indeed, in some communities, facilities have been built to accommodate new rituals created to utilize the *mikveh*, including rituals to mark life-cycle transitions such as divorce, abortion, adoption, and menopause.

Bringing Women into Spirituality, Religious Rituals, Language, and Symbols

Women are brought to the center of ritual life through changed liturgical language and liturgical symbolism, as well. For example, many Jews put up posters inviting into the *Sukkah* not only traditional patriarchal figures—*ushpizin*—but also matriarchal figures—*ushpizot* (those "invited" into the *Sukkah*). In most Conservative, Reform, and Reconstructionist congregations (which make up the vast majority of American congregations), the names of Sarah, Rebecca, Rachel, and Leah have been incorporated into the central Amidah prayer along with the names of Abraham, Isaac, and Jacob. At Passover seders, an orange is often put on the seder plate—although the origin of this symbol of Jewish feminist strivings is unclear—and some families set out a cup of water for the prophetess Miriam in addition to the cup of wine for Elijah. Many congregations have stopped using the pronoun "He" to describe God, opting instead for nouns that refer to God's attributes or activities, such as "Creator." The use of gender-sensitive language has subtly and overtly changed the prayer experience for both men and women.

Jewish Women's Education and Scholarship

The two most sweeping impacts of changing women's roles center around the relationship of women to their Jewish cultural and intellectual heritage: (1) the inclusion of females in Jewish education; (2) the inclusion of gender and women's issues in research. On an elite level, increasing numbers of women have become Judaic studies scholars, teaching and publishing in fields ranging from the Bible and the ancient Near East to rabbinics, Jewish history, ancient and modern Hebrew literature, Jewish thought, Zionism and Israel studies, and the sociology of contemporary Jewish communities. Moreover, Judaic studies fields themselves have been transformed by insights provided when gender becomes an analytical tool. Paying attention to the lives and sometimes the writings of women in historical Jewish societies has added more than an understanding of women—it has deepened the overall comprehension of the Jewish experience. As one can easily see by reviewing the notes to this chapter, feminist scholarship has illuminated the critical importance of gender as a tool for historical understandings and the centrality of Jewish domestic life to the transmission of Jewish culture historically. Perhaps the most emblematic of these intellectual challenges have been and continue to be posed by Jewish feminist theologians and philosophers, who urge a revisioning of Jewish conceptual and religious categories.

Jewish Women and Public Jewish Leadership

For many observers, the impact of Jewish feminist change was epitomized by the movement of women into public religious leadership roles. In 1972, the Reform movement ordained the first female rabbi, followed in 1974 by the Reconstructionist movement. In 1985, urged on by Ezrat Nashim and a determined group of rabbis, the Conservative movement ordained its first woman rabbi. Today, women constitute a large proportion of rabbinical and cantorial candidates and serve as professionals in numerous Conservative, Reconstructionist, and Reform American congregations.

As one female rabbi suggests, the entry of women has meant not only women themselves in rabbinical positions—"*Imah* on the *Bimah*"—but also the incorporation of women's experiences and insights into Jewish religious leadership. "I hear God say, I call you because you are a woman. You bring the pain and healing of your life," she reflects, suggesting that women may "wrestle with God" in different ways and in different settings from men. Women encounter spirituality in "daily routine and encounters with others . . . the theology of the thorn bush: transcendence in small gestures, revelations at the kitchen table . . . constructing networks, not hierarchies, bringing together diverse voices and building consensus."[14]

Jewish Women as Brokers of Increased Jewish Engagement

As we have noted, over the past half-century, the increasing involvement of American Jewish women in public Judaism, including synagogue and ritual settings, and their increasing access to Judaic texts have generated new levels of excitement and participation for both men and women. Mature women studying Hebrew, trope Torah and Haftarah reading, and Jewish history in preparation for adult bat mitzvahs, for example, have often been the impetus for innovative synagogue and communal educational programs—programs that are open to all. Women in Reform temples proudly donning Israeli hand-crafted *kippot* (head coverings) and *tallitot* (prayer shawls) have reintroduced this distinctive ritual garb in environments that discouraged their participation in religious services for decades. Contemporary feminist scholarship has shown how important women's domestic Judaism was in many earlier periods of Jewish history.

In a change from past patterns, sociological study of the American Jewish community shows that today women's involvement is powerfully influential in rescuing public Jewish rituals and customs, along with Jewish texts and traditions. In sociological language, women increasingly serve as "brokers," connecting not only other women but also men with their Jewish cultural heritage. Transformations in women's relationship to Judaism have been profound in ways not yet fully acknowledged, and this transformed relationship has deeply affected the spiritual lives of Jewish men and Jewish women. During the second half of the 20th century, Jewish women have emerged more and more as the brokers of Jewish religious and spiritual life, bringing excitement about and knowledge of Jewish religious texts, customs, and celebrations back into deeply Westernized Jewish communities. These new activities by Jewish women have not only brought Judaism to the center of women's lives and women to the center of Judaic life but have also served to ignite the religious sensibilities of the acculturated Jewish men around them. Jewish women's transformative influences on contemporary Jewish religious life have been sweeping and powerful. Now they face a new challenge: helping their sons, fathers, brothers, husbands, and friends find their own path to Jewish spiritual engagement.

Jewish Women's Challenges to the Israeli Status Quo

Jewish women in Israel face challenges different from those that face women in the Diaspora. Women have been very active across the political spectrum, mobilizing publicity both for their "dovish"—The Women in Black—and "hawkish"—The Women in Green—political causes. In addition to such right-wing and left-wing political causes, women have been crusaders for moderation in religious realms. The State of Israel has, for complicated reasons, evolved in ways that allow the religious rabbinical courts to have ultimate jurisdiction over all marriages and divorces among Jews—there are no civil marriages in Israel—and thus to exercise considerable power over the lives of both religious and irreligious Israelis. Strikingly, the activism against perceived unresponsiveness and corruption in these rabbinical courts has been led by women who are themselves part of religiously observant communities. The Orthodox feminist activist Leah Shakdiel changed the makeup of religious councils, for example, by indefatigably struggling to become the first member of her regional council. In recent years, the makeup of the councils in general has become much more diverse and reflective of the populations they serve, facts that are written about quite frequently and freely in the Israeli press. The pioneer Israeli activist Alice Shalvi for years headed up a network of Israeli feminist activists while continuing her lifestyle as a religiously observant Jew. Susan Weiss, an Orthodox attorney who serves as the executive director of the Center for Women's Justice in Jerusalem, coordinates the efforts of para-rabbinically and legally trained *to'anot* who assist women working toward divorce equity, including women whose husbands are denying them a Jewish divorce (*get*). In a new cultural development, the Ma'ale Film School in Jerusalem trains Orthodox women to write screenplays and make films that dramatize social problems, such as rape, divorce, and unwed motherhood, that affect Orthodox as well as non-Orthodox societies.[15]

In the realm of spirituality, Jewish women are leaders in helping Israeli society come to terms with modernity intellectually and systemically, as well as in ways specifically addressed to social problems. For example, the philosophy professor Tamar Ross has powerfully challenged the traditional Jewish understanding of "divine revelation." Ross writes articles and books asserting that women's subordination in the Hebrew Bible is not meant to be taken literally in contemporary societies. Using the rabbinic axiom that the "Bible speaks in the language of human beings" in order to make meaning plain to ordinary people—otherwise God would be talking just to God's-self—Ross says the Bible's acceptance of certain social norms is also a form of "speaking in the language of human beings." For example, the Bible does not outlaw slavery; it attempts instead to put boundaries around slavery to prevent its excesses. In contemporary times, most Western readers do not perceive the Bible's discussions of slavery to condone slavery because Western societies have moved beyond slavery—the "language of human beings" has changed, that is, our social norms have changed. In the same way, says Ross, no reader today should assume that the Bible's acceptance of female subordination is meant to condone female subordination. When we move beyond female subordination, we read different biblical messages, but the Bible is still "speaking in the language of human beings," in a more advanced revelation more suitable to our own times. Each generation of Jews must re-understand biblical texts, and in that way the Bible will be newly revealed to a new generation. According to the strictly Orthodox Ross, feminist struggle is thus a sacred activity.[16]

Contemporary Jewish Women's "Ownership" of American Jewishness

New research shows that today Jewish women are much more involved than Jewish men in Jewish spiritual, educational, religious, and liturgical pursuits.[17] Simply put, reversing hundreds of years of Jewish history, outside the Orthodox community today, American Jewish women have more extensive connections to Jews and Judaism than men do. These gender gaps are more pronounced among Jews under the age of forty. Similarly, the recently released Boston study of the Jewish community indicated that more than nine out of ten Jewish mothers who are married to non-Jewish men said they wanted to raise their children as Jews, while just about half of Jewish fathers married to non-Jewish women said they wanted to raise their children as Jews.[18]

The fact that men and women relate differently to Jewishness today is what one might call an "open secret," to use Malcolm Gladwell's formulation.[19] An "open secret" is some kind of challenging information that everyone sort of knows about but that has not received systematic, sustained attention and analysis. For some reason, discussing the fact that in the non-Orthodox world American girls and women today are more Jewishly connected than boys and men seems to be politically incorrect. And yet, when you ask Jewish leaders, rabbis, educators, and organizational professionals about the gender of the people who are involved in their enterprises, almost universally they reveal that far more women than men attend services on a regular basis, enroll in and attend adult education classes, take volunteer leadership positions that involve significant amounts of work and time, and participate in Jewish cultural events.

This bias toward women in Jewish life has developed at the very same time that women have become more and more overwhelmingly involved in the labor force, so the easy answer that "women have more time" does not explain the trend. And it seems likely to continue, because it is also present among girls and boys: slightly more girls than boys are enrolled in supplementary school educational settings during the pre-bar/bat mitzvah years.

These feminized patterns contradict thousands of years of Jewish history, during which, it might be argued, Jewish men, rather than Jewish women, were the "signifying Jews" (those especially recognizable as such). Over the past thirty to forty years, the American Jewish community has made dramatic strides in shifting a centuries-old Jewish gender imbalance.

Today, far more Jewish girls receive Jewish educations than did in their grandmothers' time. Bat mitzvah is ubiquitous and almost universal among Jewish-connected American families. Many adult women have reclaimed their religious and cultural heritage by studying Hebrew and Judaic texts and Jewish liturgy and having adult bat mitzvahs. Jewish women have entered and excelled in many Jewish professional positions that were once the exclusive province of men. For the first time in recorded Jewish history, the talents and voices of Jewish women can contribute publicly, as individuals and as a group, to Jewish intellectualism, art, and life. Jewish women have rediscovered their Jewish passions.

But, at the same time, outside the Orthodox community, the involvement of Jewish boys and men has undergone a steady decline. Part of the reason for this decline is that Americanized Jews, following the Protestant model, have tended more and more to think of religion and religious activities as "women's work." The work of boys and men, in contrast, is seen as being more compelling and manly: participating in sports activities and building up one's resume for boys, engaging in work-related activities and networking for men. Divested of the all-male religious and communal world that was an old-boys' network, a place to be powerful and to meet the powerful, Jewish boys and men have drifted off to other, seemingly more rewarding environments.

This chapter has taken the interpretive stance that real progress is reflected in the fact that many women are more invested in Jewish worship and education today than in the past. I certainly would not want to turn the clock back to a time, not so long ago, when many women were given no formal Jewish education. That is still the case in many European countries, where you can find women sitting high in balconies talking to each other as if they were at their kitchen tables, because they have no knowledge of Hebrew whatsoever and no knowledge of the contents of the religious services going on far below them. The Jewish education women receive today in day school and yeshiva settings and the involvement of women in all kinds of adult Jewish education are something precious not just for women. The whole Jewish community benefits when women's insights and talents become part of the communal treasure.

But it is a tragedy when men absent themselves from Jewish life, Jewish rituals, Jewish learning, and an impoverishment for the whole Jewish people. One must ask if this gendered exodus from Jewish life is simply what happens in American culture when full egalitarianism is attained.

Modern American Orthodox Jews present an alternative model. Research by Moshe Hartman and Harriet Hartman, using data from the 1990 and 2000 National Jewish Population Studies, shows that modern Orthodox couples under the age of fifty are the group most closely matched in terms of spousal equity—husbands and wives are remarkably similar in terms of educational and occupational achievement.[20] They are also most closely matched in religious attitudes and the number of religious activities, although not necessarily the exact type of activities. What both men and women in the American modern Orthodox world today have is what sociologists call "ethnic social capital." Ethnic capital is created when a group learns and teaches its children ethnic languages; eats distinctive foods; sings and listens to distinctive music; participates in distinctive rituals and ceremonies; reads distinctive literature; visits its distinctive national homeland; and pursues distinctive interests. It is also possible that one factor in Jewish ethnic capital has historically been, and in Orthodox circles continues to be, distinctively defined gender roles in our religious lives.

Perhaps some aspects of the gender differences that have emerged over the centuries provided sociological and psychological religious strength that functioned as a way of engaging boys and men in Jewish life, rituals, ceremonies, learning, and other activities. Because all Jewish men were responsible for public prayer and familiarity with Judaic religious texts, the masses of Jewish men—rather than just the elite strata, as was common in other religious societies—felt extraordinarily tied to religious life. One must ask the politically incorrect question whether there is something about completely divesting men of that exclusivity that makes many of them lose interest in Jewishness. Perhaps the next challenge to Jewish women as brokers of Jewish ethnic capital is participation in the creation of a new balance that can help to bring men into dynamic engagement with their own Jewish heritage.

NOTES

1. Sondra Henry and Emily Taitz, *Written Out of History: Our Jewish Foremothers* (New York: Biblio Press, 1990).

2. For a fuller discussion of these phenomena, see Sylvia Barack Fishman, *A Breath of Life: Feminism in the American Jewish Community* (New York: Free Press, 1993).

3. Iris Parush, *Reading Jewish Women* (New Hampshire: Brandeis University Press/University Press of New England, 2004).

4. Marion Kaplan, *The Making of the Jewish Middle Class: Women, Family and Identity in Imperial Germany* (New York: Oxford University Press, 1991).

5. Paula Hyman, "Gender and the Jewish Immigrant Experience in the United States," in *The Jewish Woman in Historical Perspective*, ed., Judith Baskin (Detroit: Wayne State University Press, 1991), pp. 222-42.

6. Betty Friedan, *The Feminine Mystique* (New York: Norton, 1963).

7. Gloria Steinem, "Humanism and the Second Wave of Feminism," *Humanist* (May/ June, 1987).

8. Shulamith Firestone, *The Dialectic of Sex* (New York: Morrow, 1971).

9. Vivian Gornick, *Women in Sexist Society: Studies in Power and Powerlessness* (New York: Harper Collins/Basic Books, 1971).

10. Sidney Goldstein, "Profile of American Jewry: Insights from the 1990 National Jewish Population Survey," *American Jewish Year Book 1992* (New York: American Jewish Committee, 1992), pp. 115–16.

11. Moshe Hartman and Harriet Hartman, *Gender Equality and American Jews* (Albany: State University of New York Press, 1996), pp. 219–25. Their update of these data is scheduled to be published in the Hadassah-Brandeis Series on Jewish Women.

12. Trude Weiss-Rosmarin, "The Unfreedom of Jewish Women," *Jewish Spectator* (October, 1970), pp. 2–6.

13. Rachel Adler, "The Jew Who Wasn't There," *Davka* (Summer, 1971), pp. 6–11.

14. Sandy Eisenberg Sasso, "Celebrating Thirty Years of Women as Rabbis," in *Reconstructionism Today* 11, no. 1 (Autumn 2003), http://www.jrf.org/rt/2003/women_as_rabbis.htm.

15. More information about Israel women's activities can be found in numerous articles available on the Internet under the names of Israel women activists, such as Sharon Shehav, Batsheva Sherman, Ruth Halperin Kadari, Susan Weiss, Leah Shakdiel, and Alice Shalvi, and the organizations Yad L'Isha, Max Morrison Legal Aid Center and Hotline, and Kolech.

16. Tamar Ross, *Expanding the Palace of Torah: Orthodoxy and Feminism* (Hanover: NH: Brandeis University Press/University Press of New England, 2005).

17. Sylvia Barack Fishman and Daniel Parmer, *Raising Jews by Gender: Men and Women Discuss the Raising of Jewish Children* (Waltham, MA: Cohen Center for Modern Jewish Studies, Brandeis University, forthcoming).

18. According to Benjamin Phillips and Graham Wright, 92 percent of children in intermarried households with a Jewish mother are being raised as Jews, but only 53 percent of children in intermarried households with a Jewish father are being raised within the Jewish religion (personal communication on the 2005 Boston study).

19. Malcolm Gladwell, "Open Secrets: Enron, Intelligence, and the Perils of Too Much Information," *The New Yorker* (January 8, 2007), pp. 44–53.

20. M. Hartman and H. Hartman, *Gender Equality and American Jews*, pp. 227, 244–48, 294.

Part IV

Literature

Women in Jewish American Literature

Sara R. Horowitz

Not long ago, the mention of Jewish American literature would bring to mind three writers whose works dominated thinking in that field but whose presence was central to 20th-century American letters more broadly: Saul Bellow, Bernard Malamud, and Philip Roth. Having earned for themselves a wide readership, these writers also occupied literary scholars who focused on what they said about the Jewish experience in America, as well as their more "universal" concerns about the human condition.[1] Aficionados might know also the works of Henry Roth or Isaac Bashevis Singer, perhaps Chaim Potok. Indeed, as late as the 1990s, when I asked a colleague who taught courses in Jewish American literature why he never included women writers in his syllabus, he asked, "Are there any good ones?" For him as for most readers, these Jewish men stood for all Jews and for all that was once referred to unself-consciously as "all men," meaning all people. Jewish women looked to find themselves reflected in both of these images.

The past quarter-century, however, has seen a sea change in the way we view Jewish American literature—that is, the texts that we read and the ways in which we read them. We have come to notice the representation of gender in the novels we read—the ways women are depicted, the ways men are depicted—and to connect those depictions with the place of women and men in the world beyond the text. In what follows, we look at two aspects of this change: new developments in the way we approach Jewish American women's writing and new trends in the growing body of Jewish American literature by women.

Literary Criticism and Women's Studies

The Minefields of Feminist Literary Studies

In a landmark and controversial 1980 essay on the state of feminist literary criticism in America, Annette Kolodny coined the phrase "dancing through the minefield" to describe her work as an American feminist literary critic and theorist.[2] The "minefield" in question is the product of a literary tradition, a university system, and a way of thinking and teaching that feminist criticism engaged, resisted, and hoped to influence with new ways of reading literature. Kolodny describes picking her way through a cultural and academic minefield in which focusing on women's writing and women's thinking can blow up in one's face. As she notes, feminist literary critics at that time had two main concerns—"what we read" and "how we read."[3] Focusing on "what we read" entailed questioning the accepted consensus on the "great works"—that is, on what we call the literary canon, which featured writing that was authored predominantly, if not exclusively, by men. Was this simply because men had written far, far better literary works than women? Or, as Kolodny and others suggested, was it because, in their roles as editors, publishers, and patrons, men exercised economic and cultural clout, functioning as tastemakers, as arbiters of excellence? Men, it was suggested, responded to literature that emerged from and spoke to men's experiences and sensibilities. Looking at "how we read" involved noticing the ways that gender was portrayed in works by both men and women and linking these portrayals to more broadly based world views assumed and conveyed in literary works. It entailed placing literary figures of gender in the wider context of the social, economic, and political systems that shape the way men and women experience their lives and in which writers ply their craft.

Addressing either of those concerns—what and how we read—from a feminist viewpoint could draw fire from more established (and mostly male) scholars. When feminist critics focused on "what we read," they often noticed an imbalance, for example, between the number of men and women writers whose works were included in high school or university courses or mandated by school curricula. To address this, women critics read with a fresh eye, bringing to light women writers whose works had been ignored or undervalued, "rediscovering a lost body of writing."[4] They introduced a new set of authors into literature classes—new in the sense of not having been studied seriously before. From Elizabethan English literature to contemporary American writing, literature courses began to take on a new shape as feminist critics chipped away at conventional ideas about whose writing "counts" and whose does not. However, such challenges to established literary judgment came at a price. Not infrequently, colleagues would accuse professors of women's studies of lowering their aesthetic standards by concentrating on inferior works. It was not uncommon, in the 1970s and 1980s—and even into the 1990s—to hear such dismissive comments as, "What should we teach—Shakespeare or _____?" with the name of any contemporary woman writer inserted in the blank.

When feminist critics focused on "how we read," offering new interpretations of acclaimed writers—interpretations that brought issues of gender to the foreground—colleagues accused them of allowing ideology to distort their reading. Rather than reading "objectively" and allowing the work of literature to speak for itself in all its richness and complexity, feminist critics, it was claimed, brought with them an externally imposed template. Their overweening concern with women's issues, it was said, brought them to produce readings of literary works that were flat, or oversimplified, or just plain wrong. For a generation largely trained in new criticism, a form of literary criticism that focuses closely on the text and ignores biographical and historical material, this was a damning assessment. Such negative evaluations of the emerging body of feminist criticism could not simply be seen as part of an open literary debate, because the disparaging remarks often came from senior professors, whose influence bore heavily on hiring, tenure, and promotion decisions that mightily affected the career paths of relatively junior feminist critics. Kolodny's essay responds to those accusations, attempting to articulate a coherent theoretical framework that grounded the diverse strands of feminist literary criticism. Moreover, she and others linked attitudes toward women's literature and feminist literary criticism with the status of women in society and the significance of women's work more broadly. Acknowledging that feminist literary scholars put their professorial careers at risk, Kolodny anticipated a more auspicious time, a future "happy circumstance," when their collective work will have dismantled the mines. She imagines generations to come dancing their way through what was once dangerous terrain.

But the minefield of Kolodny's metaphor was even more complex than she had described. By the time she published "Dancing Through the Minefield," Kolodny and other influential American feminist literary critics had come under fire not only from their skeptical and disapproving male cohorts but from other feminists, most notably women of color.[5] In a move begun by African American women but soon augmented by Latina, Asian, and other self-identified minority women in America, women of color argued that feminist theory and feminist literary criticism were not adequate to describe their cultural position. In fact, they insisted, they had been done a harsh disservice by Kolodny and others like her: white, middle-class professors writing from their own, limited experience, much as white male professors had been doing. Women of color, these critics insisted, had been doubly marginalized: first, by patriarchal traditions and privileges that either ignored or diminished women's accomplishments, and second, by white traditions and privileges—including the feminism of white women, which similarly ignored or diminished the accomplishments of people of color.

In fact, they noted, feminist literary criticism had turned a blind eye to the history, culture, and experience of women of color. When American literary scholars wrote about or taught novels and poems by women of color, they read them simply as illustrations of women's experience and women's culture. They assumed that all women shared similar experiences, struggles, and outlooks. To put it differently, they presumed that white, middle-class, or professional women could speak for all women, much as men had presumed that they could speak for all people. Women of color, then, described themselves as doubly marginalized—by men (including black men) and by whites (including white feminists). Men of color had written without taking into account the experiences of women of color *as women* and without acknowledging their own role in subjugating them. Similarly, white feminists had written without taking into account the diversity of female experience and their own relatively privileged existence. If, as Kolodny's metaphor has it, feminist critics pick their way through a minefield, women of color might be said to traverse a minefield with two layers of armaments, a double minefield. This critique of feminist literary criticism figured strongly in the way that literary theory and criticism developed from the 1980s on. Moreover, a consciousness of the dynamics that govern the relationship between women of color and more privileged women on the one hand and more privileged men on the other comes to permeate literature written by women of color.

The Minefields of Jewish Feminist Literary Studies

I would like to borrow Kolodny's metaphor of the minefield to talk about the interplay between women's studies and contemporary Jewish literature in North America. While she carefully makes her way through a single minefield—that of patriarchal assumptions, so pervasive as to be considered a natural truth—and women of color negotiate the double minefield of sexist and racist traditions, Jewish women writers on this continent and the literary critics who interpret their work confront a triple minefield, one layered upon the next and each with its own trigger points and patterns.

These explosive layers correspond to three interlinked critiques of American literary criticism and the American literary tradition. First, along with other feminist scholars, scholars of Jewish literature have developed a critique of patriarchy that is reflected in fiction and poetry by American Jewish women.[6] For example, Jewish feminist literary scholarship explores stereotypes of Jewish women that pervade Western literary traditions and Jewish literary traditions. It examines the exclusion of women's experiences and the absence of Jewish women's desires in works by non-Jewish and Jewish men. It explores the place in the American and the Jewish American literary canons of works by Jewish women writers. Second, in a movement comparable to the critique of normative feminist scholarship mounted by women of color, Jewish feminist literary scholarship points to the invisibility of Jewish experience in feminist discourse. It insists on bringing anti-Semitism and the concomitant marginality into the compass of feminist studies.[7] Third, in a twinned critique of both Judaism and secularity, it brings Jewish ritual and spirituality into the center of the conversation about contemporary Jewish literature.[8] Because these last two "layers" of the minefield represent an expansion of the concerns of feminist literary criticism, I will flesh them out further.

By insisting that normative feminist scholarship falsifies or excludes their own historical experiences and collective memories, women of color pushed feminist literary critics to pluralize feminism(s) and to rethink ideas about gender and identity. Many Jewish feminist scholars felt a deep sympathy and even a sense of kinship with the challenge to the notion of an idealized unity among women, regardless of ethnicity, social class, or religion. Jewish feminist scholarship began to develop ways of thinking about Jewish women's writing, Judaism, and gender that took issue with the invisibility or distortion of the Jewish experience in feminist criticism and theory. Many found inspiration in the boldness of academic work by women of color. They admired, for example, the way that African American women literary critics took on not only misogyny but also racism. They found that works by Latina and Asian women addressed issues of biculturalism, dual and hybrid identities, and bilingualism in ways that resonated meaningfully with Jewish experience. One particularly influential critic, Gloria Anzaldúa, focused on the writings and experiences of the "mestizas"—that is, "biologically or culturally mixed" women. Her writing is often cited in works on Jewish women writers.

While mainstream feminist critics in America acknowledged that, in not accounting for the very different experiences of women of color, their work was flawed—"parochial," one African American critic termed it[9]—the response to the Jewish critique of literary feminism was less pronounced. There were several reasons for this. A significant number of the feminist critics and theorists prominent in the 1960s and 1970s—those whose thinking weighed heavily in Kolodny's essay—were Jewish (or of Jewish descent), but their academic work did not engage Jewish experiences or sensibilities per se. Some were removed from Jewish cultural and textual traditions, which simply did not figure in their world views. Others saw these traditions as bound up in the sexist sensibilities they opposed; others associated Jewishness with middle-class, suburban values that they repudiated. Kolodny's generation of scholars included many feminists who, while Jewish, did not write as Jewish feminists. With few exceptions, they were not particularly interested in the specific experiences and history of Jewish women as such.[10]

In turn, many of the women of color whose writing came to prominence in the 1980s and 1990s were not responsive to literary critics who wished to make a place in women's studies for Jewish women's experiences. Some did not grasp the distinction between feminists who happened to be Jewish and those whose feminism engaged and embraced Judaism and Jewishness—what I mean, in other words, when I use the terms "Jewish feminism" and "Jewish feminist critic." Since so many of the influential white feminists whose insularity they criticized were Jewish, it was difficult to acknowledge that feminism had not engaged Jewish culture on its own terms, any more than it had African American culture. Others rejected the idea that Jewish women's experiences resonated with and should be in dialogue with the experiences and literatures of women of color. Anzaldúa, for example, warned Jewish women in her university seminar on mestiza feminism that they were wrong to compare themselves "more to the women-of-color group than they did to the white group." She chastised them for "not get[ting] it into their heads that this was a space and class on and about women-of-color."[11]

By the mid-1970s and early 1980s, a small cadre of Jewish women professors was publishing books that focused on Jewish American literature.
Like their male cohorts in the field, they engaged these literary works in
multiple contexts that included the Western literary tradition, the Jewish
intellectual tradition, and the Jewish experience in America. As literary
critics, they explored issues such as the immigrant experience, acculturation, Americanization, and social justice as these played out in the literature they wrote about and taught. Some developed a special interest in
writing by Jewish women. The issues they addressed and the literature
they read were deeply rooted in the Jewish experience and cast in a largely
secular venue.[12] Indeed, by then it was commonly accepted that Jewish
American literature was purely secular. Chaim Potok's novels were cited
as the exception that proves the rule, taught more often as social artifact
than as literature.

But, by the turn of the century, a constellation of circumstances had
altered the shape of Jewish American women's literary studies and, indeed, the shape of Jewish American women's writing. In all areas of Jewish Studies, there was a growing attention to the place of women. Scholars
in a wide range of fields were applying the insights and methodologies
of women's and gender studies to their work in Jewish Studies. Literary
scholars with an interest in Jewish American literature were in conversation with colleagues in other fields, including history, Bible, Talmud, and
sociology. They lent those fields the insights of literary criticism and the
contributions of literary analysis to women's studies. Correspondingly, literary scholars drew upon an expanded idea of what makes literary works
Jewish and how women figure in a broad range of Jewish texts and historical periods. In addition, a growing number of women rabbis and professors at rabbinical seminaries brought Jewish women's studies into the
sphere of religious thought, practice, and spirituality in new ways. Earlier
generations of academic scholars had been trained on ideas of strict objectivity in one's research—a sense of professional detachment and distance from what one studied, taught, and wrote about. Now, under the
influence of feminist studies, scholars learned to question the very possibility of objectivity, of a scholarship shorn of the ideological and personal
convictions and assumptions of the scholar. Furthermore, they questioned
whether such detachment was even desirable. Feminist studies developed
the concept of "standpoint theory," which maintains that knowledge and
perceptions are shaped by one's standpoint—that is, by one's place in the
world.[13] What had been regarded as "objective" analysis, more often than

not, was not so much objective as an unacknowledged reflection of the values and ideology of the dominant culture. By providing analysis from a different standpoint, reflecting different experiences and social conditions, women and oppressed minorities offered a corrective to the bias inherent in an "objective" analysis that was not really objective at all but that simply reflected a different standpoint. By incorporating other standpoints, it was argued, researchers would develop knowledge that was less distorted.

While standpoint theory was most influential in feminist analyses of science and social science, its insights were embraced also by feminist literary theorists. They encouraged literary scholars not only to bring the social conditions of the authors they studied into their analysis of literary works but also to acknowledge in a self-conscious manner their own standpoints as readers and interpreters of literature. As women and as Jews—indeed, as Jewish women—scholars of Jewish American literature brought their sensibilities, values, and concerns into their readings of literary texts. Their engagement and struggles with Jewish texts, traditions, communities, and practices shaped the kinds of literature they read and the issues they focused on. One aspect of this engagement was the movement of Judaism from the margins to the center of Jewish American women's writing.

One other significant development that affected the way that literary scholars read and understand Jewish women's writing has been in the area of queer theory, which emerged in part from within the compass of women's studies but also in part—like the critique of feminism by women of color—in opposition to some of its assumptions. Just as some women of color remarked on what they saw as a false unity that the work of Kolodny and other feminists posited among women as a category, a unity that ignored their own perspectives and experiences, so, too, some lesbian thinkers criticized "Dancing Through the Minefield" as exemplifying the subsuming of distinctly lesbian experiences in a collective vision that rendered gay women invisible or irrelevant.[14] Often referred to as a postfeminist approach, queer theory has become increasingly influential in literary criticism. In its approach to gender, queer theory deconstructs, or dismantles, the idea that women's studies can speak for all women, not only by pointing to the different standpoint of lesbians and gays but also by taking apart the very concept of gender identity.[15] Queer theory reminds us that gender identity is socially constructed and not a natural outcome of biology. Thus, according to leading theorists, we perform— rather than naturally inhabit—gender identity. Gender theory emphasizes the fluidity and complexity of gender identity and, by extension, all aspects of identity. In breaking down the binary opposition between male and female, gender theory insists on the fluidity and instability of gender and other aspects of identity. While women's studies has tended to focus on hierarchies of gendered power—how women's control of economic and cultural resources or control over their own bodies, for example, has been limited by patriarchy—queer theory focuses on the complex issues of sexuality and desire, as well as on behaviors such as mimicry and drag, through which people assert and attempt to stabilize identity.[16] Within the compass of Jewish studies, queer theory has enriched the way that scholars think about such ideas as Jewish masculinity and Jewish feminism, as well as Jewish identity and Judaism more generally.[17]

In a move that reversed the longstanding treatment by both literary authors and literary critics of the Jewish experience as secularizing and secular, the field of Jewish American women's writing took a turn to think seriously about issues of Jewish practice, texts, rituals, and spirituality. It was not a matter of simply embracing traditional Judaism, a penitential "return" from secularism. As both literary authors and literary critics, Jewish women were shaped by movements in society generally and in the university in particular, as well as by challenges in the synagogue and the seminary. Literature offered itself as a means through which to reflect, to analyze, to criticize, and to transform the position of woman in Judaism—her exclusion from certain aspects of Jewish ritual life, her diminished stature, her spiritual yearning. Rather than seeing literature as offering a backward glance at an outmoded or outgrown tradition, peppered with anger or with nostalgia, Jewish women literary authors and their readers looked to it and to literary studies to reinvent and reshape contemporary Judaism.

Contemporary Jewish American Women's Writing

These three minefields—patriarchy, feminism, and religion—marked the terrain that Jewish feminist literary scholars traversed in recent years. They are also points of pressure that increasingly occupy much of contemporary North American Jewish women's fiction. Novels, of course, are not manifestos, but fiction often responds to and prompts a particular cultural moment. I'd like to look more closely at several contemporary novels by Jewish women in terms of these concerns, to take the pulse, as it were, of contemporary North American Jewish culture.

Minefields in the 1980s

As early as the 1980s, all three areas began to show up on the radar of North American Jewish women writers, explored thematically in the fiction of a handful of writers. Three benchmark works may serve here to illustrate their presence in Jewish women's letters. Nessa Rapoport's 1979 short story "The Woman Who Lost her Names" articulates the powerlessness of a Jewish woman under a patriarchal system that determines, in large measure, who she is. Anne Roiphe's 1987 novel *Lovingkindness* articulates a trenchant challenge to feminism for neglecting, even demonizing, Judaism through the relationship of a feminist professor and her rebellious daughter who repudiates her mother's values in favor of Jewish practice. E. M. Broner's 1985 novel *A Weave of Women* defiantly embraces ritual practices traditionally reserved for men, imaginatively inventing new, feminist Jewish rituals.

In Rapoport's story, which has been anthologized in several collections of Jewish writing, the protagonist is repeatedly renamed by others. Given the name Sarah at birth, she soon acquires the middle name Josephine after an uncle who died soon after she was born. As a child, she detests her name. When she begins elementary school, her teacher Americanizes her name to Sally to help her to "integrate." Because her fiancé's mother is also named Sarah, Jewish custom dictates that she must change her name; her husband chooses Yosefa. Eventually, Sarah/Yosefa gives birth to a daughter whom she wishes to name "Ayelet Hashachar," Dawn Star, a poetic phrase from Psalms. Her husband insists that the child be named Dina after Sarah's mother, Dinsche, who had recently died. "It is the Jewish way," he tells her,[18] although Sarah objects to the biblical allusion to a victim of rape. The story ends with a vision of female invisibility and exclusion from Jewish ritual life. "When the day of the naming arrived she was numb, jabbing the pins of her head covering into her hair. She walked with her sons and her husband to the synagogue, and left them to climb the steps to the balcony for women. Below her the men were lifting the Torah, opening and closing it, dressing, undressing it, reading the day's portion. . . . The women around her moved their lips to the words. She stood still. She stood in her place, the place where the mothers always sat for their children. She closed her mouth, her lips pressed together, one on top of the other, and waited to hear her daughter's name."[19] The inability to name oneself and one's daughter serves as an emblem for the larger issue of female powerlessness, the inability to define oneself.

In Roiphe's novel, published almost ten years later, a young woman seizes the ability to rename herself, but in a movement quite different from the one Rapoport's story anticipates. *Lovingkindness* follows the struggle between Annie and her daughter Andrea, who has renamed herself Sarai after becoming a *ba'alat teshuva*, a newly Orthodox woman. Andrea had been a problem child, rebellious and self-destructive. Sarai, by contrast, lives in an ultra-Orthodox yeshiva and finds a sense of purpose in knowing that "God respects me." Annie is a single mother, a strong feminist with a flourishing career as an English professor and an attenuated sense of Jewish identity, not unlike some of Kolodny's academic cohorts. Annie believes that, in joining the ultra-Orthodox community, her daughter has succumbed to a patriarchal system that makes women invisible. Indeed, she recollects that none of her male cousins took any interest in the tales of Reb Nachman that her grandfather wished to tell. Despite her eagerness to hear his stories, he deemed them "not for you" because she was a girl, not a boy. For her part, Sarai believes her mother has bought into a secular culture that makes Judaism invisible. In a series of letters, Sarai explains her choice to her mother. "Jews make distinctions, mark things off cleanly and clearly . . . tangles and piles are not for God's people . . . I know that you did not think it important to scrub the stove or make the curtains lie straight with the pleats in place. But it is very important to do those things and to wipe and dust and iron. After breakfast we take care of chores, taking turns at each. The time goes so fast because we are busy. I used to be waiting for something to happen, for someone to come, for something to rouse me. Now I am not waiting, I am doing. When I sponge the table and the crumbs are gone and the board is again honey-colored and the patches of light from the window shine on my part of the floor, the One Above is pleased with me. I take a deep breath and smell the pine and the ammonia and I feel good."[20] While Annie's feminism leads her to reject a Judaism that had rejected her, Andrea/Sarai points to the rootlessness that is the consequence of such a repudiation.

E. M. Broner's novel offers an angry look at Jewish patriarchy, which, like all patriarchal systems, does violence to women. But implied in the novel is also a critique of a feminism that has repudiated Judaism, as the novel reclaims—or more properly refashions—Judaism. The narrative follows a period of time in the lives of fifteen women who come together in Jerusalem at moments of flux. The women create rituals and ceremonies that are both Jewish and feminist to mark significant events and to negotiate crises in their lives. The novel incorporates contemporary midrashim, or narrative commentaries on biblical episodes, building on classic rabbinic texts. For example, imagining women back into the events of the biblical exodus from Egyptian slavery, Broner elaborates on older rabbinic interpretations of the role of Miriam, the sister of Moses. "Miriam had dictated to the men of her father's generation the appropriate behavior when they all rejected their wives. Miriam told Moses to give up the ascetic ways that were upon him since he had his vision in the desert and to return physically to his wife, Tsiporah."[21] In its call for liturgical renewal, for the development of alternative rituals for Jewish women, and for the integration of feminism and Judaism, Broner's novel begins to develop a place for serious thought about religion in a literary discourse that had been regarded as purely secular.

For a greater part of the 20th century, Jewish American literature was the literature of immigrants and their children, writing their way into American culture. Their fiction captured the process of acculturation, most often marked by distancing from Jewish traditional practices. They dealt with such issues as ethics, immigration, exclusion, acculturation, assimilation, and historical trauma. When it appeared in these works at all, Judaism was presented either critically or nostalgically, viewed as a relic of a European life left behind. It built upon a body of historical or textual memories that were presented, in American literature, as oppressive or inspiring as American Jews moved into a secularized, Americanized modern future. In a sense, literature presented itself as an alternative grounding for Jewish ethics and values, taking the place of religious learning and practice and the mores of a tightly bound community. In fact, virtually all scholars understood Jewish literature in North America to be a secular discourse, however much its texts might gesture to religious texts, ritual practices, and remembered communities.

In different ways, these three works introduced a new element into Jewish American literature: the articulation of a Jewish feminist narrative in a context that sees Judaism as a source of meaningfulness, however contentious, for Jewish women. Incorporating Jewish texts, history, legends, and culture, these novels mark a reversal of a movement away from Judaism that had marked Jewish American literature up to that time. The issues at the heart of fiction by authors such as Rapoport, Roiphe, and Broner figure importantly in contemporary fiction by North American Jewish women writers.

New Wave of Jewish American Women's Writing

As part of what has been termed a "new wave" of Jewish American writing published at the turn of the century, contemporary Jewish American writers write out of a context already deeply affected by Jewish feminism. Mainstream synagogues and other Jewish communal organizations have taken on different configurations in response to feminist critiques, and, as individuals, American Jews think about such things as ethnic and religious identity differently than they had in the past. Jewish writing by both men and women reflects, probes, and challenges this changed Jewish American landscape.[22]

New-wave literature by Jewish American women writers negotiates terrain very different from the one navigated by such works as Rapoport's "The Woman Who Lost Her Names," Roiphe's *Lovingkindness*, and Broner's *A Weave of Women*. The more contemporary writers have less need to stake out their territory, as it were, and to claim it for Jewish feminism. As a result, new-wave Jewish American women's writing tends to be less polemical and more nuanced than the writing of the 1980s, which first introduced issues of Jewish feminism into a literature that had not encompassed them before. In different ways, contemporary Jewish women's writing in America explores issues that face Jewish women in a postdenominational era, when many Jews move in and out of Jewish social and religious communities. Rather than dividing neatly into definable categories, such as secular and religious, the Jewish experience in America is increasingly characterized by fluidity. This sense of flux connects to a larger cultural consciousness of the contingency and changeability of identity. As Jewish women's literature explores the variety of Jewish religious experience in America, especially as it pertains to women's lives, it also oscillates with issues of growing concern to Americans generally, such as the nonfixed quality of the boundaries of ethnic, gender, cultural, and religious identity and belonging.

Tova Mirvis, for example, explores the lives of women in Orthodox and ultra-Orthodox communities, fleshing out the religious contexts that make their actions, conflicts, and choices meaningful. In her 2004 novel *The Outside World*, she focuses on the struggles of four women to find a place of comfort as women within Judaism. Tzippy is the oldest of five daughters in a *haredi*, or ultra-Orthodox, family in Brooklyn. Rebelling against the narrowly defined path her life is expected to follow—dates arranged by a matchmaker, marriage at a young age, an elaborate wedding, married life and motherhood—Tzippy struggles to carve out her own path. At the start of the novel, she has left her parents' home to study at a religious seminary for girls in Israel. The move gains her freedom from the scrutiny of her insular community and distance from her controlling mother. Below the radar, she finds and eventually proposes to the man who will become her husband. As a married woman, Tzippy continues to push against the boundaries her community places upon women. Although still committed to ultra-Orthodox practices, she aspires to a university education, a career.

Tzippy's sister-in-law, Ilana, a high school student, has been raised in a modern Orthodox home in New Jersey, in a meshing of beliefs and behaviors that affirms the "integration of religious and secular" knowledge and values.[23] The students in her Orthodox high school date, dance, and explore their sexuality more freely than do young people in Tzippy's community. Their families expect their children to grow up retaining their ties to Jewish practice but also to complete university and professional studies. Ilana, too, rebels against her community's religious norms. Her rebellion centers on a defiance of her school's dress code, intended to uphold ideas of modesty for Jewish women. After eight weeks in summer camp, where she experiments with the pleasures of sexually suggestive clothing, she finds the long, loose skirts and baggy shirts that her school demands to be confining, even strangling. "The skirt not only covered her body; it hid who she was. . . . Suddenly she couldn't stand it. Her legs felt too constricted. She felt like they might break into a rash."[24] As Ilana and other girls use the issue of dress to push against the mores of the community, their rabbis and teachers push back, bringing the weight of Jewish tradition to bear on the adolescent girls' experience of their bodies by imposing yet a stricter dress code, marshaling the authority of Judaism, and citing texts that designate the parts of the body that are "off limits."[25] For Ilana, these texts feel like a bodily punishment that reduces her to pure flesh. She feels them as "arrows . . . landed on various parts of her body. She became nothing but an assemblage of forbidden parts: legs, elbows, arms, thighs."[26] For Ilana, the struggle against the norms of female modesty unravel her sense of natural belonging in the modern Orthodox world, moving her to question other aspects of the religious world she inhabits and to experiment with more liberal ideas of Judaism.

Although Tzippy and Ilana meet because Tzippy marries Ilana's brother, their mothers turn out to have been roommates during their college days. Tzippy's mother, Shayna, is a *ba'alat teshuva*, someone raised outside the Orthodox community who took on its strictures of her own accord. In her college years, she felt Orthodox Judaism to be a "secret kingdom" where she required "the password in order to be admitted."[27] Even after many years of living by the mores of the ultra-Orthodox community, marrying and raising children according to its norms, she feels her membership in that community is provisional. Although scrupulous in her observance of Jewish law, she worries that "her neighbors would see through her, to her past . . . would strip off her hat, her long skirt, and her stockings, and expose her as an impostor."[28] One could describe her self-consciousness and hyperattentiveness to such detail as a kind of Jewish drag, performing an identity she fears that others may question. During their college days, Ilana's mother, Naomi, who had been raised in a modern Orthodox household and felt comfortable in Jewish tradition and practice, had helped Shayna to integrate. Naomi's ease and sense of belonging to the Orthodox world remain constant throughout the novel, and her steadiness functions as an anchor to the narrative as the other central characters struggle with their place in Judaism. Yet, Naomi's relationship to Judaism is by no means static. As the dynamics within her extended family become complicated, she seeks to deepen the meaningfulness that Jewish ritual and practice bring to her life and to share that meaningfulness with her family. She participates in a Women's Pre-Passover Healing Circle, an event that draws women from a range of denominations—or no denomination—within Judaism. Using techniques introduced by the Jewish Renewal movement—meditation, breathing, guided visualization, chanting—the Healing Circle reflects a postdenominational Judaism, one that invites shared connections with the sacred and with one another. Connecting with the image of the biblical prophetess Miriam, the Healing Circle helps free up in Naomi a sense of spirituality that at once transcends and has a place in the rituals that define her Jewish life.

The different trajectories of these four female characters offer an expanded sense of the complexity and diversity of religious experience within American Orthodox Judaism. In describing these alternate paths, the novel also raises questions about belonging, identity, and community. The feminism that underlies the novel recognizes the possibility of multiple places for women in Judaism and different ways of living with or resolving the tensions that may arise between religious and secular pulls or between competing desires as a woman.

Unlike the literature by Jewish women that emerged in the 1980s and early 1990s, the new wave of writing takes it as given that women have a voice—as Jews, as women, as Americans. Rather than mount a feminist argument against patriarchal restraints, the novels of this new wave more often plunge in and depict the life of contemporary Jewish women in its full complexity. Instead of arguing against stereotypes of women, Jewish or not, these novels simply break these stereotypes in the characters they forge. The novels establish connections with Jewish women of the past in ways that go beyond simply looking at their lives as oppressed and devoid of opportunity. Instead, contextualizing them against the backdrop of their historical conditions, the novels see in them strengths and complexity.[29]

The Presence of the Past

Several novels of this new wave center on the shtetl. Journeying backward into the European past of Ashkenazic Jewry, these novels explore the Jewish past, with particular attention to the fabric of women's lives. Ranging from lovingly nostalgic to more evaluative and critical, the novels present the eastern European past not as an experience to flee or outgrow but as an important window on where we come from, the place of origin that shapes who we are today. Three novels can serve to briefly illustrate different ways in which Jewish American women's novels of the new wave make use of the shtetl. Rebecca Goldstein's 1995 novel *Mazel* juxtaposes the life of a grandmother raised in a small Polish town with the life of her granddaughter in the suburbs of contemporary New York City. Lilian Nattel's 1999 novel *The River Midnight* explores the friendship of four women in a shtetl a century earlier. Nancy Richler's 2002 novel *Your Mouth Is Lovely* looks at the effect of modernity and the Russian revolution on Jewish women at the turn of the century.

Sorel, the grandmother of Goldstein's *Mazel*, was born Shasha in the fictional shtetl of Shluftchev (in Yiddish, "Sleepy") -on-the-Puddle. Shasha was awakened into what would later be termed feminist consciousness by the tragedy that befell her older sister, Fraydel. Bristling against the restrictive possibilities for Jewish women in traditional communities of eastern Europe that dictated that "girls were all supposed to be pressed out from the same cookie cutter, anything extra trimmed away," Fraydel struggled with a sense of being "different" from other girls. Brilliant and intellectually inclined, Sorel later reflects that, had her sister "been a boy, they would have called her an *illui*, a prodigy."[30] As a girl, however, she did not fit in. Envying their freedom, Fraydel tries unsuccessfully to run away with gypsies. Eventually she commits suicide in face of an unwanted arranged marriage. When the family leaves the shtetl for the more cosmopolitan Warsaw, Sorel embraces secular Jewish culture. The Yiddish theater, in particular, gives expression to the sorrow and anger she feels and helps her deal with sister's life and death. Eventually coming to New York, Sorel passes along her rebelliousness to her daughter, who decides to become a single mother, with no particular attachment or animus toward her Jewish roots. Sorel's granddaughter, Phoebe, a gifted mathematician, chooses a different direction, returning to traditional Judaism. She marries a brilliant and sensitive Jewish young man, and the couple moves to an Orthodox suburb. Sorel sees Phoebe's choices as returning to the benighted, restrictive shtetl life that she left behind—she calls it "Shluftchev with a designer label."[31] Phoebe, by contrast, feels she has left an unrooted life for one saturated with meaning, "the very first place in which Phoebe feels quite entirely at home."[32] Having sensed a vacuum in her life, Phoebe explains to her mother and grandmother that, without knowing precisely what she was seeking, she has found it in Judaism.

In alternately framing the narrative from the viewpoint of each of the three women, the novel complicates our sense of both the Jewish past and the Jewish present. Rather than merely retracing the unidirectional journey from old to new world that occupies much of earlier Jewish American literature, the novel allows Sorel's memories to shatter the dichotomy between old-world tradition and modern secularization. Of Sorel and her cosmopolitan cohorts, the novel notes, "They were worldly men and women, dressed like any other citizens of Europe and informed by Europe's culture, and yet they were unworldly, too. What they took from the world was meshed with that sensibility which was their birthright, which they could no sooner have put off than their own faces."[33] Further, the novel also challenges a facile feminist dismissal of the contemporary Orthodox world as a retreat into parochialism and sexism. Even Sorel acknowledges that, the strictures of Jewish observance notwithstanding, Phoebe and her husband live out their joined lives in "the most perfectly egalitarian terms."[34] Their community has vibrancy, and its inhabitants are as much part of contemporary American culture as they are of Jewish culture. In contrasting the brilliant but doomed Fraydel with her brilliant great-niece Phoebe, who is permitted to satisfy her intellect and choose her life partner, the novel points to a reinvention of Judaism in contemporary America.

Set in the fictional shtetl of Blaszka, Poland, in 1894, Nattel's *The River Midnight* is a novel of magical realism, drawing on the style that characterizes the works of Toni Morrison on the one hand and Isaac Bashevis Singer on the other. From a 20th-century perspective, the novel finds the lives of shtetl women bounded and burdened. "[A] woman doesn't do what she wants, only what she has to," the narrator observes.[35] The novel examines the ways in which these restrictions cause grief to women's lives—restrictions not lost in the distant past but carried into the present, such as the dead-end faced by the *aguna*, the anchored woman whose husband has abandoned her without having presented her with a valid *get*, or religious bill of divorcement. The four central characters of the novel draw strength from their friendship with one another, offering a vision of female solidarity and the existence of a community of women. Nattel's shtetl is a benign place, and the women remain deeply attached to its culture. One woman, for example, decides to become a writer, to write stories in Yiddish, because what she wants to express "can only be said in the mama-loshen" or mother tongue.[36] Ultimately, Nattel's story about the Jewish past is about the Jewish present. It offers an affirmation of the connection of present world—the world of Nattel's readers—and the world of their past. The struggles of contemporary Jewish women are a continuation of those of their female ancestors, and their rootedness in Jewish culture derives from lives lived long ago on the other side of an ocean.

Set around the time of the Russian revolution, Nancy Richler's *Your Mouth Is Lovely* centers on a political assassin—a Jewish woman from a Russian shtetl whose life is swept up in ongoing events. The novel begins in Siberia in 1911, with a letter written by a mother, twenty-seven-year-old Miriam, to the six-year-old daughter, Hayya, she does not know; upon Miriam's arrest, in 1905, the baby was taken by Miriam's stepmother's sister, to be raised in Montreal.

The novel looks backward at Miriam's life, tracing the events that have brought her to the desolate Russian prison. Written in a historically realistic style and faithful to historical detail, the novel explores the effects of turn-of-the-century political and cultural movements on a group of eastern European Jewish women. The narrative captures the rhythms of the Russian seasons and of the Jewish calendar. In tracing the life of a woman who was left motherless in early childhood, the novel introduces a variety of women—religious, secular, educated, superstitious, and political activists. In so doing, it breaks down conventional ideas of what women, and particularly Jewish women, were and are. Poised on the edge of the modernity moving eastward into Russia, the women live lives that reflect changing religious practices and understanding. Some are superstitious and unlettered, others wise and educated. Some hold fast to Jewish practice; others plunge into the world of free-thinkers. Miriam's stepmother, Tsili, for example, rejects the superstitions to which many of the other women in her shtetl subscribe. Intelligent and widely read, she knows Torah as well as medicinal practices. Teaching Miriam to read, she promises her, "Knowledge will be your mother."[37] Tsili, who eventually brings her family to the New World, breaks down the false divide between religious observance and modernization.

Through the lives of women, Richler's novel gives a sense of the diversity of Jewish life under the promise of the century to come. Neither sentimentally nostalgic nor flatly critical, the novel offers a complex view of women grappling with competing visions of religious and political life and with complicated psychological responses to life events, such as pregnancy and the death of children. In many ways, women function as sources of wisdom, knowledge, tradition, and values. The novel captures the excitement and seductiveness that the promise of Russian revolution held out for Jews, yearning for social integration and justice, equality and modernization. Bayla, the step-aunt who will later raise Miriam's daughter, thwarts the community's norms. She cohabits, unmarried, with her revolutionary lover, repudiating the community she came from. She tells Tsili, "I have no parents. I am a child of the revolutionary ideals that birthed me" (p. 258). The baby, Hayya, successfully rescued and brought to Canada, symbolizes the beginning of the author's world. The complex dynamic between past and present is emblemized by the complicated portraits of mother-daughter relations. Daughters in the novel may have more than one mother, or no mother at all. In a sense, the novel points to the women of the novel as our place of origin, to the world of the shtetl as mother world.

In focusing on the place of women in the Jewish past and present, new-wave North American Jewish writers also find a means to explore profound philosophical issues. Their novels look at the displacement inherent in the Jewish immigration to North America, the legacy of the Holocaust, the impact of modernity on Jewish life, the relevance of Jewish spirituality, and questions of identity, community, and belonging. The novels reflect the shifts in contemporary North American society and the development of uniquely American modes of Jewishness. They push readers to expand the ways in which we think about these ideas and engage them in our lives.

NOTES

1. I wish to thank Yedida Eisenstat for her valuable assistance.

2. Annette Kolodny, "Dancing Through the Minefield: Some Observations on the Theory, Practice and Politics of a Feminist Literary Criticism," *Feminist Studies* v. 6, no. 1 (Spring, 1980): 1–25.

3. Ibid., p. 12.

4. Ibid., p. 6.

5. In fact, a cluster of criticism of Kolodny's essay was published in "An Interchange on Feminist Criticism: On 'Dancing Through the Minefield,'" *Feminist Studies*, vol. 8, no. 3 (Autumn, 1982): 629–75, featuring responses by Judith Kegan Gardiner, Elly Bulkin, and Rena Grasso Patterson. According to Bulkin, "Kolodny is simply reinforcing the limited angle of vision that has itself too often been passed along from one white, nonlesbian academic woman critic to another" (p. 636); Patterson sees in the essay "an uncritical acceptance of one's privilege" (p. 663). In her response to her critics, Kolodny correctly notes that these remarks "are directed no so much at my essay per se as at some imagined monolith of established white feminist criticism within academe, of which they take me and my work to be representative" (p. 664).

6. See, for example, Joyce Antler, *Talking Back: Images of Jewish Women in American Popular Culture* (Waltham, MA: Brandeis University Press, 1998); Janet Burstein, *Writing Mothers, Writing Daughters: Tracing the Maternal in Stories by American Jewish Women* (Chicago: University of Illinois Press, 1996) and *Telling the Little Secrets: American Jewish Writing Since the 1980s* (Madison: University of Wisconsin Press, 2006); Sylvia Barack Fishman, *Follow My Footprints: Changing Images of Women in American Jewish Fiction* (Waltham, MA: Brandeis University Press, 1992); Lois E. Rubin, *Connections and Collisions: Identities In Contemporary Jewish-American Women's Writing* (Newark: University of Delaware Press, 2005); Ellen Serlen Uffen, *Strands of the Cable: The Place of the Past in Jewish American Women's Writing* (New York: Peter Lang, 1993); as well as the essays collected in Ann Shapiro et. al., eds., *Jewish American Women Writers: A Bio-Bibliographical and Critical Sourcebook* (Boston: Greenwood Press, 1994); Jay L. Halio and Ben Siegel, eds., *Daughters of Valor: Contemporary Jewish American Women Writers* (Newark: University of Delaware Press, 1996); Daniel Walden, ed., *Jewish Women Writers and Women in Jewish Literature* (Studies in American Jewish Literature no. 3; Albany: State University of New York Press, 1984); and the section on literature in T. M. Rudavsky, ed., *Gender and Judaism: The Transformation of Tradition* (New York: New York University Press, 1995).

7. See, for example, Evelyn Torton Beck, *Between Invisibility and Overvisibility: The Politics of Anti-Semitism in the Women's Movement and Beyond* (Madison: University of Wisconsin Working Paper Series—Women's Studies Research Center, 1984), and "Judaism, Feminism and Psychology: Making the Links

Visible," in *Jewish Women Speak Out: Expanding the Boundaries of Psychology*, ed. Kayla Wiener and Arinna Moon (Seattle: Canopy Press, 1995).

8. See, for example, Sylvia Barack Fishman, "American Jewish Fiction Turns Inward," *American Jewish Yearbook* 91 (1991), and Sara R. Horowitz, "Portnoy's Sister—Who's Complaining? Contemporary Jewish American Women's Writing on Judaism," in *Jewish Book Annual*, vol. 51, ed. Jacob Kabakoff (1993–94), pp. 26-41.

9. Hazel Carby, "It Jus Be's Dat Way Sometime: The Sexual Politics of Women's Blues," in *Gender and Discourse*, ed. Alexandra D. Todd and Sue Fisher (Norwood, NJ: Ablex, 1988).

10. Some examples of influential critics are Nina Auerbach, Susan Gubar, Carolyn Heilbrun, Nancy K. Miller, Elaine Schowalter, and Eve Sedgwick.

11. Gloria Anzaldúa, *Making Face, Making Soul = Haciendo Caras: Creative and Critical Perspectives by Feminists of Color* (San Francisco: Aunt Lute Books, 1990), p. xx.

12. Some examples are Evelyn Avery, Sarah Blacher Cohen, Carole Kessner, S. Lillian Kremer, Ellen Schiff, and Ann Shapiro.

13. See, for example, Patricia Hill Collins, *Black Feminist Thought: Knowledge, Consciousness, and the Politics of Empowerment* (New York: Routledge,1990); Donna Haraway, "Situated Knowledges: The Science Question in Feminism and the Privilege of Partial Perspective," *Feminist Studies* 14 (Fall 1988): 575–99; and Sandra Harding, *Whose Science? Whose Knowledge? Thinking From Women's Lives* (Ithaca: Cornell University Press, 1991).

14. See, for example, Elly Bulkin's remarks in Judith Kegan Gardiner, Elly Bulkin, Rena Grasso Patterson, and Annette Kolodny, "An Interchange on Feminist Criticism: On Dancing Through the Minefield," *Feminist Studies* 8:3 (Autumn 1982): 629–75.

15. Particularly important to the development of queer theory has been the theoretical underpinning provided by Jacques Derrida and Michel Foucault, especially the latter's *The History of Sexuality: The Will to Knowledge* (London: Penguin, 1976).

16. Literary theorists particularly influential to the development of queer theory include Judith Butler, *Gender Trouble, Feminism and the Subversion of Identity* (New York: Routledge, 1990); Eve Kosofsky Sedgwick, *Tendencies* (Durham, NC: Duke University Press, 1993); and Teresa de Lauretis, *The Practice of Love: Lesbian Sexuality and Perverse Desire* (Bloomington: Indiana University Press, 1994).

17. Works that bring queer theory to bear on Jewish studies include Daniel Boyarin, Daniel Itzkovitz, and Ann Pellegrini, *Queer Theory and the Jewish Question* (New York: Columbia University Press, 2004); Lori Lefkovitz, "Passing as a Man: Narratives of Jewish Gender Performance," in *Narrative* 10 (January 2002): 91–103; and some of the essays in Miriam Peskowitz and Laura Levitt,

eds., *Judaism Since Gender* (New York: Routledge, 1997). Also significant in complicating ideas of Jews and gender is Harry Brod's work on Jewish masculinity, "Of Mice and Supermen: Images of Jewish Masculinity," in T. M. Rudavsky, ed., *Gender and Judaism*, pp. 279–93. For examples of the ways in which the tools of queer theory elucidate readings of Jewish American literature, see my "Mediating Judaism: Mind, Body, Spirit, and Contemporary North American Jewish Fiction," *AJS Review* 30 (2006): 231–53, and Wendy Zierler, "A Dignitary in the Land? Literary Representation of the American Rabbi," *AJS Review* 30 (2006): 255–76.

18. Nessa Rapoport, "The Woman Who Lost Her Names," in Julia Mazow, ed., *The Woman Who Lost Her Names: Selected Writings by American Jewish Women* (New York: Harper and Row, 1980), p. 235.

19. N. Rapoport, "The Woman Who Lost Her Names," p. 236.

20. Anne Roiphe, *Lovingkindness* (New York: Summit, 1987), p. 48.

21. E. M. Broner, *A Weave of Women* (Bloomington: Indiana University Press, 1985), p. 23.

22. For treatment of new-wave Jewish American women's writing, see Janet Burstein, "Recalling Home: American Jewish Women Writers of the New Wave," *Contemporary Literature* 42:4 (Winter 2001): 800–24; S. R. Horowitz, "Mediating Judaism: Mind, Body, Spirit, and Contemporary North American Jewish Fiction"; and W. Zierler, "A Dignitary in the Land? Literary Representation of the American Rabbi."

23. Tova Mirvis, *The Outside World* (New York: Knopf, 2004), p. 26.

24. Ibid., pp. 194–95.

25. Ibid., p. 198.

26. Ibid., p. 198.

27. Ibid., p. 90.

28. Ibid., p. 16.

29. Other Jewish American women novelists to engage these issues include Pearl Abraham, Allegra Goodman, Dara Horn, and Cynthia Ozick.

30. Rebecca Goldstein, *Mazel* (New York: Viking, 1995), p. 127.

31. Ibid., p. 333.

32. Ibid., p. 8.

33. Ibid., p. 309.

34. Ibid., p. 36.

35. Lilian Nattel, *The River Midnight* (Toronto: Knopf Canada, 1999), p. 26.

36. Ibid., p. 100.

37. Nancy Richler, *Your Mouth Is Lovely* (Toronto: Harper Collins Canada, 2002), p. 38.

‖‖‖

Text, Nation, and Gender in Israeli Women's Fiction

Nehama Aschkenasy

As a group producing imaginative narratives in the Hebrew language, Israeli women have had to contend with two overarching cultures: the patriarchy-based writings authored by Jewish males throughout history and the macho-intoned, hero-worshipping Israeli national tradition. Although neither one of these speaks in a uniform voice, they share the premise of masculine supremacy. Women writers have engaged in an uneasy love-hate dialogue with both.

In Jewish tradition, men have been the interpreters of the holy writ and its law, much of which pertains to female existence and conduct. Zionist thought no longer measured male supremacy by mastery of the text and its interpretation; instead, it ushered in a new Jewish era that judged men as builders and fighters for the (mother)land and defenders of its women and children. In an ironic development, Zionist writers, trying to reinforce the connection between masculinity and nation building, tended to characterize the traditional male as effeminate and passive. Thus, the European Jewish man, who in the past had held a superior status in his own culture and family, was seen as being in dire need of reform and of a different gender self-image.[1]

The older image was the product of the faith-bound community, whereas the newer was imbued with progressive ideas that originated in the Enlightenment and, in its Labor-Zionist manifestation, was markedly egalitarian. Yet, they both muffled the feminine voice, even while assigning a mythic role to the feminine principle. In traditional Jewish writings, the feminine appears as either the manifestation of cosmic powers, often expressed as forces within man, or the embodiment of the entire people.

In Zionist literature, the feminine is the newly emerging nation that needs to be defended and protected by the male hero.

The suppression of the female voice during the years of rabbinic creativity is easily understandable as the result of a strong patriarchy, an age-old view of the work of the mind as a male occupation, and a perception of the authorship of texts as the male domain, attitudes that have been prevalent throughout Western culture. The discouragement and marginalization of female creativity in the era of Zionist nation building may have been less plausible but were equally real. Despite the avowed egalitarianism of Labor Zionism, which was the most influential social ideology through the first three decades of Israel's existence, women were not perceived as equal partners in either the collective enterprise of rebuilding the motherland or the effort to create a new literary expression to buttress the national spirit. Instead, Labor Zionism, which openly rejected the traditional mold of Judaism and the Jewish family, recognized two urgent needs: (1) to offset the image of the cowering shtetl Jew with a new paradigm of a tough Jewish man, able to defend his country and family, and (2) to indoctrinate generations of young people with ideals of heroism, militarism, and a masculinist ethos. But the traditional status of woman as the mythic representation of the land continued in Zionist discourse and imaginative reflections. As such, she received male protection, passively kept domestic fires, and was worth dying for. Yet, women were also seen as an obstacle to the military effort needed to redeem the land. For instance, the literature of the generation of the Palmach, the acclaimed prestatehood combat elite unit, saw women as concerned with *petit bourgeois* values that distracted noble-minded heroes from their commitment to fight for the collective good.[2]

In the context of the pressing needs of nation building, both male and female Hebrew writers encountered the problem of the need to immerse the individual voice in the collective "we." But that especially complicated the dilemma of women writers, who were struggling to emerge from both a long tradition that silenced female voices and the ideological and political reality, which demanded the surrender of individual creativity to the national effort and collective destiny. Just as women pioneers could not claim parity on the basis of military dexterity, women writers found nationalist Zionism's militant-masculinist symbolism inhospitable to their creative aspirations.[3]

Thus, women's marginal role in both Jewish literary tradition and the overwhelming Zionist national narrative created an emotional disincentive for women writers in the first several decades of Hebrew nationalist literature. As a result, they contributed mostly lyrical, personal poetry that was more amenable to the smaller canvas of personal feelings. The prose works of female writers who were born before the establishment of the state and started to publish in the 1950s, such as Amalia Kahana-Carmon (b. 1926), Yehudit Hendel (b. 1926), Shulamit Hareven (b. 1931), Rachel Eytan (b. 1931), Shulamit Lapid (b. 1934), and Ruth Almog (b. 1936), reflect the conflict between their inclination to portray intimate relationships and an environment steeped in the cult of physical heroism. These writers often betray self-doubts about their artistic orientation at a time when the nation was in the throes of momentous events. As a result of this low self-image, they tend to present women as victims, prone to mental disintegration and depression, and often retreating to the sphere of the subconscious, even madness.

Amalia Kahana-Carmon created female characters of shaky mental condition who are in constant need of male approval. Her prose works, such as the stories in *Under One Roof*[4] and the novels *And the Moon in the Valley of Ayalon*,[5] *Magnetic Fields*,[6] and *Up in Montifer*,[7] are lyrical in tone, presenting heroines who possess romantic souls and crave ideal love relationships but whose search for pure, perfect love often ends in disillusionment and despair. As has long been noted, her works resemble Virginia Woolf's novels *Mrs. Dalloway* and *To the Lighthouse*, which also revolve around women protagonists.[8] In fact, her novels share many elements with those modern works that Leon Edel has called "subjective" or "psychological" novels.[9] However, Kahana-Carmon sees the acute awareness and the flow of consciousness that takes over the linear progression of events as characteristic mainly of woman's experience.

The protagonist of *And the Moon in the Valley of Ayalon*, Noa Talmor, lives in an idealistic past, a reality that perhaps has always existed only in her imagination. Her husband, Asher, is securely anchored in the here and now; he is a successful businessman, who constantly looks for new projects and advantageous connections. By contrast, when Noa's eyes are turned outward, it is only to see in other characters new illuminations, or alter egos, of her inner being. When episodes and scenes from the past intrude into the present, they are not conveyed as "flashbacks" but become the present moment of the narrative. In one such instance, we see the two young students, Noa and Asher, falling in love with each other in prestatehood Jerusalem. Asher, we gradually understand, is responsible for placing explosives in an Arab market as part of the Jewish Underground.

If the youthful Asher is shrouded with a heroic, mysterious, and romantic halo, which seems to envelop Noa's complete existence at the time, the adult Asher, like his countrymen and the state of Israel itself, is no longer a dashing idealist but a pragmatist whose life focuses on material success. Yet, Noa seems frozen in the romantic past, slowly receding from participation in everyday life.

The disruption of chronology—the novel is a series of moments and glimpses that never become a coherent whole—comes to be emblematic of the feminine being. The elliptical style, with its suggested yet unsaid words, and the language that simultaneously records real events and inner images, exterior landscapes, and inner impressions, enhance the image of the woman as possessing an acute intuition and as the keeper of the absolute truth that is constantly being compromised and trampled upon by modern life. The shifting narrative voice mirrors the sense of the relativity of existence and its lack of harmony and coherence. It also reflects the protagonist's fragmented psyche and heightened consciousness, as well as her inner rifts, which she fails to reconcile. The novel's lexicon, replete with archaic words and grammatical structures, reveals the narrator's painful sense of the loss of glorious times.

Kahana-Carmon's protagonist is filled with anguish at the diminished reality that surrounds her and encroaches on her almost mystical, private sphere. In her rebellion against the "male" world, the narrator defeats the reader's expectations of a coherent, logical sequence of events or of syntactically complete sentences, which she associates with the masculine perception of reality. For Kahana-Carmon, the most appropriate method of conveying the feminine experience of the world is with the use of an elliptical technique of incomplete sentences as well as simultaneity, which situates the narrative in different landscapes and different times all at once.

Kahana-Carmon's works also give voice to the female writer's other dilemma, mentioned earlier, that of women's painful interaction with the masculine Jewish tradition. Through Noa and her other female protagonists, she explores the paradox of the love-hate relationship between her sensitive (and often learned) protagonists and the Jewish literary heritage, which they admire despite its history of suppressing woman's voice. Noa integrates many quotes from the Bible and other ancient documents into her language, often in an ironic manner that reverses their original meanings. She has a long memory that is steeped in the rich tradition of Judaic letters but regrets the incongruity between the ancient sources and modern reality. That leads to an intense sense of existential estrangement. Paradoxically, the language of tradition becomes a solace to the female protagonist; her ability to manipulate and relish it turns into another form of escape.

Kahana-Carmon's protagonists often retreat from the coherent grammar of everyday communication into new linguistic creations. They enjoy the subjective magic that Hebrew words hold for them. This is true of Osnat, another prototypical Kahana-Carmon protagonist, in the short story "Impoverishment."[10] Osnat draws on the age-old male tradition that associates cities with women as she recounts an unhappy meeting with a former lover on a rainy day in Tel Aviv. The spirit of the Book of Lamentations permeates the narrative and enhances the woman's mourning over the treacherous man, whom she still loves. Lamentations likens the city of Jerusalem, abandoned by God and ransacked by the enemy, to a widow. Osnat sees a projection of her own faded youth and lost vitality in the dreary and shabby scenes of Tel Aviv. Although Tel Aviv is relatively new, with a name that implies spring and renewal, Osnat's eyes soak in only bleak, depressing sights of a city in decline; these mirror her own state of mind and her present self-image.

Osnat finds solace in her current occupation, preparing indexes for scholarly books. The last part of the story abandons sentence and syntax, offering instead a long list of ancient titles. Although the list carries no meaning to the reader or the protagonist, the archaic titles' almost mystical flavor, the old cities where they were published, and the long-gone scholars who wrote them become sources of comfort. The titles and places retain the glory of bygone years, tying the heroine to the long, noble tradition of Hebrew learning. Osnat forgets the present moment as she immerses herself in the charm of the ancient words and savors their esoteric sounds. The city and its everyday reality now recede to the background as a "masculine" sphere, where people compete and are engaged in power struggles. Ironically, the old titles, which testify to male scholarship, become the new reality for the heroine, who now feels revitalized and purified.

Another modern female protagonist, Aviva in Rachel Eytan's *Pleasures of Man*,[11] also sails away from the modern city and its noisy, oppressive, male-dominated ambience. Eytan's novel does not resort to innovative styles and techniques in order to reveal the feminine predicament, but her protagonist, like Kahana-Carmon's, tends to juxtapose male and female modes of relating to the world and experiences deep estrangement. The novel satirically portrays the life of the glittering circles of Tel Aviv society, where Aviva is victimized by her successful but ruthless and unscrupulous husband. Eytan's landscapes are mainly exterior; where Kahana-Carmon's Noa escapes to archaic language and lets scenes from the past take over, Aviva runs away to France with her French lover but then returns home. After her escape to another geographical landscape proves futile, Aviva flees to a different mode of reality: she conveys her feminine frailty with concepts from Jewish mystical literature. Like the Shechinah, the female element of the deity according to the Zohar, Aviva sees herself as needing light from the masculine domain. She views herself as an empty vessel that derives fullness and substance from the masculine sphere. At the end of the novel, Aviva feels victimized and defeated; she attempts to write a play but senses that she is traveling away from reality, taking a trip into herself, into "a dark hole."

Kahana-Carmon's and Eytan's protagonists turn to their inner selves, leaving husbands and sanity behind. Their departures express their wish for self-annihilation. The males in their stories enfold the sum total of the world's imperfections and its attempts to defeat these sensitive, frail, and idealistic women. Although some of Kahana-Carmon's male protagonists are as introspective and oppressed by life as their female counterparts, most of her works are told from the woman's point of view and identify the male world as oppressive. In Kahana-Carmon's and Eytan's novels, the ills of the modern city and life are inextricably tied to man's flawed, callous nature.

By contrast, the female protagonist in Shulamit Hareven's first novel, *City of Many Days* (1972),[12] displays a stronger personality and a well-defined feminist sensibility. This novel, which was largely ignored in Israel when it first came out, is a *bildungsroman* of sorts, tracing an independent woman's coming of age. Hareven depicts the Jerusalem of the British mandate in a richly detailed, colorful way and presents a broad and intricate panorama of British as well as Sephardi and European Jewish characters. She was ahead of her times in critiquing the Zionist ideology and, in many ways, spearheaded the trend of strong female characters who voiced "feminist" opinions. These two features were undoubtedly the reason why Hareven's works did not initially receive the attention they deserved.

Ruth Almog's *Roots of Air*,[13] which returns to the theme of female mental breakdown, has been read as a rewriting of Charlotte Bronte's *Jane Eyre*.[14] As such, it belongs to the modern literary corpus that has given a feminist twist to this 19th-century novel, recovering and focusing on the demented first Mrs. Rochester. Mira, Almog's protagonist, lives under the threat of what she sees as a genetically determined journey into madness that originated in a male ancestor. Her struggle to free herself from her fate expands into political activism, mainly in Europe. While Almog examines her own artistic ego in this novel, the story collection *Artistic Mending*[15] focuses on children, mainly second-generation Holocaust survivors, who seek ways to understand and "mend" the damaging effects of growing up with parents haunted by horrific memories. The image of mending becomes a central feminist metaphor in women's writings, going beyond the context of the Holocaust. In *The Inner Lake*,[16] Almog is at her most innovative and daring, abandoning the linear story line and defying the concept of the traditional "plot."

Shulamit Lapid's nostalgic novel *Gei Oni* (Valley of My Suffering)[17] embodies a different feminine vision. In narrating the story of the Galilean settlement Rosh Pinah, she reconstructs an epic chapter in Zionist history, inserting the female voice and presence into a story that is imprinted in the national memory with heroic masculinity. The novel enjoyed wide popularity in the country, responding, it appears, to pent-up longings in the Israeli reading public for a romantic, idealistic past.

The dramatic change in Israeli mood that occurred around the third decade of the state's history led to a revision in Zionist poetics, which had earlier relegated literary art to boosting patriotism.[18] The series of military conflicts, the constant state of siege, and the onset of materialism and corruption in the country eroded the Zionist vision of an ideal society and created a spirit of disillusionment among Israelis. Both male and female writers sought a more private vision that was less committed to the collective voice of ardent nationalism. Some of the women writers who had encountered an inhospitable environment in the early years of the state became bolder as their careers developed, gaining success both critically and among the general reading public. Ruth Almog achieved mainstream status within contemporary Hebrew letters. Amalia Kahana-Carmon carved out a central position as a feminist writer and innovative stylist, receiving the 1985 Brenner Prize for *belles lettres*; Gershon Shaked considered her the heir to S. Yizhar, the stylistically innovative, prominent writer of the generation of the War of Independence.[19] Shulamit Lapid, though less original as a craftswoman, won great popularity for her widely read historical novel, and Shulamit Hareven published numerous books of poetry, fiction, and essays, despite the critical community's dismissal of her first novel. After gaining increasingly in popularity and respect, she published an autobiography in 2002.[20]

Yehudit Hendel also received major literary awards, and her works have been adapted for the stage and the screen. Hendel's career, as well as her "rediscovery" and "reinstatement" by the critical community, is especially telling. She broke into the literary scene with her collection of short stories *They Are Different People*[21] and her first major novel, *The Street of Steps*.[22] Yet, despite her popularity, she remained a marginal literary figure for decades. The main reason for this was undoubtedly her being a pioneer in foregrounding the mental disability of Holocaust survivors and the poverty and underprivileged status of the Sephardi community in Israel that would only later come to the fore. While she had published continuously since the 1950s, she was not considered "mainstream" until the 1990s, when new editions of her older works were reprinted and met with renewed success and admiration from her reading public. In 2003, she won the Israel Prize for literature.

Ideological and political themes eclipsed gender concerns in the culture at large as well as within the literary criticism of the first decades of statehood. But Israeli culture was changing, and attitudes toward the Zionist ideology transformed into critique and even disillusionment. In that environment, gender issues, along with other social concerns, came to the fore of Israeli public discussion as well as in fiction.

Over the past three decades or so, women's issues have become a central social concern, and the literary/critical establishment has opened its doors to women writers. As a result, women have felt freer to express themselves in fiction and to introduce the feminine dimension into the national culture without the earlier generations' sense of inferiority or estrangement. Several cultural trends have contributed to this development. Both male and female writers have turned away from the Zionist master story, experimenting with themes and techniques that reflect personal choices and inclinations rather than a national consensus. Openness to Western literary and cultural trends, especially the modern women's movement, also helped legitimize gender issues as well as women's writing and stylistic preferences. Israeli receptiveness to the postmodern spirit, which rejects any master narrative and prefers minorities of all sorts, also emboldened female writers to claim a central position for their own visions.[23]

More recently, in the past twenty years or so, women writers such as Savyon Liebrecht (b. 1948), Michal Govrin (b. 1950), Nava Semel (b. 1954), Zeruya Shalev (b. 1959), Ronit Matalan (b. 1959), Orly Castel-Bloom (b. 1960), and Yehudit Katzir (b. 1963) have been recognized by the country's literary/critical establishment as the very core of current Israeli literature.

These writers are no longer seen as trespassers; if they still seem to produce "counternarratives," it is because they identify with the postmodern preference for "minority" narratives.

These women were born after the establishment of the state, some to Holocaust survivors, and they came of age as writers within the liberating environment of postmodernism and post-Zionism.[24] They were also empowered by the country's women's movement and the legitimizing presence of academic research into theories of gender and women's lives. Most of them seem to be free of the psychological and social issues that plagued the older generation. Their sense of autonomy as writers comes through even as they record their feminist grievances. They do not record dramatic changes in the social environment or cultural attitudes in Israel so much as write boldly and more openly about the female existence. They do not fear placing gender issues and feminine consciousness at the nerve center of their works, from which they view and assess the entire culture.

The most intriguing and iconoclastic among these women writers is Orly Castel-Bloom, whose dark style envisions contemporary life in the image of depleted selves, grotesque actions, and broken-down social and familial structures. Gershon Shaked heralded her acceptance as a central literary voice in Israel, proclaiming her style as a new Israeli literary experience.[25]

I here give special attention to the writings of Savyon Liebrecht, Zeruya Shalev, and Michal Govrin. These writers share several traits, despite their differences in style and literary sensibility. They seem closely and unapologetically attuned to their inner feminine selves, while simultaneously allowing their protagonists (mainly in the works of Liebrecht and Govrin) to be free agents, commenting on issues at the heart of the country's public debate. Their protagonists also share the need to "mend" the female psyche while repairing deficiencies, cracks, and ruptures in the life of Israeli society at large. Another element predominant in the work of these three writers (most radically in that of Shalev and Govrin) is women's deliberate attempt to "break borders," to use a phrase from Govrin's *Snapshots*.[26] Giving unabashed centrality to women's voice, these writers view the condition of the contemporary female protagonist as that of breaking the boundaries of sexual taboos, ethnic considerations, and national creed, actions hitherto identified with the male exploration of life and art.

The works of these writers also touch upon several issues that are at the heart of gender inquiry today, such as the roots of women's sympathy with minorities, the question of whether women are propelled by a sense of justice or by an innate drive for caring and nurturing,[27] and the gendered nature of the politics of military confrontation.[28] At the same time, contemporary Hebrew female writers have opened a bold dialogue with male-authored texts, both old and new, that is entwined with issues that are particularly Israeli and specifically feminine.

Savyon Liebrecht's prose is written in a realistic vein, offering an open-eyed, direct, and sober look at central problems that plague contemporary Israeli society. These include the debate over the treatment of Palestinians, the psychological issues of children of Holocaust survivors, the supremacy given to men and the male point of view, and the cult of machismo that still suffuses the Israeli public. Her writings braid social realism, feminist sensibility, and major public issues in present-day Israel together with the private, feminine point of view. She centers on the psychology of modern, educated women who allow themselves to be dominated by their accomplished husbands, on the everyday economic and emotional plight of Palestinian laborers, and on Holocaust survivors' estrangement from their environment and the younger generation's reluctance to share in their memories. These issues appear to be natural domains for an Israeli and a woman writer. Liebrecht's works voice various forms of social protest, but the discomfort and self-doubts transmitted by earlier women writers about trespassing into the male domain or about the very legitimacy of female creativity are no longer heard in her works. Indeed, her short-story collection *Apples From the Desert* (1986)[29] offers a panorama of the multiple aches in contemporary Israel.

Liebrecht's story "A Room on the Roof" from that collection is in some ways a response to and revision of "Nomad and Viper" (1963) by Amos Oz,[30] a writer separated from her by less than a decade in age but who has achieved a canonical stature in the history of Israeli writing. Both stories exhibit the inextricable link between gender politics and geopolitics; in both, a young, progressive Israeli woman encounters the ethnic other and comes to realize unspoken truths about her culture and her own life. The stories take place in different times in Israel's history and in very different social and political environments. Oz's story is set in the kibbutz of the early 1960s, while Liebrecht's is an urban tale, set more than two decades later. A comparative reading of these two stories highlights the intricate web of the geopolitical conflict between Israelis and Palestinians and how it connects with gender relations in Israeli society. It reveals that these two sets of conflicts mirror each other and that the regional strife, with its ethnic biases, mutual hostility, and state of constant anxiety, parallels

Israeli society's sociosexual dynamic. Oz centers on the geopolitical re-percussions of Israel's moral dilemma, while Liebrecht raises the issue of inequality, even in thoroughly "modern" marriages. She puts the female protagonist at the center; for Oz, the woman's otherness highlights the Ar-ab's otherness. His tale further converts the moral dilemma of the kibbutz and, by extension, of modern Israel into an existential encounter with in-ternal demons and subterranean, dark, irrational forces in the psyche of the woman protagonist, Ge'ula, as well as in the minds of her compatriots. Liebrecht's tale, less powerful and less inclined to probe the subconscious, is effective as a feminist protest. Its young protagonist becomes poignantly aware of her inferior marital position through her dealings with a Pales-tinian construction worker, whom she first suspects and denigrates but later comes to appreciate.

Some of Liebrecht's other works are less focused on social issues in contemporary Israel than on the individual woman's sphere of emotional and spiritual uncertainty and conflict. Her novel *A Man, a Woman, and a Man* (1998)[31] appears at first glance, and well into its narrative, to be a psychological novel written from the perspective of its female protago-nist. Hamutal is in the throes of marital crisis, compounded by the near-ing death of her decrepit mother as well as the sudden realization that she lacks the self-knowledge and the strong inner core to be able to deal satisfactorily with her husband, her daughters, or her mother. The need for "mending" at all levels appears early yet only indirectly; it applies to a new psychiatric technique in which dreamers are required to mend their nightmares by constructing alternate endings to these disturbing dreams while fully awake. Hamutal, a professional editor, is working on a collec-tion of these narrated dreams and their "repairs." Very soon, it becomes clear that she herself is in the midst of a bad dream that she can mend only if she is willing to probe territories that she was determined to never visit.

Hamutal's journey to repair her life takes the form of a decision to have an affair with another person who is also waiting for the death of a parent in the same hospital, a man who had left the country and made a life for himself in Chicago. She assesses this affair as a voluntary and clear deci-sion to assert her own personal freedom by breaking conventional bound-aries. In so doing, she seems blind to her husband's and daughters' well-meaning attempts to connect with her and unable to understand that the affair will not lead to a lasting commitment. Hamutal's greatest ignorance lies in what unfolds as the true core of the novel: her mother's Holocaust experience and the way it shaped her style of mothering Hamutal. Like the protagonists in many of Liebrecht's earlier stories, Hamutal reveals herself as a person who chose, in both her childhood and her adulthood, to ignore her mother's Holocaust experience and to turn a deaf ear to the stories of horrors in her immediate environment.

Liebrecht's own story as a child of Holocaust survivors underlies many of the tales she spins. She knows that the inclination to suppress or reject knowledge of the immediate past is not the only route taken by Hamutal's contemporaries. For instance, Tzipi, Hamutal's cousin with whom she grew up, opts for being open to the stories of her parents and other family members. Hamutal's strategy for emotional survival, however, is to suppress this nightmare, an attitude that reappears in her dealings with other crises in her life. This cold aloofness is the underlying cause of her husband's and daughters' later resentment and gradual estrangement from her.

Once her dying mother's Holocaust experience comes to the fore in a shocking way, forcing itself on the reluctant Hamutal, other elements and puzzles in her current situation begin to clarify. As much as Hamutal tried to concentrate on her own inner life and the close circle of family and work, she has realized time and again that public life in Israel is unavoidable, forcing its imprint on the narrow parameters of individuals' lives. Her second daughter, Hilah, was conceived when her husband returned home for a short furlough during the Lebanon war, and each of them, independently, decided to create a new life. As Liebrecht has shown in her other stories, geopolitical events and personal decisions always collide and often merge in the realities of life in Israel.

The critical factor in Hamutal's life and the inner workings of her psyche has always been her mother's cold, strict, and demanding style of childrearing. Hamutal repeats this style involuntarily with her own daughters. In a moment of rare lucidity, shortly before her death, Hamutal's mother explains her seemingly harsh treatment of her daughter in childhood as her way of making her daughter ready for brutal reality. On her deathbed, Hamutal's mother explains that she learned in the Holocaust that only the tough people survive.

Liebrecht views Hamutal's awakening to the true reality of her life as a compromise, yet it is the only sane and healing option available. The decidedly nontragic, noncatastrophic ending sets Liebrecht's writing apart from that of some of her contemporaries. For instance, with the help of a simple practical nurse, Hamutal comes to understand that her husband's style of finding the humorous in dark situations is the necessary and potentially healing antidote to her own darkness of spirit. In a conversation with her lover, Hamutal explains that she felt that her brooding parents imposed the role of comforter and healer on her. In a way, she gives voice to a generational grievance: Holocaust survivors created new lives to cure their own existential despair without understanding the immense burden this put on their Israeli-born children.

Several contemporary works add another image to that of the woman who is called upon to "mend": that of the woman as architect. A woman architect is at the heart of Liebrecht's novella "Hiroshima" as well as Michal Govrin's *Snapshots* (1998). Interestingly, one of the most prominent feminist scholars of our time, Carol Gilligan, whose academic work probes the issue of women's moral decisions, has also chosen a female architect as the protagonist of her recent novel, *Kyra*.[32]

Liebrecht's short story "Hiroshima" is part of a collection titled *A Good Place for the Night* (2002),[33] which takes on a darker hue than her other works. The stories are linked by the centrality of place. Their protagonists escape from one place to another that seems safer, with mostly destructive results. The female architect in "Hiroshima," Idit, escapes from Israel to Hiroshima. Carrying the emotional burden of a childhood with a father who was a Holocaust survivor, she finds herself in a deadlocked relationship with her boyfriend. As an architect, she feels the need to design new structures, change old ones, or rebuild those shattered by human activity. Her father's conduct, imprinted by his Holocaust experience, merges with that of an old Japanese woman who had witnessed the bombing of Hiroshima. The Jewish Holocaust and the Japanese calamity become one and the same in Idit's mind; she has chosen to spend nine years in Hiroshima instead of visiting her father's childhood town.

Idit is one of several postmodern protagonists in current Hebrew female writings who submit to the attraction of the other (in this case, Hiroshima, Japanese culture, and a Christian man) in order to break the geographic and mental boundaries that limit them. Yet, at the end, Idit realizes that she cannot repair and rebuild alone, nor can she solve all the human problems she encounters. The story, in fact, ends in a somewhat traditionally romantic vein: after a traumatic event in Hiroshima, Idit is ready to return to her old boyfriend and repair her own private life in her natural habitat, Israel.

The story "Kibbutz" in this collection is both an indictment of kibbutz culture and an exploration of women's sense of justice. A retarded young couple, who had chosen the kibbutz as a place that would treat them fairly, have been killed after a joke played on them went horribly wrong. The woman protagonist in this story, wife of one of the tricksters, chooses for many years to ignore the truth about the accident and, instead, to raise the couple's child as her own. Despite having been an antiwar activist who fought against social and political wrongs, her sense of justice takes a backseat to the drive to protect and nurture the orphaned child, just as Gilligan suggests about women in general. Only at the end of the tale does she allow herself, very slowly and painfully, to face the injustice that caused the young couple's tragic death. In this collection, as in her other stories, Liebrecht attributes to women a deeper sensitivity to injustice of any kind, including the oppression of minorities and the resort to violence as a way of solving problems. Woman is often the moral compass, the mirror that reflects these forms of injustice most sharply; yet she is also inadequate when it comes to solving injustice and often resorts to the maternal role where she can be more effective.

If Liebrecht's plotlines and psychological underpinnings merge the private and the public, Zeruya Shalev's two novels _Love Life_ (1997)[34] and _Husband and Wife_ (2000)[35] engage in a textual dialogue with some of the major works of the Hebrew canon. I read _Love Life_ as a postmodern, pornographic, subversive rewriting of Agnon's "In the Prime of Her Life" (1923).[36] Both describe young women who pursue their mothers' lost love. However, the daring nature of Shalev's narrative can be understood as a grotesque, scatological rewriting of Agnon's sexually tame style. The tone underlying the narrative can be gloomy and nightmarish; however, some of the scenes, especially those where the female protagonist Ya'ara is kept hostage, naked, in her lover's bedroom, take on the form of slapstick, mocking Agnon's more delicate sexual innuendoes in a dark way.

While Shalev is engaged in a kind of dialogue with Agnon, her fictional protagonist Ya'ara is conversing with an ancient canonical Jewish text, the bodies of midrashim revolving around the destruction of the First Temple (_midreshei akeda_). Ya'ara exists within a textual web provided by Agnon's modern masterpiece and the older midrash. Paradoxically, there is no sense of physical reality in Ya'ara's experiences, even though the sexual act is depicted in minute detail, often as if in slow motion, with graphic depictions of the male and female anatomies. The body seems to reign supreme, but Ya'ara exists in a dreamlike, hallucinatory haze; even her most graphically recounted sexual encounters take on an aura of unreality. In fact, Ya'ara lives within the text and deals with life around her through the prism of text.

Where Liebrecht's stories mesh the shared life of the Israeli public with the inner life of the female observer/narrator/protagonist, Zeruya Shalev sifts and filters the rhythm of life, with people coming and going and individuals possessing distinct personalities, as through a fog, totally subjugated to the internal, impressionistic prism of her female protagonist. Ya'ara is also in need of mending, because she is filled with a sense of destruction and senses that life around her is slowly dismantling and breaking apart. She is mentally steeped in the ancient tales of the Temple's destruction, while, like Agnon's protagonist, Tirtsa, she is, in her waking hours, on a mission to reconstruct another ruined temple, that of her mother's first love.

Love Life has been interpreted as a feminine rewriting of Bruno Bettelheim's readings of the children's stories "Sleeping Beauty" and "Snow White."[37] Yet, Shalev's active dialogue with Judaic texts is undeniable. The name Ya'ara recalls the Hebrew idiom *ya'arat devash* ("honeycomb," 1 Sam 14:27). Her older sex partner is Arye (lion). Together, their names evoke the biblical image of Samson, who tore the lion and then found honey in its carcass. That became the basis for the riddle that Samson posed to his wedding guests, honey and contest around riddles being age-old sexual images. Arye is sexually voracious and, it seems, very skillful; yet, like Samson, he will remain childless, having been rendered infertile by a combat injury.

Shalev's daring, quasi-incestual, and hallucinatory tale about Ya'ara is thus nourished by a male-authored intertextual web that includes the Samson cycle, the midrashic legends of destruction, and Agnon's story. By creating her own midrash (about the Temple priest and his daughter) and claiming that it is part of the ancient midrashim, Shalev asserts the power and legitimacy of her own imaginative creativity, even as she iconoclastically and even mockingly revises earlier male models.

In *Husband and Wife*, Shalev also focuses on the narrow confines of a couple's disintegrating marriage. Although she leaves out the broader issues of contemporary Israeli life within which the story is placed, she engages in active conversation with the master canon itself, the Bible. The husband of the title, Udi, is attached to the Bible, though in its geopolitical and territorial implications. As a tour guide, he identifies ancient sites that are linked to specific biblical tales. His wife, Na'ama, on the other hand, sees the biblical story, especially of the separation between the kingdom of Judah and the kingdom of Israel, as a parable of the intimate relationship between herself and her husband. Thus, she converts the Bible, the national epic that earlier gave validity to the Zionist enterprise and legitimized the prestatehood generation's territorial aspirations, into a paradigm of the private, conjugal relationship between a man and a woman. Once again, Zeruya Shalev boldly and unabashedly claims the Judaic masterpiece from the center of the Jewish patriarchal tradition, where it validates the nation's territorial ambition, as the female's space. The Bible thus directs the woman protagonist's everyday concerns of love and family relationship and even illuminates the path to mending her broken relationship.[38]

Michal Govrin's two major novels, *The Name* (1995)[39] and *Snapshots* (2002),[40] demonstrate very different ways in which female writers invade and conquer the traditional male territory of Jewish writ. Both are imbued with references to the Jewish literary tradition. In each novel, the female protagonist's existence is defined within the framework of a distinctly biblical concept or law. In the former, it is the custom of the counting of the *Omer*, which marks the time span between the holidays of Passover and Shavuot; in the latter, it is the law of the sabbatical year (*shemitah*). Amalia, the woman protagonist in *The Name*, is in the process of retracting into herself, withdrawing from the larger issues of modern Israel and gradually shrinking her own private time in a suicidal journey to self-annihilation. By contrast, the female protagonist of *Snapshots*, Ilana, is spearheading an ambitious architectural and political program with broad repercussions for public life and, indeed, for the course of the future history of the region.

The Name is set in contemporary Jerusalem, yet there is no specific reference to date or political or military events. The flavor is of the 1990s, around the time the novel was published. The heroine lives on the outskirts of the city, a place populated mostly by Arabs. Amalia has returned from New York city, where she led a promiscuous life as an artist/photographer. Before that, she was in Europe, where she had a German lover, who was also a photographer. The novel is structured along the time period of forty-nine days, the seven weeks (*sheva shabbatot*) of the counting of the *Omer*. During this time, Amalia weaves a Torah curtain, which she must complete on the eve of Shavuot, the holiday of the giving of the Torah. She shuttles back and forth in her memory between the present and the events that have occurred at around the same time in the previous year. She also moves internally between flashbacks from her old life, including childhood and young adulthood, her career as a photographer and the promiscuity of New York life, and the events that brought her now to Jerusalem. Her greatest trauma has been her work on a photographic exhibit that necessitated her to stay in Europe; the exhibit, left unfinished, was to commemorate her father's first wife, who was lost in the Holocaust,.

The Name represents three aspects of the modern Israeli novel. Socioculturally, it captures contemporary Israel's post-Zionist mentality, reflecting the ideological and psychological crisis of a generation disillusioned with the Zionist idea. The heroine's tale also belongs to the genre of the "second-generation" Holocaust narratives, because her parents' past and her upbringing as a "replacement child" are a large part of what brings Amalia to her present suicidal mood. Finally, the novel can be read as a "woman's fiction" in the feminist sense, since it focuses on the protagonist's "feminine space" and records her interior consciousness. The image of the woman as weaver and the theme of redemption are dominant in all three perspectives.

The story opens in the aftermath of a period of nihilism and deep disillusionment in Amalia's life. Her search for meaning and fulfillment has been futile; not only has Zionism failed her, but so have all her other ventures, professional and personal. Leaving Israel, she roams in the United States, Germany, and various other European locales. In the end, the only solution to her hungry soul is to resort to the domain that Zionism itself has long rejected: the old-fashioned world of mysticism, messianic fervor, and other-worldliness. The novel deflates the Zionist idea in surprising, unexpected ways. For instance, it depicts Jerusalem as a bizarre, mystical space, a haven for lost souls, spiritual seekers, and cultic figures, rather than as the modern city that it is. Where Zionism preached the return from text to territory, Amalia reverses the Zionist story, turning from territory to text within the current narrow confines of her existential and physical space.

For Amalia, who has been all over the world, Jerusalem is a place of mental refuge because of the Orthodox seminary, not because of its Zionist context. She lives close to the Arab quarter of the city and, significantly, is oblivious to "Yom Yerushalayim," which celebrates the 1967 unification of the Old and New parts of Jerusalem. Israel is her birthplace and her country, but she does not give much thought to the complexity of the Zionist claim to this land or the ongoing political and ideological debate. I believe it is a mistake to attribute this lack of interest to Amalia's femininity; it belongs to her personal brand of postmodern sensibility.

Amalia's geographic frame of reference is not modern Israel, but old-world, pre-Zionist Jerusalem, where Jews came to study, pray, repent, and die, which is Amalia's own intent! For her, Jerusalem is a spiritual domain, not a real city with a busy modern life. It is mainly the hub for the religious life, the cycle of holidays, the celebration of the Sabbath, and the counting of the *Omer*. While Zionism sought to redeem not only the people and the land, but also the dispirited Jewish mentality, Amalia is seeking redemption in ways that are akin to the traditional Jewish spiritual sense of pre-Zionist times.

The predicament of the children of Holocaust survivors is a major theme in the works of both men and women writers of this generation. Amalia is a replacement, expected to fill the gap in her father's life that was left by her namesake, his first wife, Mala. The latter, a brilliant and famous Warsaw pianist who committed suicide in Auschwitz, was a haunting presence in Amalia's childhood. The dead Mala continues to overshadow Amalia's adult life when another Holocaust survivor commissions Amalia to reconstruct Mala's life by collecting documents and photographs that survived in the various European countries where Mala lived or performed.

The novel's power and uniqueness lies in Govrin's ability to set spiritual seeking within the framework of gender by using concepts and myths from traditional Jewish lore to represent the essence of the feminine experience.[41] She places Amalia at the center of a mystical-spiritual journey for redemption, an effort that earlier literature epitomized as an essentially masculine endeavor. The linguistic texture of Govrin's novel is "dialogic," as described by Mikhail Bakhtin.[42] Not only does its heroine conduct a dialogue with a variety of Judaic literary and theological sources, but the narrative itself converses with S. Y. Agnon's short story "The Tale of the Scribe."[43] Amalia and her creator occupy the space of the male writer Agnon and his creation, Raphael the scribe; thus, it is the females who now become the mythmakers, the spiritual seekers, and the designers of sacred artifacts.

Agnon's tale starts with a pseudo-midrash, which envisions God as engaged in the traditionally female occupation of weaving a cosmic prayer shawl (*tallit*), which falls into disrepair every time the people of Israel commit a sin. Amalia, too, weaves prayer shawls. In Agnon's story, Raphael, the scribe, writes a Torah scroll as homage to the wife that he wronged, at the completion of which he dies. This exclusively male activity is paralleled by Amalia's engagement in the feminine activity of weaving. She is frantically weaving a Torah curtain that needs to be completed at the end of the *Omer* as a way to expiate her sins before she dies. Evoking the mystical concept of correspondences, Amalia describes the Torah curtain as a replica of heaven, recalling the heavenly *tallit* that God weaves in Agnon's midrash. At the end of the novel and as the mark of the end of her own life, Amalia covers herself with the Torah curtain, just as Agnon's scribe covers himself with the Torah cover, which is fused with his wife's wedding gown and the shroud in which he will soon be buried.[44]

Exploring the woman's psyche, Govrin shows Amalia measuring a variety of traditional values and concepts. She simultaneously challenges, adopts, and adjusts these ideas that originated in the male mind to her female sensibility and understanding of life. Among the ideas that she evaluates and absorbs are the concepts of *tikkun* (repair), *teshuvah* (repentance), and mystical union with God. In her quest to repair her soul and cleanse herself of her troubled past, Amalia shuttles between Maimonides' rational, therapeutic option and Rabbi Avuya's mystical alternative, with its self-denial and self-annihilation. Amalia's multiple, fragmented identities combine the "replacement child" syndrome and the feminine condition with the postmodern conception of the human as an indeterminate entity. The loom at which she busies herself symbolizes woman's existence and her creativity as the spinner of both yarn and tales.

Govrin converts various other Judaic images into signs of the female existence. Amalia is an embodiment of Jerusalem or the Shechinah, God's bride, relating to God in erotic terms and imbuing sexuality with the duality of sinfulness and sanctity. Thus, Amalia and her creator, Michal Govrin, boldly and comfortably employ Jewish symbols and lore to describe the female's private state of mind and unique lexicon, giving supremacy and legitimacy to the woman's internal turmoil and fractured concept of reality and self, while at the same time challenging some of the leading figures and concepts in Jewish life and letters.

The woman's space and feminine vision in *Snapshots* stand in marked opposition to those in Govrin's *The Name*. From Amalia, the woman as agent of mystical repair, Govrin moves to Ilana, the woman as builder of new architectural and perceptional constructions. Like Amalia, Ilana, the novel's protagonist, also reaches Jerusalem, but her program and agenda there are not only a quest for emotional and mystical salvation; they also embrace geopolitics as she attempts to transform the course of history in a tangible, pragmatic way.

Ilana sees herself as the breaker of all boundaries. In her private life, she violates all the truths and taboos she has grown up with. She betrays her father's Zionist fervor by leaving the country and embarking on a love affair with a Palestinian who had been close to the engineer of the Munich massacre. She works for an international peace group, designing a structure based on the concept of the *sukkah* (hut), which commemorates the ancient Hebrews' wanderings in the desert. As "architecture of nomads," as she names this project, it physically embodies the concept of place as temporary and fluid and thus owned by all and by none. Ilana merges her architectural/political plan with the feminist language of women as free agents. Just as it is primitive and passé to own a woman, so too is the concept of conquering and owning a geographic place. Ilana hopes that this *sukkah* will be an antimonument of sorts, teaching peace, tolerance, understanding, and "letting go" of the sense of owning and dominating a geographic territory.

Ilana's far-reaching activist vision makes her a postfeminist protagonist. Her maternal care is central in a large part of the novel, but her political efforts challenge the feminist paradigm that women's peace leanings are derived from their maternal instincts.[45] Seeing herself as an agent of peace, Ilana, ironically, fails and betrays her own two sons. In this sense, Govrin's novel adds to current discussions regarding women and activism.

But the physical structure and the concept behind Ilana's program remain incomplete. The Palestinians lose interest, and Ilana dies in a car accident. I see in this novel Govrin's post-Zionist conversation with Agnon's *Temol Shilshom* (*Only Yesterday*, 1945, rev. 1953). The latter glorifies and sharply critiques the Zionist dream; the former promotes as well as questions post-Zionist efforts. In both sagas, the protagonists-dreamers end in failure and death. In both, the protagonists' love interests are expressions of their ideological shuffling. *Snapshots* is framed by Ilana's imaginary correspondence with her Zionist father; she tries to explain her own views to him and to come to terms with his, to both challenge and understand him. At the same time, Govrin is conducting a conversation with another father, S. Y. Agnon, the greatest figure in modern Hebrew literature. She mirrors his exploration of Zionism with her scrutiny of post-Zionism, using the female sensibility as the natural setting for this existential and political probing.

Contemporary Israeli women authors have thus found a variety of ways to create a new vocabulary within Hebrew, a language that had been inextricably tied to male dominant systems. During the first several decades of the state, Hebrew women writers were marginalized by the traditionally emblematic role of the female in the culture and the new nationalist image of masculine heroism. In their attempts to break out of this imposed silence, writers like Kahana-Carmon and Yehudit Hendel formed female spaces outside the mainstream, private domains that were considered unimportant to their immediate culture. In the current psychological and political environment, the female sensibility seems best suited to express the postmodern spirit. The women's sense of time and space, once deemed irrelevant to the culture, has progressed to epitomize the postmodern and post-Zionist spirit. Postmodernism, which rejects master stories of any kind, has freed women writers to claim legitimacy for their own narratives, which were heretofore considered "minor" or "subjective." The fragmentation of the self is no longer a psychotic female symptom but rather the epitome of the postmodern condition. Israeli female protagonists tend to sympathize with any minority, attempt to build consensus, try to mend that which masculine thinking has damaged, and construct innovative new structures, both conceptually and physically. They also give themselves license to break boundaries, the intensity of which escalates dramatically from Liebrecht to Shalev to Govrin.

Current Israeli female writers proudly exhibit their own thorough immersion in the traditional Jewish writings and wrest them from male hegemony. In the process, they are able to convert hallowed images and concepts of the male canonical writings into feminine symbolism and codes. Further, contemporary women writers expand their challenging dialogue to include not only the ancient male sources but also some of the male giants of modern Hebrew literature, in a state of mind free of the "anxiety of [male] influence."[46] Israeli women's narratives have thus progressed from expressing self-doubt and marginality to protesting gender inequality, and finally, to placing the feminine zone at the very heart of the culture.

NOTES

1. On the cultivation of the masculine image for the "new Jew," starting with Zionist ideology and nation-building efforts, see Tamar Mayer, "From Zero to Hero: Masculinity in Jewish Nationalism" in *Gender Ironies of Nationalism: Sexing the Nation*, ed. Tamar Mayer (New York: Routledge, 2000) pp. 283–307.

2. See Esther Fuchs, "The Enemy as Woman: Fictional Women in the Literature of the Palmach," *Israel Studies* 4.1 (1999) 212–33.

3. For an extensive discussion, see Yael Feldman, *No Room of Their Own: Gender and Nation in Israeli Women's Fiction* (New York: Columbia University Press, 1990).

4. *Bi-Khefifah Aḥat* (Merhaviah: Sifriyat Po'alim, 1966).

5. *Ve-Yareah Be-Emek Ayalon* (Tel Aviv: HaKibbutz HaMeuchad, 1971).

6. *Sadot Magnetiyim: Triptikhon* (Tel Aviv: HaKibbutz HaMeuchad, 1977).

7. *LeMa'alah Be-Montifer* (Tel Aviv: HaKibbutz HaMeuchad, 1984).

8. See Nehama Aschkenasy, *Eve's Journey, Feminine Images in Hebraic Literary Tradition* (Philadelphia: University of Pennsylvania Press, 1986), pp. 226–27.

9. Leon Edel, *The Modern Psychological Novel* (New York: Grosset and Dunlap, 1964).

10. In *Under One Roof* (*Bi-Khefifah Ahat*), pp. 152–74.

11. *Shidah Ve-Shidot* (Tel Aviv: Am Oved, 1974).

12. Trans. Hillel Halkin and Shulamit Hareven (San Francisco: Mercury House, 1993). *City of many Days*

13. *Shorshei Avir* (Tel Aviv: HaKibbutz HaMeuchad; Jerusalem: Keter, 1987).

14. See Yael Feldman, *No Room of Their Own*, pp. 197–98.

15. *Tikkun Omanuti* (Jerusalem: Keter, 1993).

16. *HaAgam HaPenimi* (Tel Aviv: HaKibbutz HaMeuchad, 2000).

17. Jerusalem: Keter, 1993.

18. On the permutations of the Zionist meta-narrative in Israeli fiction, see Gershon Shaked, "Fiction and the Zionist Metanarrative: Hebrew Fiction's Dialectical Encounter With a Changing Reality" (Hebrew) in *Independence: The First Fifty Years*, ed. Anita Shapira (Jerusalem: Zalman Shazar Center, 1998), pp. 487–511.

19. Gershon Shaked, *A New Wave in Israeli Writings* (Hebrew; Tel Aviv: Poalim, 1974), p. 222.

20. *Yamim Rabim* (*Many Days*) (Tel Aviv: Bavel, 2002).

21. *Anashim Aherim Hem* (Merhaviyah: Sifriat Poalim, 1950).

22. *Rehov HaMadregot* (Tel Aviv: HaKibbutz HaMeuchad, 1955).

23. For more on the postmodern rejection of meta-narratives of any kind, see Jean-Francois Lyotard, *The Postmodern Condition: A Report on Knowledge*, trans. Geoff Bennington and Brian Massumi (Manchester: Manchester University Press, 1984).

24. The term "post-Zionism" has been used for different purposes. Here it means the tendency by Israeli thinkers and writers to reevaluate the Zionist "master story," meaning the major tenets of the Zionist idea as they were formulated by the early Zionists, often also revising Zionist history as it had been accepted and taught in Israel. Some post-Zionists also posit that the Israeli state should move toward a more inclusive, less nationalist definition of the state.

25. Gershon Shaked, *Literature Then, Here and Now* (Hebrew; Tel Aviv: Zemorah-Bitan, 1993), p. 76.

26. Trans. Barbara Harshav (New York: Riverhead, 2007), p. 46.

27. The renowned Harvard scholar Carol Gilligan has suggested that a person's moral orientation is a function of gender and that women's judgments are predominantly oriented toward the value of care, whereas those of men skew

toward the value of justice (*In a Different Voice: Psychological Theory and Women's Development* [Cambridge, MA: Harvard University Press, 1982]). For more on women's moral orientation and development, see *Women and Moral Theory*, ed. Eva Feder Kittay and Diana T. Meyers (New Jersey: Rowman and Littlefield, 1987).

28. See Nira Yuval-Davis, *Gender and Nation* (London: Sage, 1997).

29. Trans. Marganit Wienberger-Rotman (New York: The Feminist Press, 1998).

30. In *Where the Jackals Howls*, trans. Nicholas de Lange (New York: Harcourt, 1981), 21–38.

31. Trans. Marsha Pomerantz (New York: Persea Books, 2001).

32. New York: Random House, 2008.

33. Trans. Sondra Silverston (New York: Persea Books, 2005).

34. Trans. Dalya Bilu (New York: Grove, 2000).

35. Trans. Dalya Bilu (New York: Grove, 2001).

36. In *Eight Great Hebrew Short Novels*, ed. Alan Lelchuk and Gershon Shaked (New York: New American Library, 1983).

37. Yigal Schwartz, "The Frigid Option: A Psychological Study of the Novel *Love Life* by Zeruya Shalev," in *History and Literature: New Readings of Jewish Texts in Honor of Arnold J. Band*, ed. William Cutter and David C. Jacobson (Providence: Brown Judaic Studies, 2000), pp. 479–88.

38. For more on this novel, see Vered Shemtov, "The Bible in Contemporary Literature: Text and Place in Zeruya Shalev's *Husband and Wife* and Michal Govrin's *Snapshots*," *Hebrew Studies* 47 (2006): 363–84. For Zeruya Shalev's own interpretation of the Bible's role in this novel, see "Literary Protagonists read the Bible," *Hebrew Studies* 47 (2006): 389–93.

39. *HaShem*, trans. Barbara Harshav (New York: Riverhead, 1999).

40. Trans. Barbara Harshav (New York: Riverhead, 2007).

41. For an exhaustive study of the wealth of Judaic materials, symbols, and concepts incorporated in this novel as well as its feminist symbolism, see Nitza Keren, "In the Name of the Mother: Women's Discourse-Women's Prayer in Michal Govrin's *The Name*," *Nashim: A Journal of Jewish Women's Studies and Gender Issues* 10 (Fall, 2005): 126–54.

42. On Mikhail Bakhtin's theory of dialogism, see *The Dialogic Imagination: Four Essays*, ed. Michael Holquist, trans. Caryl Emerson and Michael Holquist (University of Texas Press Slavic Series 1; Austin: University of Texas Press, 1981).

43. In *Twenty-One Stories*, ed. Nahum N. Glatzer, trans. Isaac Franck (New York: Schocken, 1970), pp. 7–25.

44. For more on Agnon's story, see Nehama Aschkenasy, *Eve's Journey*, pp. 150–53.

45. A common denominator in the Western feminist peace literature locates women's peace activism in the practice of mothering; see Sara Riddick, *Maternal*

Thinking: Towards a Politics of Peace (New York: Ballantine, 1989). Several feminist scholars have challenged this link; see N. Yuval-Davis, *Gender and Nation*, p. 112. For more on women and peace, see Karen Warren and Duane Cady, "Feminism and Peace: Seeing Connections," *Hypatia* 9:2 (1994): 4–20.

46. A term coined by Harold Bloom to describe the relationship between male poets and their precursors in *The Anxiety of Influence: A Theory of Poetry* (New York: Oxford University Press, 1973).

Epilogue

|||||||||||||||||||||||||||||||||||||||||||||||||||||

Women and Judaism:
From Invisibility to Integration

Frederick E. Greenspahn

The past century has been witness to a remarkable number of changes. Many of the most dramatic innovations have been technological; computers, the automobile, and even space travel have affected our lives in countless ways. However, social changes have left imprints that are every bit as profound. The most notable of these have been the breakdown of cultural barriers that had come to be taken for granted. The most obvious examples relate to race, religion, and gender. Not only did these changes challenge accepted ideas, but their effects reached into almost every aspect of our lives and our society.

This book is the product of developments in two of these realms—gender and religion—that took place more or less concurrently. Over the past generation, Jews have come to be accepted within American society in a way that was previously inconceivable. One example of that process is the widespread acceptance of the term "Judeo-Christian tradition," which began to take root toward the end of World War II, when it replaced references to America as a Christian nation.[1] The significance of this phenomenon is not simply rhetorical. Its implications are dramatically captured in the title of a book—*How Jews Became White Folks*.[2] It means that Jews and Jewish tradition were no longer considered outsiders or oddities but an accepted part of the American mainstream. That recognition would eventually pave the way for a more rigorous examination of Jewish history and culture.

At the same time that this was taking place, women's role in our society was also changing. The most visible effects of that process have been in the workplace; however, its ramifications have extended into a host of other arenas, including the home and politics, health care, and even our views about the genetic and social bases of behavior. One result was to awaken interest in women's experiences and concerns, including those in the various fields that make up Jewish Studies, beginning with the Bible and continuing to modern sociology.

These two developments converged on the campuses of American universities, where women's studies and Jewish studies blossomed simultaneously. Although they developed separately and were driven by different dynamics,[3] it was only a matter of time before these two fields intersected, with feminist scholars beginning to think about Judaica and Jewish Studies scholars exploring women's issues. These processes were furthered by the emergence of a cadre of female Judaic scholars, who found in women's studies the intellectual tools with which to address their areas of expertise and interest. The fact that previous generations had avoided these topics strengthened their motivation, as did the tension they experienced by not being fully accepted within either Jewish Studies, which saw them as women, or women's studies, where they were perceived as Jews.

Marilyn Schuster and Susan Van Dyne have studied the process through which women's concerns have come to be incorporated into many different academic disciplines. They break it down into six stages, starting with total absence and proceeding to complete integration: (1) At first, women are invisible. Their absence from the curriculum is not even recognized; those who do notice attribute it to the insignificance of women's contributions. (2) That explanation eventually loses credibility, leading to a search for the missing women. This compensatory stage typically turns into a quest for women who act like men and results in the "discovery" of figures like Cleopatra and Madame Curie. (3) As it becomes clear that these women were exceptional, attention shifts to examining the field itself and the way it treats women. (4) That culminates in a recognition of the biases that were built into previous inquiries, which in turn motivates scholars to reconsider the entire subject from the feminine point of view and to examine the actual experience of women and the roles that they played. (5) One product of that effort is a heightened awareness of how gender has affected the way the subject has been approached, which includes the very definitions and paradigms that underlie research and thus what is seen and what is overlooked. (6) With these theoretical perspectives in mind, it becomes possible to reconceive the entire discipline, fashioning a broader and more inclusive curriculum that incorporates this new knowledge.[4]

The chapters of this book, which focus on wide array of topics, illustrate how this process has played out in the various fields that make up Jewish Studies and its impact on our understanding of Jewish civilization.

(1) The first stage is evident in Sara Horowitz's observation about the longstanding tendency to use Philip Roth, Bernard Malamud, and Saul Bellow as the yardstick against which American Jewish literature can be measured. That same kind of mindset has governed our approach to the entirety of Jewish history, resulting in the traditional focus on philosophers and kings, prophets and rabbis—all of whom are men. That does not mean that women have been ignored, but those who are mentioned usually turn out to be wives and mothers, in other words, women who were related to or had an impact on the men who are the real center of attention. The most obvious examples include biblical figures such as Esther and Eve or Jezebel and Bathsheba. Even the famous "woman of valor," who is described in the last chapter of Proverbs, is portrayed in terms of the way she cares for her family. The consequences of this approach are apparent in the custom, which prevails to the present day, whereby Jewish husbands recite that passage to their wives on Sabbath eve, as if to promote the role that it prescribes.[5] In this androcentric (male-centered) orientation, women are looked at from a male point of view, so that it is always their impact on someone else that matters. They are the "other," to use modern, scholarly parlance.

(2) As the apparent imbalance resulting from that approach became apparent, people began to look for women who were as wise as Maimonides or as powerful as King David. That led to a (usually short) list of exceptional women, including figures like Beruriah in the Talmud, Doña Gracia Nasi of Spain, and Israeli prime minister Golda Meir. Such women are real but rare. Putting them alongside their male counterparts had the ironic, if unintended consequence of highlighting their rarity, thereby creating the impression that women were less important in Jewish history than men. It also ignored the experience of most women throughout Jewish history. In other words, this compensatory approach left the larger story of Jewish culture untold.

(3) Before that broader picture can be painted, Schuster and Van Dyne point out that there must be an intermediate step—an examination of how women are portrayed from within the prevailing androcentric point of view. Dvora Weisberg provides an example of that process when she observes rabbinic literature's presentation of women as manipulative tricksters.[6] In fact, the rabbis did not invent that image; it reaches all the

way back to the Bible, which repeatedly presents women as seducing men away from God.[7]

This image is so pervasive that one cannot help but wonder, "Why": why would a tradition that was constructed by men present women in this way? Framing the question in these terms can actually help us get at the reality of women's experience. It can also illustrate the relevance and the value of raising these issues for understanding the culture as a whole. We can see an example of that in Esther Fuchs's "critical" approach to the Bible, which leads her to the conclusion that even passages that are not patently misogynistic support a patriarchal social order. In much the same way, blaming women for male disloyalty to God enabled the men who wrote the Bible to abdicate responsibility for their own short-comings. Similarly, rabbinic literature's portrayal of women as seductive suggests that its male authors saw women as threatening their ability to give the Torah the attention they believed it required. In other words, this motif is evidence that the men responsible for it believed that they were being tempted away from their "real" partner, a threat they felt compelled to resist. Nowadays, women rabbis who reject the their male counterparts' longstanding tendency to put their jobs (Torah) ahead of their families may have exposed a similar dynamic in traditional rabbinic behavior.

(4) Identifying the ways that women have been portrayed within the (androcentric) Jewish tradition brings gender to the fore, making it an issue that must be taken into account in understanding *all* of Jewish history and life. That, in turn, makes it possible to move to the next stage and to seek out information about women's actual experience.

In fact, that is often less difficult than one might suppose. There are sources, such as the memoirs of Glikl of Hameln, the financial records of Wuhsha, and the *tkhines* by Leah Horowitz, in which women describe their perceptions and record their experiences. Even documents that were composed by and focus on men, such as the letters from ancient Elephantine or the laws about wife-beating that Judith Hauptman describes, can teach us a great deal about women once we examine them through the lens of gender.

Surprisingly, many of these documents have been known for a long time, even if the idea of contemplating their implications regarding the lives of Jewish women is new. In that same spirit, scholars have begun to scour the Bible for repressed traces of femininity and have tried to reconstruct female biographies on the basis of material preserved in rabbinic literature. Such efforts have led to the recovery of many roles that women played in earlier periods—as godmothers (*sandaqi-ot*) and prayer leaders (*firzogerins*), circumcisers (*mohalot*) and slaughterers (*shohatot*).

Reexamining existing sources from this new point of view can sometimes have unexpected consequences. For example, there are ancient synagogue inscriptions that have been known for generations that mention female leaders; however, only in the past thirty years have scholars fully considered their implications for understanding the role women played in synagogue life.[8] Regarding an earlier age, it is often said that the Bible does not mention female priests. That might seem reasonable, in light of the Roman Catholic and Eastern Orthodox priesthoods with which we are most familiar; however, it is dissonant with other ancient Near Eastern societies, where women did serve as religious officiants.[9] That difference has sometimes been attributed to the Bible's rejection of the ritual sexuality in which priestesses of other ancient cultures engaged;[10] however, more careful scrutiny may lead in an entirely different direction.

In fact, the Bible does know of several ritual functions in which women could serve.[11] They sang at both festive and tragic occasions[12] and even offered sacrifices.[13] They also served as prophets[14] and at the entrance to the tent of meeting.[15] To be sure, the Bible never mentions female counterparts to the *kohanim*, who were the primary priests in ancient Israel, but it does speak of *qedeshot*.[16] Although that word is commonly translated "cult prostitute," there is absolutely no support for such a rendering. Its root (*q-d-sh*) occurs in many Semitic languages, where it consistently means "sacred." The office of *qedeshah* itself existed in Babylon, but there is no evidence that it entailed sexual activity.[17] What's more, the Bible also mentions the masculine equivalent (*qedeshim*), which is also known in other ancient cultures, again with no indication of a sexual role.[18] In short, these terms appear to designate some kind of religious officiant, in other words, priests, who could be either male or female. That means that there may have been female priests in ancient Israel. To be sure, we do not know what they did, just that the authors of the Bible didn't always approve, any more than they approved of their male counterparts. The assumption that their job involved sexual activity may owe more to scholars' imaginations—or, perhaps, to the androcentric view of women as seductresses—than to either history or philology.

In order to hear *from* women rather than just *about* them, as Renée Levine Melammed puts it, we often do need new sources of information. On occasion, unexpected discoveries can provide previously unavailable insights. The records found in the Cairo Geniza opened up a whole "world of women" about which we would otherwise have known nothing. But there is also much to be learned by looking in places no one previously bothered to check, such as the histories of women's organizations mentioned by Pamela Nadell or the rituals created (or revived) by women in our own time.

(5) Wherever we find them, new data can affect our understanding of Jewish culture as a whole and even challenge the field of Jewish Studies itself. They force us to look inward, providing a stimulus to consider why we were previously satisfied with accounts that spoke only of men or presented women solely as their adjuncts. For example, we ought to think about why modern scholars were so sure that the reason ancient synagogues had two stories was to provide a place where women could sit when there is simply no evidence that they had to sit separately at all.[19] For the same reason, it is important that we not just evaluate the nature of the society in which women were beaten as callously as the rabbis describe, but also explain why it took so long for us to wonder.

(6) This process can be carried one step further if we ask not simply why women have been treated the way that they have or how they might be treated better but what should we make of a system that leaves the decisions on such matters to men alone.[20] In that way, exploring the place of women in Jewish history and culture can lead to a rethinking of "Judaism" itself, since so much of what we have in mind by that term represents the beliefs, the practices, and even the point of view of just one segment of the Jewish population.

In practice, such a rethinking often leads well beyond women's concerns. Nehama Aschkenasy demonstrates that when she describes how so much of modern Israeli feminist literature has been concerned with the "macho" culture that has long dominated that society and how its female authors struggle for the kind of attention so readily available to their male counterparts. That may be one reason why recovering the feminine Jewish experience has so often led to thinking about other outsiders. In the case of biblical studies, for example, feminist research has paved the way for paying attention to other marginalized groups, such as those with disabilities. Similarly, Israeli feminists have drawn attention to ethnic minorities, and the ordination of women in America clearly paved the way for ordaining homosexuals. A similar dynamic may account for the way in which a study of Jewish women in the American West demonstrated how much the Jewish experience in that part of the country differed from that in the East.[21] That is a reminder about the importance of using caution when making statements about "American Jewry" as a whole on the basis of evidence from just one region of the country. Phenomena that actually originated somewhere else may not be considered important until they reach the dense center of Jewish population. Such studies may also provide a valuable reminder of the ways in which Jewish culture has been influenced by broader social trends; after all, it was in Wyoming that American women first attained the right to vote and Montana that sent the first woman to Congress.[22]

The point of these observations is to illustrate how thinking about gender can lead to insights that extend far beyond the status of women. The pages of this book are filled with examples of that possibility. We might, for example, speculate about why it took the Reform movement more than half a century from the time it endorsed the principle that women could be rabbis until it actually ordained a woman. Or we might ponder the significance of the fact that it is within the Orthodox community that one finds the highest level of educational and occupational equity between husbands and wives. Sylvia Barack Fishman suggests that it may be better for women to have discrete realms of control than to gain access to roles that were previously reserved for men. That raises questions about the consequences of American synagogues' elimination of women's galleries in the 19th century. Is it possible that the result was to deprive women of their distinct identity? Men sometimes retreat from arenas in which women gain power. Harriet Pass Friedenreich traces the contemporary feminization of Judaism back to the 19th century. Perhaps the growing prominence of women in Jewish life correlates with religion's loss of prestige; then again, it is difficult to know which is the cause and which the effect.

If having to choose between equality and segregation seems unsatisfying, we should not overlook how often Jewish life has been enriched by the contributions of women. Chava Weissler illustrates this with her description of the ways in which women "translated" the spirituality that had developed in 16th-century Safed into Yiddish. The same process may be at work today with the growing interest in spirituality expressed by contemporary American Jews. Something similar may be taking place in academia, where the presence of female scholars has forced academics in any number of disciplines to rethink their own fields. Perhaps that is one reason why the chapters of this book are able to draw on the insights of scholars such as Avraham Grossman, Howard Adelman, and Jacob Neusner, who have addressed issues that were first raised by women. In short, the growth of women's studies may have had a salutary effect that reaches far beyond its own specific concerns.

We might do well to remember that all of this has taken place in 20th- and 21st-century America, the same place where the bat mitzvah cere- mony was invented, women first ordained, oranges put on Passover plates, and organizations like Edah and Ezrat Nashim created. Of course, it is also the environment that produced the women's movement as a whole. Nor can that be accidental. As Judith Baskin points out, Jewish culture and Jewish life have always been influenced by their environment. And part of that influence has been the kind of scholarship reflected in these pages, which, like ritual and communal life, has been profoundly affected by the dramatic steps toward egalitarianism which have taken place over the past century. Contributing to that process have been the enhanced ed- ucational opportunities open to women, which is the ultimate source for the cadre of female scholars who have done so much to raise our aware- ness of women's contributions to Jewish culture and civilization. In this, contemporary America is reminiscent of 6th-century Sassanian Babylon, where, as we have seen, women were better educated than were women in 2nd-century Palestine.[23]

At the same time, it bears noting that the relationship between femi- nism and American Judaism has been reciprocal. It is surely no acci- dent that Betty Friedan, Bella Abzug, and Gloria Steinem were all Jew- ish. As much as American culture has shaped Jewish women, they have also helped shape it. Moreover, their impact has reached far beyond this country. Israeli feminism, too, owes much to American Jewry. Thus, the issues and developments described in these pages are the product of a complex interaction among Judaism, Jewish women, and the communi- ties in which they live. Making sure that women are included in the study of Jewish civilization thus broadens our awareness in many different ways, enriching our appreciation for both Jewish civilization and the larger cul- tures in whose midst it has unfolded.

NOTES

1. Mark Silk, *Spiritual Politics, Religion and America Since World War II* (New York: Simon and Schuster, 1988) pp. 40–53.

2. Karen Brodkin, *How Jews Became White Folks and What That Says About Race in America* (New Brunswick, NJ: Rutgers University Press, 1998).

3. For some of the differences, see Frederick E. Greenspahn, "Have We Arrived? The Case of Jewish Studies in U.S. Universities," *Midstream* 52:4 (September-October 2006): 16–17.

4. "Placing Women in the Liberal Arts: Stages of Curriculum Transformation," *Harvard Educational Review* 54 (1984): 413–28, reprinted as chapter 2 of their *Women's Place in the Academy: Transforming the Liberal Arts Curriculum* (Totowa, NJ: Rowman and Allanheld, , 1985), pp. 13–29.

5. Ironically, the practice originated in 15th-century Safed, where the passage was understood as referring to the Shechinah/Sabbath; see Yael Levine, "'The Woman of Valor' in Jewish Ritual" (Hebrew), *Beth Hamikra* 31 (1985–86): 344.

6. According to Tal Ilan, even Beruriah turns out to be "a fantasy and nightmare of the guilty male conscience of the rabbis" ("The Quest for the Historical Beruriah, Rachel, and Imma Shalom," *AJS Review* 22 [1997]: 8).

7. E.g., Num 25:1 and Prov 7:6-27, 9:13-18, and Ezra 9:2. Ecclesiastes observes, "I find woman more bitter than death; she is all traps, her hands are fetters and her heart is snares" (7:26). Several biblical stories highlight the danger women can cause to men: Lot is seduced by his daughters, Samson by Delilah, and Judah by his daughter-in-law Tamar. King Solomon's downfall is attributed to "his foreign wives [who] turned his heart away" from God (1 Kgs 11:3). Jezebel and Potiphar's wife play similar roles. In such an environment, it is no wonder that the prophets so frequently associate pagan practices with women (e.g., 2 Kgs 23:7; Jer 7:18, 44:15-17; Ezek 8:14 and 13:18), who are often seen as loose (e.g., Isa 1:21; Jer 3:1-3, 4:30; Ezek 16 and 23; Hos 2:4-7); cf. Gale A. Yee, *Poor Banished Children of Eve, Woman as Evil in the Hebrew Bible* (Minneapolis: Fortress Press, 2003).

8. Bernadette J. Brooten, *Women Leaders in the Ancient Synagogue: Inscriptional Evidence and Background Issues* (Atlanta: Scholars Press, 1982).

9. Richard A. Henshaw, *Female and Male: The Cultic Personnel, The Bible and the Rest of the Ancient Near East* (Allison Park, PA: Pickwick Publications, 1994).

10. Cf. Lev 21:9.

11. Many of these involve disapproved practices, such as necromancy (1 Sam 28:3-8) and pagan rituals (e.g., 2 Kgs 23:7, Jer 7:18, 44:15-19, Ezek 8:14 and 13:17-18).

12. Exod 15:20, Judg 5:1, 11:34, 1 Sam 18:6-7, 2 Sam 1:20-24, Jer 9:16-21, 31:15, 49:3, Ezek 32:16, Ps 68:12,26, Ezra 2:65, Neh 7:67, 2 Chron 35:25.

13. Lev 12:6, 15:28-29; 1 Sam 1:24-25.

14. Exod 15:20, Judg 4:4, 2 Kgs 22:14-20, Neh 6:14, and possibly Isa 8:3 and Ezek 13:17-23.

15. Exod 38:8, 1 Sam 2:22; similar roles are elsewhere assigned to the Levites (Num 4:23, 8:24).

16. Gen 38:21-22, Deut 23:18, Hos 4:14.

17. See Joan Goodnick Westenholz, "Tamar, *Qĕdēšâ, Qadištu*, and Sacred Prostitution in Mesopotamia," *Harvard Theological Review* 82 (1989): 249–55, and Mayer I. Gruber, "The Hebrew *Qĕdēšâ* and Her Canaanite and Akkadian

Cognates," in his *The Motherhood of God and Other Studies* (Atlanta: Scholars Press, 1992), pp. 17–47.

18. Deut 23:18, 1 Kgs 14:24, 15:12, 22:47, 2 Kgs 23:7; it is also found in Ugarit and Phoenicia. It is only in Israel that both the male and the female terms are found.

19. Lee I. Levine, *The Ancient Synagogue: The First Thousand Years* (New York: Yale University Press, 2000); Shmuel Safrai, "Did Ancient Synagogues Have a Women's Gallery" (Hebrew), in his *In Times of Temple and Mishnah, Studies in Jewish History* (2nd edition, Jerusalem: Magnes Press, 1996), vol. 1, pp. 168–69; and Brooten, *Women Leaders in the Ancient Synagogue*, pp. 103–38.

20. Cf. Judith Plaskow, "Beyond Egalitarianism," *Tikkun* 5 (November-December 1990), 79–80; reprinted in *The Coming of Lilith, Essays on Feminism, Judaism, and Sexual Ethics, 1972–2003*, ed. Judith Plaskow with Donna Berman (Boston: Beacon Press, 2005), pp. 128–33.

21. Jeanne E. Abrams, *Jewish Women Pioneering the Frontier: A History in the American West* (New York: New York University Press, 2006).

22. Ibid., pp. 17–18.

23. David Goodblatt, "The Beruriah Traditions," *Journal for Jewish Studies* 26 (1975): 84.

Contributors

NEHAMA ASCHKENASY is Professor of Comparative Literary and Cultural Studies at the University of Connecticut and Founding Director of the Center for Judaic and Middle Eastern Studies at its Stamford campus. She is author of three books, including the award-winning *Eve's Journey: Feminine Images in Hebraic Literary Tradition*, as well as numerous book chapters and essays in the fields of biblical influences on Western literature, Hebraic literary tradition, the Bible as literature, and women in the Bible and Judaic literature.

JUDITH R. BASKIN is Knight Professor of Humanities, Head of the Department of Religious Studies, and Director of the Harold Schnitzer Family Program in Judaic Studies at the University of Oregon. Her books include *Pharaoh's Counsellors; Job, Jethro, and Balaam in Rabbinic and Patristic Tradition*; *Midrashic Women: Formations of the Feminine in Rabbinic Literature*; and the edited collections *Jewish Women in Historical Perspective* and *Women of the Word: Jewish Women and Jewish Writing*.

SYLVIA BARACK FISHMAN is Professor of Contemporary Jewish Life in the Near Eastern and Judaic Studies Department at Brandeis University and co-director of the Hadassah-Brandeis Institute. She is the author of *Follow My Footprints: Changing Images of Women in American Jewish Fiction; A Breath of Life: Feminism in the American Jewish Community; Jewish Life and American Culture*; and *Double or Nothing? Jewish Families and Mixed Marriage*.

HARRIET PASS FREIDENREICH is Professor of History at Temple University and the author of *The Jews of Yugoslavia, Jewish Politics in Vienna*, and *Female, Jewish, and Educated*.

ESTHER FUCHS is Professor of Near Eastern Studies and Judaic Studies at the University of Arizona in Tucson. She is the author of numerous publications on gender and biblical studies, including *Cunning Innocence: The Irony of S. Y. Agnon*; *Israeli Mythogynies: Women in Contemporary Hebrew Fiction*; *Women and the Holocaust: Narrative and Representation*; *Sexual Politics in the Biblical Narrative: Reading the Hebrew Bible as a Woman*; she recently co-edited, with Alice Bach and Jane Schaberg, *Wisdom on the Cutting Edge: The Study of Women in Biblical Worlds*.

FREDERICK E. GREENSPAHN is Gimelstob Eminent Scholar in Judaic Studies, Florida Atlantic University. He is the editor of *Essential Papers on Israel and the Ancient Near East*, as well as author or editor of numerous other titles, including *The Hebrew Bible: New Insights and Scholarship*; *When Brothers Dwell Together: The Preeminence of Younger Siblings in the Hebrew Bible*; *An Introduction to Aramaic*; *Uncivil Religion: Interreligious Hostility in America* (edited with Robert Bellah); and *Pushing the Faith: Proselytism and Civility in a Pluralistic World* (edited with Martin Marty).

JUDITH HAUPTMAN is the E. Billi Ivry Professor of Talmud and Rabbinic Culture at The Jewish Theological Seminary. Her books include *Development of the Talmudic Sugya: Relationship Between Tannaitic and Amoraic Sources*; *Rereading the Mishnah: A New Approach to Ancient Jewish Texts*; and *Rereading the Rabbis: A Woman's Voice*.

SARA R. HOROWITZ is Director of the Centre for Jewish Studies at York University and the author of *Voicing the Void: Muteness and Memory in Holocaust Fiction*, co-editor of the journal *Kerem: Creative Explorations in Judaism*, and editor of the Azrieli Series of Holocaust Memoirs.

RENÉE LEVINE MELAMMED is Associate Professor of Jewish History at the Schechter Institute of Jewish Studies, Jerusalem, and the author of *Heretics or Daughters of Israel: The Crypto-Jewish Women of Castile* and *A Question of Identity: Iberian Conversos in Historical Perspective*. She is also academic editor of *Nashim, Journal of Jewish Women and Gender Studies* and editor of *"Lift up Your Voice": Women's Voices and Feminist Interpretation in Jewish Studies*.

PAMELA S. NADELL is Professor of History and Director of the Jewish Studies Program at American University. Among her books are *Women Who Would Be Rabbis: A History of Women's Ordination, 1889–1985* and *American Jewish Women's History: A Reader.*

DVORA E. WEISBERG is Associate Professor of Rabbinics at Hebrew Union College-Jewish Institute of Religion, Los Angeles. She received her Ph.D. in Talmud and Rabbinics from the Jewish Theological Seminary. Her publications deal with Levirate marriage and gender issues in rabbinic texts.

CHAVA WEISSLER is Professor of Religion Studies at Lehigh University, where she holds the Philip and Muriel Berman Chair of Jewish Civilization. Her book on the religious lives of Jewish women, *Voices of the Matriarchs,* was a National Jewish Book Award Finalist in 1999 and won the Koret Foundation Book Award in Jewish History in 2000.

Index